D1588546

THE DAILY STUDY BIBLE

THE LETTER TO THE ROMANS

REVISED EDITION

THE LETTER TO THE
ROMANS

REVISED EDITION

WILLIAM BARCLAY

THE SAINT ANDREW PRESS
EDINBURGH

To
G. H. C. M.
WHOM IT WAS MY HONOUR
TO CALL MY CHIEF
AND MY PRIVILEGE
TO CALL MY FRIEND

Published by
THE SAINT ANDREW PRESS
121 George Street, Edinburgh

© William Barclay 1975
First Edition 1955
Revised Edition 1975

For copyright reasons not for sale in the USA

ISBN 0 7152 0277 4 (Limp)
ISBN 0 7152 0294 4 (Cased)

Photoset by R. & R. Clark Ltd., Edinburgh
Printed and Bound by McCorquodale (Scotland) Ltd., Glasgow

GENERAL INTRODUCTION

The Daily Study Bible series has always had one aim—to convey the results of scholarship to the ordinary reader. A. S. Peake delighted in the saying that he was a " theological middleman ", and I would be happy if the same could be said of me in regard to these volumes. And yet the primary aim of the series has never been academic. It could be summed up in the famous words of Richard of Chichester's prayer—to enable men and women " to know Jesus Christ more clearly, to love him more dearly, and to follow him more nearly ".

It is all of twenty years since the first volume of *The Daily Study Bible* was published. The series was the brain-child of the late Rev. Andrew McCosh, M.A., S.T.M., the then Secretary and Manager of the Committee on Publications of the Church of Scotland, and of the late Rev. R. G. Macdonald, O.B.E., M.A., D.D., its Convener.

It is a great joy to me to know that all through the years *The Daily Study Bible* has been used at home and abroad, by minister, by missionary, by student and by layman, and that it has been translated into many different languages. Now, after so many printings, it has become necessary to renew the printer's type and the opportunity has been taken to restyle the books, to correct some errors in the text and to remove some references which have become outdated. At the same time, the Biblical quotations within the text have been changed to use the Revised Standard Version, but my own original translation of the New Testament passages has been retained at the beginning of each daily section.

There is one debt which I would be sadly lacking in courtesy if I did not acknowledge. The work of revision and correction has been done entirely by the Rev. James Martin, M.A., B.D., Minister of High Carntyne Church, Glasgow. Had it not been for him this task would never have been undertaken, and it is impossible for me to thank him enough for the selfless toil he has put into the revision of these books.

It is my prayer that God may continue to use *The Daily Study Bible* to enable men better to understand His word.

Glasgow   WILLIAM BARCLAY

CONTENTS

viii

CONTENTS

A GENERAL INTRODUCTION
TO THE LETTERS OF PAUL

THE LETTERS OF PAUL

There is no more interesting body of documents in the New Testament than the letters of Paul. That is because of all forms of literature a letter is most personal. Demetrius, one of the old Greek literary critics, once wrote, " Every one reveals his own soul in his letters. In every other form of composition it is possible to discern the writer's character, but in none so clearly as the epistolary." (Demetrius, *On Style*, 227.) It is just because he left us so many letters that we feel we know Paul so well. In them he opened his mind and heart to the folk he loved so much; and in them, to this day, we can see that great mind grappling with the problems of the early church and feel that great heart throbbing with love for men, even when they were misguided and mistaken.

THE DIFFICULTY OF LETTERS

At the same time there is often nothing so difficult to understand as a letter. Demetrius (*On Style*, 223) quotes a saying of artemon, who edited the letters of Aristotle. Artemon said that a letter ought to be written in the same manner as a dialogue, because it was one of the two sides of a dialogue. In other words, to read a letter is like listening to one side of a telephone conversation. So when we read the letters of Paul we are often in a difficulty. We do not possess the letter which he was answering; we do not fully know the circumstances with which he was dealing; it is only from the letter itself that we can deduce the situation which prompted it. Before we can hope to understand fully any letter Paul wrote, we must try to reconstruct the situation which produced it.

THE ANCIENT LETTERS

It is a great pity that Paul's letters were ever called *epistles*. They are in the most literal sense *letters*. One of the great lights shed on the interpretation of the New Testament has been the discovery and the publication of the *papyri*. In the ancient world, *papyrus* was the substance on which most documents were written. It was composed of strips of the pith of a certain bulrush that grew on the banks of the Nile. These strips were laid one on top of the other to form a substance very like brown paper. The sands of the Egyptian desert were ideal for preservation, for papyrus, although very brittle, will last forever so long as moisture does not get at it. As a result, from the Egyptian rubbish heaps, archaeologists have rescued hundreds of documents, marriage contracts, legal agreements, government forms, and, most interesting of all, private letters. When we read these private letters we find that there was a pattern to which nearly all conformed; and we find that Paul's letters reproduce exactly that pattern. Here is one of these ancient letters. It is from a soldier, called Apion, to his father Epimachus. He is writing from Misenum to tell his father that he has arrived safely after a stormy passage.

" Apion sends heartiest greetings to his father and lord Epimachus. I pray above all that you are well and fit; and that things are going well with you and my sister and her daughter and my brother. I thank my Lord Serapis [his god] that he kept me safe when I was in peril on the sea. As soon as I got to Misenum I got my journey money from Caesar—three gold pieces. And things are going fine with me. So I beg you, my dear father, send me a line, first to let me know how you are, and then about my brothers, and thirdly, that I may kiss your hand, because you brought me up well, and because of that I hope, God willing, soon to be promoted. Give Capito my heartiest greetings, and my brothers and Serenilla and my friends. I sent you a little picture of myself painted by Euctemon. My military name is Antonius Maximus. I pray for your good health. Serenus sends good wishes, Agathos Daimon's boy, and Turbo, Gallonius's son." (G. Milligan, *Selections from the Greek Papyri*, 36.)

Little did Apion think that we would be reading his letter to his father 1800 years after he had written it. It shows how little human nature changes. The lad is hoping for promotion quickly. who will Serenilla be but the girl he left behind him? He sends the ancient equivalent of a photograph to the folk at home. Now that letter falls into certain sections. (i) There is a greeting. (ii) There is a prayer for the health of the recipients. (iii) There is a thanksgiving to the gods. (iv) There are the special contents. (v) Finally, there are the special salutations and the personal greetings. Practically every one of Paul's letters shows exactly the same sections, as we now demonstrate.

   (i) *The Greeting*: *Romans* 1: 1; 1 *Corinthians* 1: 1; 2 *Corinthians* 1: 1; *Galatians* 1: 1; *Ephesians* 1: 1; *Philippians* 1: 1; *Colossians* 1: 1, 2; 1 *Thessalonians* 1: 1; 2 *Thessalonians* 1: 1.

   (ii) *The Prayer*: in every case Paul prays for the grace of God on the people to whom he writes: *Romans* 1: 7; 1 *Corinthians* 1: 3; 2 *Corinthians* 1: 2; *Galatians* 1: 3; *Ephesians* 1: 2; *philippians* 1: 3; *Colossians* 1: 2; 1 *Thessalonians* 1: 1; 2 *Thessalonians* 1: 2.

   (iii) *The Thanksgiving*: *Romans* 1: 8; 1 *Corinthians* 1: 4; 2 *Corinthians* 1: 3; *Ephesians* 1: 3; *Philippians* 1: 3; 1 *Thessalonians* 1: 3; 2 *Thessalonians* 1: 3.

   (iv) *The Special Contents*: the main body of the letters.

   (v) *Special Salutations and Personal Greetings*: *Romans* 16; 1 *Corinthians* 16: 19; 2 *Corinthians* 13: 13; *Philippians* 4; 21, 22; *Colossians* 4: 12–15; 1 *Thessalonians* 5: 26.

   When Paul wrote letters, he wrote them on the pattern which everyone used. Deissmann says of them, " They differ from the messages of the homely papyrus leaves of Egypt, not as letters but only as the letters of Paul." When we read Paul's letters we are not reading things which were meant to be academic exercises and theological treatises, but human documents written by a friend to his friends.

THE IMMEDIATE SITUATION

   With a very few exceptions, all Paul's letters were written to meet an immediate situation and not treatises which he sat down to write in the peace and silence of his study. There was some threatening situation in Corinth, or Galatia, or Philippi, or Thessalonica, and he wrote a letter to meet it. He was not in the least thinking of us when he wrote, but solely of the people to whom he was writing. Deissmann writes, " Paul had no thought of adding a few fresh compositions to the already extant Jewish epistles; still less of enriching the sacred literature of his nation. . . . He had no presentiment of the place his words would occupy in universal history; not so much that they would be in existence in the next generation, far less that one day people would look at them as Holy Scripture." We must always remember that a thing need not be transient because it was written to meet an immediate situation. All the great love songs of the world were written for one person, but they live on for the whole of mankind. It is just because Paul's letters were written to meet a threatening danger or a clamant need that they still throb with life. And it is because human need and the human situation do not change that God speaks to us through them today.

THE SPOKEN WORD

One other thing we must note about these letters. Paul did what most people did in his day. He did not normally pen his own letters but dictated them to a secretary, and then added his own authenticating signature. (We actually know the name of one of the people who did the writing for him. In *Romans* 16: 22 Tertius, the secretary, slips in his own greeting before the letter draws to an end.) In 1 *Corinthians* 16: 21 Paul says, " This is my own signature, my autograph, so that you can be sure this letter comes from me " (cp. *Colossians* 4: 18; 2 *Thessalonians* 3: 17).

This explains a great deal. Sometimes Paul is hard to understand, because his sentences begin and never finish; his grammar breaks down and the construction becomes involved. We must not think of him sitting quietly at a desk, carefully polishing each sentence as he writes. We must think of him striding up and down some little room, pouring out a torrent of words, while his secretary races to get them down. When Paul composed his letters, he had in his mind's eye a vision of the folk to whom he was writing, and he was pouring out his heart to them in words that fell over each other in his eagerness to help.

INTRODUCTION TO THE
LETTER TO THE ROMANS

THE EPISTLE THAT IS DIFFERENT

There is an obvious difference between Paul's *Letter to the Romans* and any other of his letters. Anyone coming from, say, a reading of the *Letters to the Corinthians*, will immediately feel that difference, both of atmosphere and of method. A very great part of it is due to one basic fact—when Paul wrote to the Church at Rome he was writing to a Church with whose founding he had had nothing whatever to do and with which he had had no personal contact at all. That explains why in *Romans* there are so few of the details of practical problems which fill the other letters. That is why *Romans*, at first sight, seems so much more impersonal. As Dibelius put it, " It is of all Paul's letters the least conditioned by the momentary situation."

We may put that in another way. *Romans*, of all Paul's letters, comes nearest to being a theological treatise. In almost all his other letters he is dealing with some immediate trouble, some pressing situation, some current error, some threatening danger, which was menacing the Church to which he was writing. *Romans* is the nearest approach to a systematic exposition of Paul's own theological position, independent of any immediate set of circumstances.

TESTAMENTARY AND PROPHYLACTIC

Because of that, two great scholars have applied two very illuminating adjectives to *Romans*. Sanday called *Romans* " *testamentary*." It is as if Paul was writing his theological last will and testament, as if into *Romans* he was distilling the very essence of his faith and belief. Rome was the greatest city in the world, the capital of the greatest Empire the world had ever seen. Paul had never been there, and he did not know if he ever would be there. But, in writing to such a Church in such a city, it was fitting that he should set down the very centre and core of his belief. Burton called *Romans "prophylactic."* A prophylactic is something which guards against infection. Paul had seen too often what harm and trouble could be caused by wrong ideas, twisted notions, misguided conceptions of Christian faith and belief. He therefore wished to send to the Church in the city which was the centre of the world a letter which would so build up the structure of their faith that, if infections should ever come to them, they might have in the true word of Christian doctrine a powerful and effective defence. He felt that the best protection against the infection of false teaching was the antiseptic of the truth.

THE OCCASION OF PAUL'S WRITING TO ROME

All his life Paul had been haunted by the thought of Rome. It had always been one of his dreams to preach there. When he is in Ephesus, he is planning to go through Achaea and Macedonia again, and then comes a sentence obviously dropped straight from the heart, " After I have been there, *I must also see Rome* " (*Acts* 19: 21). When he was up against things in Jerusalem, and the situation looked threatening and the end seemed near, he had one of those visions which always lifted up his heart. In that vision the Lord stood by him and said, " Take courage, Paul. For as you have testified about me at Jerusalem, *so you must bear witness also at Rome* " (*Acts* 23: 11). In the very first chapter of this letter Paul's desire to see Rome breathes out. " I long to see you that I may impart to you some spiritual gift to strengthen you " (*Romans* 1: 11). " So, I am eager to preach the gospel to you also who are in Rome " (*Romans* 1: 15). It might well be said that the name *Rome* was written on Paul's heart.

When he actually wrote the *Letter to the Romans*, the date was sometime in the year A.D. 58, and he was in Corinth. He was just about to bring to its completion a scheme that was very dear to his heart. The Church at Jerusalem was the mother Church of them all, but it was poor, and Paul had organized a collection throughout the younger churches for it (1 *Corinthians* 16: 1ff; 2 *Corinthians* 9: 1ff). That collection was two things. It was an opportunity for his younger converts to put Christian charity into Christian action, and it was a most practical way of impressing on all Christians the unity of the Christian Church, of teaching them that they were not members of isolated and independent congregations, but of one great Church, each part of which had a responsibility to all the rest. When Paul wrote *Romans* he was just about to set out with that gift for the Jerusalem Church. " At present, however, I am going to Jerusalem with aid for the saints " (*Romans* 15: 25).

THE OBJECT OF PAUL'S WRITING

Why, then, at such a moment should he write?

(*a*) Paul knew that the journey to Jerusalem was not without its peril. He knew that he had enemies there, and that to go to Jerusalem was to take his life and liberty in his hands. He desired the prayers of the Roman Church before he set out on this expedition. " Now I appeal to you brethren, by our Lord Jesus Christ and by the love of the Spirit, to strive together with me in your prayers to God on my behalf, that I may be delivered from the unbelievers in Judaea " (*Romans* 15: 30, 31). He was mobilizing the prayers of the Church before he embarked on this perilous undertaking.

(*b*) Paul had great schemes simmering in his mind. It has been said of him that he was " always haunted by the regions beyond." He never saw a ship at anchor but he wished to board her and to carry the good news to men across the sea. He never saw a range of mountains, blue in the distance, but he wished to cross them, and to bring the story of the Cross to men who had never heard it. At this time Paul was haunted by the thought of Spain. " I hope to see you in passing as I go to Spain " (*Romans* 15: 24). " When I have completed this [that is, when he had delivered the collection to the Church in Jerusalem] I shall go on by way of you to Spain " (*Romans* 15: 28).

Why this great desire to go to Spain? Rome had opened up that land. Some of the great Roman roads and buildings still stand there to this day. And it so happened that, just at this time, there was a blaze of greatness in Spain. Many of the great figures who were writing their names on Roman history and literature were Spaniards. There was Martial, the master of the epigram. There was Lucan, the epic poet. There were Columella and Pomponius Mela, great figures in Roman literature. There was Quintilian, the master of Roman oratory. And, above all, there was Seneca, the greatest of the Roman Stoic philosophers, the tutor of the Emperor Nero, and the Prime Minister of the Roman Empire. It was most natural that Paul's thoughts should go out to this land which was producing such a scintillating galaxy of greatness. What might happen if men like that could be touched for Christ? As far as we know Paul never got to Spain. On that visit to Jerusalem he was arrested and he was never freed again. But, when he was writing *Romans*, that was his dream.

Paul was a master strategist. He had an eye for the layout of territory like a great commander. He felt that by this time he could move on from Asia Minor and for the time being leave Greece behind. He saw the whole west lying in front of him, virgin territory to be won for Christ. But, if he was to launch a campaign in the west, *he needed a base of operations*. There was only one such base possible—*and that was Rome*.

That was why Paul wrote this letter to Rome. He had this great dream in his heart and this great plan in his mind. He needed Rome for a base for this new campaign. He was aware that the Church in Rome must know his name. But he was also aware, for he was a realist, that the reports which reached Rome would be mixed. His opponents were not above spreading slanders and false accusation against him. So he wrote this letter to set out for the Church at Rome an account of the very essence of his belief, in order that, when the time came for action, he might find in Rome a sympathetic Church from which the lines of communication might go out to Spain and the west. It was with such a plan and such an intention, that in A.D. 58 Paul sat down in Corinth to write his letter to the Church at Rome.

THE LAYOUT OF THE LETTER

Romans is at once a very complicated and a very carefully constructed letter. It will therefore help us to find our way through it, if we have in our minds an idea of its framework. It falls into four definite divisions.

(i) Chapters 1–8, which deal with the problem of righteousness.

(ii) Chapters 9–11, which deal with problem of the Jews, the chosen people.

(iii) Chapters 12–15, which deal with practical questions of life and living.

(iv) Chapter 16, which is a letter of introduction for Phoebe, and a list of final personal greetings.

(i) When Paul uses the word *righteousness*, he means *a right relationship with God*. The man who is righteous is the man who is in a right relationship with God, and whose life shows it.

Paul begins with a survey of the Gentile world. We have only to look at its decadence and corruption to know that it had not solved the problem of righteousness. He looks at the Jewish world. The Jews had sought to solve the problem of righteousness by meticulous obedience to the law. Paul had tried that way himself, and it had issued in frustration and defeat, because no man on earth can ever fully obey the law, and, therefore, every man must have the continual consciousness of being in debt to God and under his condemnation.

So Paul finds the way to righteousness in the way of utter trust and utter yieldedness. The only way to a right relationship with God is to take him at his word, and to cast oneself, just as one is, on his mercy and love. It is the way of faith. It is to know that the important thing is, not what we can do for God, but what he has done for us. For Paul the centre of the Christian faith was that we can never earn or deserve the favour of God, nor do we need to. The whole matter is one of grace, and all that we can do is to accept in wondering love and gratitude and trust what God has done for us.

That does not free us, however, from obligations or entitle us to do as we like; it means that for ever and for ever we must try to be worthy of the love which does so much for us. But we are no longer trying to fulfil the demands of stern and austere and condemnatory law; we are no longer like criminals before a judge; we are lovers who have given all life in love to the one who first loved us.

(ii) The problem of the Jews was a torturing one. In a real sense they were God's chosen people, and yet, when his Son had come into the world, they had rejected him. What possible explanation could there be for this heart-breaking fact?

The only one Paul could find was that, in the end, it was all God's doing. Somehow the hearts of the Jews had been hardened; but it was not all failure, for there had always been a faithful remnant. Nor was it for nothing, for the very fact that the Jews had rejected Christ opened the door to the Gentiles would bring in the Jews and all men would be saved.

Paul goes further. The Jew had always claimed that he was a member of the chosen people in virtue of the fact that he was a Jew. It was solely a matter of pure racial descent from Abraham. But Paul insists that the real Jew is not the man whose flesh and blood descent can be traced to Abraham. He is the man who has made the same decision of utter yieldedness to God in loving faith which Abraham made. Therefore, Paul argues, there are many pure-blooded Jews who are not Jews in the real sense of the term at all; and there are many people of other nations who are really Jews in the true meaning of that word. The new Israel was not a racial thing at all; it was composed of those who had the same faith as Abraham had had.

(iii) The twelfth chapter of *Romans* is so great an ethical statement that it must always be set alongside the Sermon on the Mount. In it Paul lays down the ethical character of the Christian faith. The fourteenth and fifteenth chapters deal with an ever-recurring problem. In the Church there was a narrower party who believed that they must abstain from certain foods and drinks, and who counted special days and ceremonies as of great importance. Paul thinks of them as the weaker brethren because their faith was dependent on these external things. There was a more liberal party, who had liberated themselves from these external rules and observances. He thinks of them as the brethren who are stronger in the faith. He makes it quite clear that his sympathies are with the more liberal party; but he lays down the great principle that no man must ever do anything to hurt the conscience of a weaker brother or to put a stumbling block in his way. His whole point of view is that we must never do anything which makes it harder for someone else to be a Christian; and that that may well mean the giving up of something, which is right and safe for us, for the sake of the weaker brother. Christian liberty must never be used in such a way that it injures another's life or conscience.

(iv) The fourth section is a recommendation on behalf of Phoebe, a member of the Church at Cenchreae, who is coming to Rome. The letter ends with a list of greetings and a final benediction.

TWO PROBLEMS

The sixteenth chapter has always presented scholars with a problem. Many have felt that it does not really form part of the *Letter to the Romans* at all; and that it is really a letter to some other Church which became attached to *Romans* when Paul's letters were collected. What are their grounds? First and foremost, in this chapter Paul sends greetings to twenty-six different people, twenty-four of whom he mentions by name and all of whom he seems to know very intimately. He can, for instance, say that the mother of Rufus has also been a mother to him. Is it likely that Paul knew intimately twenty-six people in *a Church which he had never visited*? He, in fact, greets far more people in this chapter than he does in any other letter, and yet he had never set foot in Rome. Here is something that needs explanation.

If this chapter was not written to Rome, what was its original destination? It is here that Prisca and Aquila come into the argument. We know that they left Rome in A.D. 52 when Claudius issued his edict banishing the Jews (*Acts* 18: 2). We know that they went with Paul to Ephesus (*Acts* 18: 18). We know that they were in Ephesus when Paul wrote his letter to Corinth, less than two years before he wrote *Romans* (1 *Corinthians* 16: 19). And we know that they were still in Ephesus when the Pastoral Epistles were written (2 *Timothy* 4: 19). It is certain that if we had come across a letter sending greeting to Prisca and Aquila we should have assumed that it was sent to Ephesus, if no other address was given.

Is there any other evidence to make us think that chapter sixteen may have been sent to Ephesus in the first place? There is the perfectly general reason that Paul spent longer in Ephesus than anywhere else, and it would be very natural for him to send greetings to many people there. Paul speaks of Epaenetus, *the first-fruits of Asia*. Ephesus is in Asia, and such a reference, too, would be very natural in a letter to Ephesus, but not so natural in a letter to Rome. *Romans* 16: 17 speaks about *difficulties, in opposition to the doctrine which you have been taught*, which sounds as if Paul was speaking about possible disobedience to his own teaching, and he had never taught in Rome.

It can be argued that the sixteenth chapter was originally addressed to Ephesus, but the argument is not so strong as it looks. For one thing, there is no evidence that the chapter was ever attached anywhere except to the *Letter to the Romans*. For another thing, the odd fact is that Paul does *not* send personal greetings to churches which he knew well. There are no personal greetings in *Thessalonians*, *Corinthians*, *Galatians*, and *Philippians*, all of them letters to churches he knew well; whereas there *are* personal greetings in *Colossians*, although Paul had never set foot in Colosse.

The reason is really quite simple. If Paul had sent personal greetings to churches he knew well, jealousies might well have arisen; on the other hand, when he was writing to churches he had never visited, he liked to establish as many personal links as possible. The very fact that Paul had never been in Rome makes it likely that he *would* try to establish as many personal connections as possible. Again, it is to be remembered that

Prisca and Aquila *were banished by edict* from Rome. What is more likely than that, after the trouble was over, six or seven years later, they would return to Rome and pick up the threads of their business after their stay in other towns? And is it not most likely that many of the other names are names of people who shared in this banishment, who took up temporary residence in other cities, who met Paul there, and who, when the coast was clear, returned to Rome and their old homes? Paul would be delighted to have so many personal contacts in Rome and to seize hold of them.

Further, as we shall see, when we come to study chapter 16 in detail, many of the names—the households of Aristobulus and Narcissus, Amplias, Nereus and others—well suit Rome. In spite of the arguments for Ephesus, we may take it that there is no necessity to detach chapter sixteen from the *Letter to the Romans*.

But there is a more interesting, and a much more important, problem. The early manuscripts show some very curious things with regard to chapters 14, 15 and 16. The only natural place for a doxology is at *the very end. Romans* 16: 25–27 is a doxology, and in most good manuscripts it comes at the end. But in a number of manuscripts it comes at the end of chapter 14; two good manuscripts have it in *both places*; one ancient manuscript has it at the end of chapter 15; two manuscripts have it in *neither place*, but leave an empty space for it. One ancient Latin manuscript has a series of section summaries. The last two are as follows:

50: On the peril of him who grieves his brother by meat.

That is obviously *Romans* 14: 15–23.

51: On the mystery of the Lord, kept secret before his passion but after his passion revealed.

That is equally clearly *Romans* 16: 25–27, the doxology. Clearly, these summaries were made from a manuscript which did not contain chapters fifteen and sixteen. Now there is one thing which sheds a flood of light on this. In one manuscript the mention of Rome in *Romans* 1: 7 and 1: 15 is *entirely omitted*. There is no mention of any destination.

All this goes to show that *Romans* circulated in two forms—one form as we have it with sixteen chapters, and one with fourteen chapters; and perhaps also one with fifteen chapters. The explanation must be this. As Paul wrote it *to Rome*, it had sixteen chapters; but chapters 15 and 16 are private and personal to Rome. Now no other letter gives such a compendium of Paul's doctrine. What must have happened was that *Romans* began to circulate among all the churches, *with the last two local chapters omitted*, except for the doxology. It must have been felt that *Romans* was too fundamental to stop at Rome and so the purely local references were removed and it was sent out to the Church at large. From very early times the Church felt that *Romans* was so great an expression of the mind of Paul that it must become the possession not of one congregation, but of the whole Church. We must remember, as we study it, that men have always looked on *Romans* as the quintessence of Paul's gospel.

ROMANS

A CALL, A GOSPEL AND A TASK

Romans 1: 1—7

> This is a letter from Paul, a slave of Jesus Christ, called to be an
> apostle, set apart to serve the good news of God. This good news
> God promised long ago, through his prophets, in the sacred
> writings. It is good news about his Son, who in his manhood was
> born of David's lineage, who, as a result of his Resurrection from
> the dead, has been proved by the Holy Spirit to be the mighty Son
> of God. It is of Jesus Christ, our Lord, of whom I am speaking,
> through whom we have received grace, and an apostleship to
> awaken a faithful obedience for his sake amongst all the Gentiles.
> You are included amongst these Gentiles, you who have been
> called to belong to Jesus Christ. This is a letter to all the beloved
> in Rome who belong to God, those who have been called to be
> dedicated to him. Grace be to you and peace from God our
> Father, and from the Lord Jesus Christ.

WHEN Paul wrote his letter to the Romans he was writing to a
church which he did not know personally and in which he had
never been. He was writing to a church which was situated in
the greatest city in the greatest empire in the world. Because of
that he chose his words and thoughts with the greatest care.

He begins by giving his own credentials.

(i) He calls himself the slave (*doulos*) of Jesus Christ. In this
word slave there are two backgrounds of thought.

(*a*) Paul's favourite title for Jesus is LORD (*kurios*). In
Greek the word *kurios* describes someone who has undisputed
possession of a person or a thing. It means *master* or *owner* in
the most absolute sense. The opposite of LORD (*kurios*) is
slave (*doulos*). Paul thought of himself as the slave of Jesus
Christ, his Master and his Lord. Jesus had loved him and given
himself for him, and therefore Paul was sure that he no longer

belonged to himself, but entirely to Jesus. On the one side *slave* describes the utter obligation of love.

(*b*) But slave (*doulos*) has another side to it. In the Old Testament it is the regular word to describe the great men of God. Moses was the *doulos* of the Lord (*Joshua* 1: 2). Joshua was the *doulos* of God (Joshua 24: 29). The proudest title of the prophets, the title which distinguished them from other men, was that they were the slaves of God (*Amos* 3: 7; *Jeremiah* 7: 25). When Paul calls himself the slave of Jesus Christ he is setting himself in the succession of the prophets. Their greatness and their glory lay in the fact that they were slaves of God, and so did his.

So then, *the slave of Jesus Christ* describes at one and the same time the obligation of a great love and the honour of a great office.

(ii) Paul describes himself as *called to be an apostle*. In the Old Testament the great men were men who heard and an-swered the call of God. Abraham heard the call of God (*Genesis* 12: 1–3). Moses answered God's call (*Exodus* 3: 10). Jeremiah and Isaiah were prophets because, almost against their will, they were compelled to listen to and to answer the call of God (*Jeremiah* 1: 4, 5; *Isaiah* 6: 8, 9). Paul never thought of himself as a man who had aspired to an honour; he thought of himself as a man who had been given a task. Jesus said to his men, " You did not choose me, but I chose you " (*John* 15: 16). Paul did not think of life in terms of what he wanted to do, but in terms of what God meant him to do.

(iii) Paul describes himself as *set apart to serve the good news of God*. He was conscious of a double setting apart in his life. Twice in his life this very same word (*aphorozein*) is used of him.

(*a*) He was set apart *by God*. He thought of God as separating him for the task he was to do even before he was born (*Galatians* 1: 15). For every man God has a plan; no man's life is purposeless. God sent him into the world to do some definite thing.

(*b*) He was set apart *by men*, when the Holy Spirit told the leaders of the Church at Antioch to separate him and Barnabas for the special mission to the Gentiles (*Acts* 13: 2). Paul was conscious of having a task to do for God and for the Church of God.

(iv) In this setting apart Paul was aware of having received two things. In verse 5 he tells us what these two things were.

(*a*) He had received *grace*. *Grace* always describes some gift wh ch is absolutely free and absolutely unearned. In his pre-Christian days Paul had sought to earn glory in the eyes of men and merit in the sight of God by meticulous observance of the works of the law, and he had found no peace that way. Now he knew that what mattered was not what he could do, but what God had done. It has been put this way, " The law lays down what a man must do; the gospel lays down what God has done." Paul now saw that salvation depended not on what man's effort could do, but on what God's love had done. All was of grace, free and undeserved.

(*b*) He had received *a task*. He was set apart to be the apostle to the Gentiles. Paul knew himself to be chosen not for special honour, but for special responsibility. He knew that God had set him apart, not for glory, but for toil. It may well be that there is a play on words here. Once Paul had been a Pharisee (*Philippians* 3: 5). *Pharisee* may very well mean *The Separated One*. It may be that the Pharisees were so called because they had deliberately separated themselves from all ordinary people an would not even let the skirt of their robe brush against an ordinary man. They would have shuddered at the very thought of the offer of God being made to the Gentiles, who to them were " fuel for the fires of hell." Once Paul had been like that. He had felt himself *separated* in such a way as to have nothing but contempt for all ordinary men. Now he knew himself to be *separated* in such a way that he must spend all his life to bring the news of God's love to every man of every race. Christianity always separates us, but it separates us not for privilege and self-glory and pride, but for service and humility and love for all men.

Besides giving his own credentials Paul, in this passage, sets out in its most essential outline the gospel which he preached. It was a gospel which centred in Jesus Christ (verses 3 and 4). In particular it was a gospel of two things.

(*a*) It was a gospel of the *Incarnation*. He told of a Jesus who was really and truly a man. One of the great early thinkers of the Church summed it up when he said of Jesus, " He became what we are, to make us what he is." Paul preached of someone who was not a legendary figure in an imaginary story, not a demi-god, half god and half man. He preached of one who was really and truly one with the men he came to save.

(*b*) It was a gospel of *the Resurrection*. If Jesus had lived a lovely life and died an heroic death, and if that had been the end of him, he might have been numbered with the great and the heroic, but he would simply have been one among many. His uniqueness is guaranteed forever by the fact of the Resurrection. The others are dead and gone, and have left a memory. Jesus lives on and gives us a presence, still mighty with power.

THE COURTESY OF GREATNESS

Romans 1: 8–15

To begin with, I thank my God for you all through Jesus Christ. I thank him that the story of your faith is told throughout the whole world. God, whom I serve in my spirit in the work of spreading the good news of his Son, is my witness that I continually talk to him about you. In my prayers I am always asking that somehow, soon, at last, I may by God's will succeed in finding a way to come to you. For I yearn to see you, that I may give you a share of some gift which the Spirit gives, so that you may be firmly founded in the faith—what I mean is, that you and I may find encouragement together, I through your faith and you through mine. I want you to know, brothers, that I have often planned to come to you—and up until now I have been prevented from doing so—that I might have some fruit among you too, as I have amongst the rest of the Gentiles. I am under a duty to Greeks and to barbarians, to wise and to foolish. So, then, it is my eager wish to preach the good news to you too in Rome.

AFTER almost nineteen hundred years the warm affection of this passage still breathes through it, and we can feel Paul's great heart throbbing with love for the Church which he had never seen. Paul's problem in writing this letter was that he had never been in Rome and had had no share in founding the Roman Church. He had to make them feel that he was not a trespasser on their preserves, interfering where he had no right to intervene. Before he could do anything else, he had to get alongside them so that the barriers of strangeness and suspicion might be broken down.

(i) Paul, in wisdom and love combined, began with a compliment. He told them that he thanked God for that Christian faith of theirs which all the world knew. There are some people whose tongues are tuned to praise, and others whose tongues are tuned to criticize. There are some people whose eyes are focused to find faults, and others whose eyes are focused to discover virtues. It was said of Thomas Hardy that, if he went into a country field, he would always see, not the wild flowers, but the dung-heap in the corner. But the fact remains that we will always get far more out of people by praising them than by criticizing them. The men who get the best out of others are the men who insist on seeing them at their best.

There never was, and never has been, anything quite so beautiful as the civilization of the Greeks at its highest and its best, and T. R. Glover once said that it was founded on " a blind faith in the average man." One of the great figures of the 1914–18 war was Donald Hankey, who wrote *The Student in Arms*. He saw men at their best and at their worst. He once wrote home, " If I survive this war I want to write a book called ' The Living Goodness,' analysing all the goodness and nobility inherent in plain people, and trying to show how it ought to find fulfilment and expression in the Church." He also wrote a great essay entitled *The Beloved Captain*. He describes how the beloved captain picked out the awkward ones and taught them himself. " He looked at them and they looked at him, and the men pulled themselves together and determined to do their best."

No one can ever even begin to save men unless he first believes in them. A man is a hell-deserving sinner, but he has also a sleeping hero in his soul, and often a word of praise will awaken that sleeping heroism when criticism and condemnation will only produce resentment and despair. Aidan was the apostle to the Saxons. Away back in A.D. 630 the Saxon king had sent to Iona a request that a missionary should be sent to his kingdom to preach the gospel. The missionary came back talking of the " stubborn and barbarous disposition of the English." " The English have no manners," he said, " they behave like savages." He reported that the task was hopeless, and then Aidan spoke. " I think, brother," he said, " that you may have been too severe for such ignorant hearers, and that you should have led them on gently, giving them first the milk of religion before the meat." So Aidan was sent to Northumbria, and his gentleness won for Christ that very people whom the critical severity of his brother monk had repelled.

(ii) Although Paul did not know the people at Rome personally he nevertheless constantly prayed to God for them. It is ever a Christian privilege and duty to bear our loved ones and all our fellow-Christians to the throne of grace. In one of his sermons on the Lord's Prayer, Gregory of Nyssa has a lyrical passage on prayer:

> " The effect of prayer is union with God, and, if someone is with God, he is separated from the enemy. Through prayer we guard our chastity, control our temper and rid ourselves of vanity. It makes us forget injuries, overcomes envy, defeats injustice and makes amends for sin. Through prayer we obtain physical well-being, a happy home, and a strong, well-ordered society.... Prayer is the seal of virginity and a pledge of faithfulness in marriage. It shields the wayfarer, protects the sleeper, and gives courage to those who keep vigil.... It will refresh you when you are weary and comfort you when you are sorrowful. Prayer is the delight of the joyful as well as the solace of the afflicted.... Prayer is intimacy with God and contemplation of the invisible.... Prayer is the enjoyment of things present and the substance of the things to come."

Even if we are separated from people, and even if there is no other gift which we can give to them, we can surround them with the strength and the defence of our prayers.

(iii) Paul, in his humility, was always ready to receive as well as to give. He began by saying that he wished to come to Rome that he might impart to the Roman Church some gift which would confirm them in the faith. And then he changed it. He wished to come to Rome that he and the Roman Church might comfort and strengthen each other, and that each might find precious things in the faith of the other. There are two kinds of teachers. There are those whose attitude is that they are standing above their scholars and telling them what they should and must accept. And there are those who, in effect, say, " Come now, let's learn about this together." Paul was the greatest thinker the Early Church ever produced, and yet, when he thought of the people to whom he longed to preach, he thought of himself not only as giving to them but also as receiving from them. It takes humility to teach as it takes humility to learn.

(iv) Verse 14 has in Greek a double meaning that is almost untranslatable. The Revised Standard Version has it, " I am under obligation both to Greeks and to barbarians." Paul was thinking of two things when he wrote that. He was under obligation because of all the kindness that he had received, and he was under obligation to preach to them. This highly compressed sentence means, " Because of all that I have received from them and because of all it is my duty to give to them, I am under an obligation to all sorts of men."

It may seem strange that Paul speaks of *Greeks* when he is writing to *Romans*. At this time the word Greek had lost its racial sense altogether. It did not mean a native of the country of Greece. The conquests of Alexander the Great had taken the Greek language and Greek thought all over the world. And a Greek was no longer only one who was a Greek by race and birth; he was one who knew the culture and the mind of Greece. A barbarian is literally a man who says *bar-bar*, that is to say a man who speaks an ugly and an unharmonious tongue in contrast with the man who speaks the beautiful, flexible language of Greek. To be a Greek was to be a man of a certain mind and spirit and culture. One of the Greeks said of his own people, " The barbarians may stumble on the truth, but it takes a Greek to understand."

What Paul mean was that his message, his friendship, his obligation was to wise and simple, cultured and uncultured, lettered and unlettered. He had a message for the world, and it was his ambition some day to deliver that message in Rome too.

GOOD NEWS OF WHICH TO BE PROUD

Romans 1: 16, 17

> I am proud of the good news, for it is the power of God which produces salvation for every one who believes, to the Jew first and to the Greek. The way to a right relationship with God is revealed in it when man's faith responds to God's fidelity, just as it stands written, " It is the man who is in a right relationsip with God as a result of his faith who will live."

WHEN we come to these two verses, the preliminaries are over and the trumpet call of Paul's gospel sounds out. Many of the great piano concertos begin with a crashing chord and then state the theme which they are going to develop. The reason is that they were often first performed at private gatherings in great houses. When the pianist first seated himself at the piano, there was still a buzz of conversation. He played the crashing chord to attract the attention of the company, and then, when attention was obtained, the theme was stated. Up to these two verses, Paul has been making contact with the people to whom he was writing; he has been attracting their attention. Now the introduction is over, and the theme is stated.

There are only two verses here, but they contain so much of the quintessence of Paul's gospel that we must spend some considerable time on them.

Paul began by saying that he was proud of the gospel which

it was his privilege to preach. It is amazing to think of the background of that statement. Paul had been imprisoned in Philippi, chased out of Thessalonica, smuggled out of Beroea, laughed at in Athens and in Corinth his message was foolishness to the Greeks and a stumbling-block to the Jews. Out of that background he declared that he was proud of the gospel. There was something in the gospel which made Paul triumphantly victorious over all that men could do to him.

In this passage we meet three great Pauline watchwords, the three foundation pillars of his thought and belief.

(i) There is the conception of *salvation* (*sōtēria*). At this time in history salvation was the one thing for which men were searching. There had been a time when Greek philosophy was speculative. Four and five hundred years before this men had spent their time discussing the problem—what is the one basic element of which the world is composed? Philosophy had been speculative philosophy and it had been natural philosophy. But, bit by bit, as the centuries passed, life fell in. The old landmarks were destroyed. Tyrants and conquerors and perils surrounded men; degeneracy and weakness haunted them; and philosophy changed its emphasis. It became, not speculative, but practical. It ceased to be *natural* philosophy, and became *moral* philosophy. Its one aim was to build " a ring-wall of defence against the advancing chaos of the world."

Epictetus called his lecture room " the hospital for the sick soul." Epicurus called his teaching " the medicine of salvation." Seneca, who was contemporary with Paul, said that all men were looking, *ad salutem*, towards salvation. What we needed, he said, was " a hand let down to lift us up." Men, he said, were overwhelmingly conscious of " their weakness and their inefficiency in necessary things." He himself, he said, was *homo non tolerabilis*, a man not to be tolerated. Men loved their vices, he said with a sort of despair, and hated them at the same time. In that desperate world, Epictetus said, men were seeking a peace " not of Caesar's proclamation, but of God's."

There can seldom have been a time in history when men were more universally seeking for salvation. It was precisely that salvation, that power, that escape, that Christianity came to offer men.

Let us see just what this Christian *sōtēria*, this Christian salvation was.

(*a*) It was *salvation from physical illness*. (*Matthew* 9: 21; *Luke* 8: 36.) It was not a completely other-worldly thing. It aimed at rescuing a man in body and in soul.

(*b*) It was *salvation from danger*. (*Matthew* 8: 25; 14: 30.) It was not that it gave a man a life free from perils and dangers, but it gave him a security of soul no matter what was happening. As Rupert Brooke wrote in the days of the First World War in his poem *Safety*:

> " Safe shall be my going,
>   Secretly armed against all death's endeavour;
>   Safe though all safety's lost; safe where men fall;
>   And if these poor limbs die, safest of all."

And as Browning had it in *Paracelsus*:

> " If I stoop,
>   Into a dark tremendous sea of cloud,
>   It is but for a time; I press God's lamp
>   Close to my breast; its splendour, soon or late,
>   Will pierce the gloom: I shall emerge one day."

The Christian salvation makes a man safe in a way that is independent of any outward circumstance.

(*c*) It was *salvation from life's infection*. It is from a crooked and perverse generation that a man is saved (*Acts* 2: 40). The man who has this Christian salvation has a kind of divine antiseptic which keeps him from infection by the evil of the world.

(*d*) It was *salvation from lostness* (*Matthew* 18: 11; *Luke* 19: 10). It was to seek and to save the lost that Jesus came. The unsaved man is the man who is on the wrong road, a road that leads to death. The saved man is the man who has been put on the right way.

(*e*) It was *salvation from sin* (*Matthew* 1: 21). Men are like slaves in bondage to a master from whom they cannot escape.

The Christian salvation liberates them from the tyranny of sin.

(*f*) It was salvation from *the wrath of God* (*Romans* 5: 9). We shall have occasion in the next passage to discuss the meaning of this phrase. It is sufficient to note at the moment that there is in this world an inexorable moral law and in the Christian faith an inevitable element of judgment. Without the salvation which Jesus Christ brings a man could only stand condemned.

(*g*) It was *a salvation which is eschatological.* That is to say it is a salvation which find its full meaning and blessedness in the final triumph of Jesus Christ (*Romans* 13: 11; 1 *Corinthians* 5: 5; 2 *Timothy* 4: 18; 1 *Peter* 1: 5).

The Christian faith came to a desperate world offering a salvation which would keep a man safe in time and in eternity.

(ii) There is the conception of *faith.* In the thought of Paul this is a rich word.

(*a*) At its simplest it means *loyalty.* When Paul wrote to the Thessalonians, he wished to know about their *faith.* That is, he wished to know how their loyalty was standing the test. In 2 *Thessalonians* 1: 4 *faith* and *steadfastness* are combined. Faith is the enduring fidelity which marks the real soldier of Jesus Christ.

(*b*) *Faith* means *belief.* It means the conviction that something is true. In 1 *Corinthians* 15: 17 Paul tells the Corinthians that if Jesus did not rise from the dead, then their faith is vain, all that they have believed is wrecked. Faith is the assent that the Christian message is true.

(*c*) *Faith* sometimes means *the Christian Religion* (*The Faith*). In 2 *Corinthians* 13: 5 Paul tells his opponents to examine themselves to see if they are *holding to their faith*, that is, to see if they are still within the Christian Religion.

(*d*) *Faith* is sometimes practically equivalent to *indestructible hope.* " We walk," writes Paul, " by *faith* and not by sight " (2 *Corinthians* 5: 7).

(*e*) But, in its most characteristic Pauline use, *faith* means *total acceptance* and *absolute trust.* It means " betting your life that there is a God." It means being utterly sure that what Jesus said is true, and staking all time and eternity on that assurance.

" I believe in God," said Stevenson, " and if I woke up in hell I would still believe in him."

Faith begins with *receptivity*. It begins when a man is at least willing to listen to the message of the truth. It goes on to *mental assent*. A man first hears and then agrees that this is true. But mental assent need not issue in action. Many a man knows very well that something is true, but does not change his actions to meet that knowledge. The final stage is when this mental assent becomes *total surrender*. In full-fledged faith, a man hears the Christian message, agrees that it is true, and then casts himself upon it in a life of total yieldedness.

(iii) There is the conception of *justification*. Now there are no more difficult words to understand than justification, justify, justice and just, in all the New Testament. We shall have much occasion in this letter to meet them. At this point we can only lay down the broad lines on which all Paul's thought proceeds.

The Greek verb that Paul uses for *to justify* is *dikaioun*, of which the first person singular of the present indicative—*I justify*—is *dikaioō*. We must be quite clear that the word *justify*, used in this sense, has a different meaning from its ordinary English meaning. If we justify ourselves, we produce reasons to prove that we were right; if someone justifies us, he produces reasons to prove that we acted in the right way. But all verbs in Greek which end in *oō* do not mean to *prove* or to *make* a person or thing to be something; they always mean to *treat*, or *account* or *reckon* a person as something. If God justifies a sinner, it does not mean that he finds reasons to prove that he was right—far from it. It does not even mean, at this point, that he makes the sinner a good man. It means that *God treats the sinner as if he had not been a sinner at all*. Instead of treating him as a criminal to be obliterated, God treats him as a child to be loved. That is what *justification* means. It means that God reckons us not as his enemies but as his friends, not as bad men deserve, but as good men deserve, not as law-breakers to be punished, but as men and women to be loved. That is the very essence of the gospel.

That means that *to be justified* is to enter into a new

relationship with God, a relationship of love and confidence and friendship, instead of one of distance and enmity and fear. We no longer go to a God radiating just but terrible punishment. We go to a God radiating forgiving and redeeming love. Justification (*dikaiosunē*) is the right relationship between God and man. The man who is just (*dikaios*) is the man who is in this right relationship, and—here is the supreme point—he is in it not because of anything that he has done, but because of what God has done. He is in this right relationship not because he has meticulously performed the works of the law, but because in utter faith he has cast himself on the amazing mercy and love of God.

In the Authorized Version we have the famous and highly compressed phrase, *The just shall live by faith.* Now we can see that in Paul's mind this phrase meant—It is the man who is in a right relationship with God, not because of the works of his hands, but because of his utter faith in what the love of God has done, who really knows what life is like in time and in eternity. And to Paul the whole work of Jesus was that he had enabled men to enter into this new and precious relationship with God. Fear was gone and love had come. The God whom men had thought an enemy had become a friend.

THE WRATH OF GOD

Romans 1: 18–23

> For the wrath of God is being revealed from Heaven, directed against all impiousness and wickedness of men, who, in their wickedness, wilfully suppress the truth that is struggling in their hearts, for, that which can be known about God is clear within them, for God has made it clear to them, because, from the creation of the world, it has always been possible to understand the invisible things by the created things—I mean his invisible power and divinity—and things have been so ordered in order to leave them without defence, because, although they knew God, they did not glorify God and they did not give him thanks, but

they have involved themselves in futile speculations and their senseless mind was darkened. They alleged themselves to be wise, but they have become fools, and they have exchanged the glory of the immortal God for the image of the likeness of mortal man, and of winged creatures, and of four-footed animals, and of creeping reptiles.

IN the previous passage Paul was thinking about the relationship with God into which a man can enter through the faith which is utter yieldedness and trust. In contrast with that he sets the wrath of God which a man must incur, if he is deliberately blind to God and worships his own thoughts and idols instead of him.

This is difficult and must give us seriously to think, for here we meet the conception of *the wrath of God*, an alarming and a terrifying phrase. What is its meaning? What was in Paul's mind when he used it?

In the early parts of the Old Testament the wrath of God is specially connected with the idea of the covenant people. The people of Israel were in a special relationship with God. He had chosen them and offered them this special relationship, which would obtain so long as they kept his law (*Exodus* 24: 3–8). That meant two things.

(*a*) It meant that within the nation any breach of the law provoked the wrath of God for it broke the relationship. *Numbers* 16 tells of the rebelliousness of Korah, Dathan and Abiram, and at the end of it Moses bade Aaron make special atonement for the sin of the people " for wrath has gone forth from the Lord " (*Numbers* 16: 46). When the Israelites were led away into Baal worship, " The anger of the Lord was kindled against Israel " (*Numbers* 25: 3).

(*b*) Further, because Israel stood in a unique relationship to God, any other nation which treated her with cruelty and injustice incurred the wrath of God. The Babylonians had ill-treated Israel, and " because of the wrath of the Lord she shall not be inhabited " (*Jeremiah* 50: 13).

In the prophets, the idea of the wrath of God occurs, but the emphasis has changed. Jewish religious thought from the prophets onwards was dominated by the idea of the two ages. There was this age which was altogether bad, and there was the golden age which was altogether good, the present age and the age to come. These two ages were separated by the Day of the Lord. That was to be a day of terrible retribution and judgment, when the world would be shattered, the sinner destroyed and the universe remade before God's Kingdom came. It was then that *the wrath of the Lord* would go into terrible action. " Behold the day of the Lord comes, cruel, with wrath and fierce anger, to make the earth a desolation " (*Isaiah* 13: 9). " Through the wrath of the Lord of hosts " (*Isaiah* 9: 19). *Ezekiel* (7: 19) speaks of " the day of the wrath of the Lord." God will pour out upon the nations " his indignation and all the heat of his anger " (*Zephaniah* 3: 8).

But the prophets did not regard the wrath of God as being postponed until that terrible day of judgment. They saw it continuously in action. When Israel strayed away from God, when she was rebellious and unfaithful, then the wrath of God operated against her and involved her in ruin, disaster, captivity and defeat.

To the prophets the wrath of God was continually operating, and would reach its peak of terror and destruction on the coming Day of the Lord.

A modern scholar has put it this way. Because he is God, because he is characteristically holy, God cannot tolerate sin, and *the wrath of God* is his " annihilating reaction " against sin.

That is hard for us to grasp and to accept. It is in fact the kind of religion that we associate with the Old Testament rather than with the New. Even Luther found it hard. He spoke of God's love as *God's own work*, and he spoke of his wrath as *God's strange work*. It is for the Christian mind a baffling thing.

Let us try to see how Paul understood this conception. Dr C. H. Dodd writes very wisely and profoundly on this matter. Paul speaks frequently of this idea of wrath. But the strange thing is that although he speaks of the wrath of God, *he never speaks of God being angry*. He speaks of God's love, and he speaks of God loving. He speaks of God's grace, and of God graciously giving. He speaks of God's fidelity, and of God being faithful to his people. But, very strangely, although he speaks of the wrath of God, he never speaks about God being angry. So then there is some difference in the connection with God of love and wrath.

Further, Paul speaks of the wrath *of God* only three times. He does so here, and in *Ephesians 5: 6 and Colossians* 3: 6 where, in both passages, he speaks of the wrath of God coming upon the children of disobedience. But quite frequently Paul speaks about *the wrath*, without saying it is the wrath *of God*, as if it ought to be spelled with capital letters—The Wrath—and was a kind of impersonal force at work in the world. In *Romans* 3: 5 the literal translation is, " God who brings on men The Wrath." In *Romans* 5: 9 he speaks about being saved from the wrath. In *Romans* 12: 19 he advises men not to take vengeance but to leave evil-doers to the wrath. In *Romans* 13: 5 he speaks about the wrath as being a powerful motive to keep men obedient. In *Romans* 4: 15 he says that the law produces wrath. And in 1 *Thessalonians* 1: 10 he says that Jesus delivered us from The Wrath to come. Now there is something very strange here. Paul speaks about the wrath, and yet from that very wrath Jesus saves men.

Let us go back to the prophets. Very often their message amounted to this, " If you are not obedient to God, the wrath of God will involve you in ruin and disaster." Ezekiel put this in another vivid way—" The soul that sins shall die " (*Ezekiel* 18: 4). If we were to put this into modern language we would say, " There is a moral order in this world, and the man who transgresses it soon or late is bound to suffer." That is exactly what J. A. Froude the great historian said: " One lesson, and one lesson only, history may be said to repeat with distinctness, that the world is built somehow on moral foundations, that, in the long run, it is well with the good, and, in the long run, it will be ill with the wicked."

The whole message of the Hebrew prophets was that there is a moral order in this world. The conclusion is clear—*that moral order is the wrath of God at work.* God made this world in such a way that we break his laws at our peril. Now if we were left solely at the mercy of that inexorable moral order, there could be nothing for us but death and destruction. The world is made in such a way that the soul that sins must die—if the moral order is to act alone. But into this dilemma of man there comes the love of God, and that love of God, by an act of unbelievable free grace, lifts man out of the consequences of sin and saves him from the wrath he should have incurred.

Paul goes on to insist that men cannot plead ignorance of God. They could have seen what he is like from his world. It is always possible to tell something of a man from his handiwork; and it is possible to tell something about God from the world he made. The Old Testament writers knew that. *Job*, chapters 38 to 41, is based on that very idea. Paul knew it. It is from the world that he starts when he is speaking to the pagans at Lystra (*Acts* 14: 17). Tertullian, the great early Christian Father, has much about this conviction that God can be seen in his world. " It was not the pen of Moses that initiated the knowledge of the Creator.... The vast majority of mankind, though they had never heard the name of Moses—to say nothing of his book— know the God of Moses none the less." " Nature," he said, " is the teacher; the soul is the pupil." " One flower of the hedgerow by itself, I think—I do not say a flower of the meadows; one shell of any sea you like—I do not say a pearl from the Red Sea; one feather of a moor fowl—to say nothing of a peacock—will they speak to you of a mean Creator? " " If I offer you a rose, you will not scorn its Creator."

In the world we can see God. It is Paul's argument—and it is completely valid—that if we look at the world we see that *suffering follows sin.* Break the laws of agriculture—your harvest fails. Break the laws of architecture—your building collapses. Break the laws of health—your body suffers. Paul was saying ' Look at the world! See how it is constructed! From a world like that you know what God is like." The sinner is left without excuse.

Paul goes on another step. What did the sinner do? *Instead of looking out to God, he looked into himself.* He involved himself in vain speculations and thought he was wise, while all the time he was a fool. Why? He was a fool because he made *his* ideas, *his* opinions, *his* speculations the standard and the law of life, instead of *the will of God*. The sinner's folly consisted in making " man the master of things." He found his standards in his own opinions and not in the laws of God. He lived in a self-centred instead of a God-centred universe. Instead of walking looking out to God he walked looking into himself, and, like any man who does not look where he is going, he fell.

The result of this was *idolatry*. The glory of God was exchanged for images of human and animal forms. The root sin of idolatry is that it is *selfish*. A man makes an idol. He brings it offerings and addresses prayers to it. Why? *So that his own schemes and dreams may be furthered.* His worship is for his own sake and not for God's.

In this passage we are face to face with the fact that the essence of sin is to put self in the place of God.

MEN WITH WHOM GOD CAN DO NOTHING

Romans 1: 24, 25

> So then God abandoned them to uncleanness in their hearts' passionate desires for pleasure, desires which made them dishonour their bodies among themselves, for they are men who have exchanged the truth of God for falsehood, and who worship and serve the creation more than they do the Creator, who is blessed for ever.   Amen.

THE word translated *desires* (*epithumia*) is the key to this passage. Aristotle defined *epithumia* as *a reaching out after pleasure*. The Stoics defined it as a reaching after pleasure *which defies all reason*. Clement of Alexandria called it an unreasonable reaching for that which will gratify itself. *Epithumia* is the passionate desire for forbidden pleasure. It is the desire which makes men do nameless and shameless things. It is the way of life of a man who has become so completely immersed in the world that he has ceased to be aware of God at all.

It is a terrible thing to talk of God *abandoning* anyone. And yet there are two reasons for that.

(i) God gave man free-will, and he respects that free-will. In the last analysis not even he can interfere with it. In *Ephesians* 4: 19 Paul speaks of men who have abandoned themselves to lasciviousness; they have surrendered their whole will to it. *Hosea* (4: 17) has the terrible sentence: " Ephraim is joined to idols; let him alone." Before man there stands an open choice; and it has to be so. Without choice there can be no goodness and without choice there can be no love. A coerced goodness is not real goodness; and a coerced love is not love at all. If men deliberately choose to turn their backs on God after he has sent his Son Jesus Christ into the world, not even he can do anything about it.

When Paul speaks of God *abandoning* men to uncleanness, the word *abandon* has no angry irritation in it. Indeed, its main note is not even condemnation and judgment, but wistful, sorrowful regret, as of a lover who has done all that he can and can do no more. It describes exactly the feeling of the father when he saw his son turn his back on his home and go out to the far country.

(ii) And yet in this word *abandon* there is more than that—there is judgment. It is one of the grim facts of life that the more a man sins the easier it is to sin. He may begin with a kind of shuddering awareness of what he is doing, and end by sinning without a second thought. It is not that God is punishing him; he is bringing punishment upon himself and steadily making himself the slave of sin. The Jews knew this, and they had certain great sayings upon this idea. " Every fulfilment of duty is rewarded by another; and every transgression is punished by another." " Whosoever strives to keep himself pure receives the power to do so; and whosoever is impure, to him is the door of vice thrown open." " He who erects a fence around himself is fenced, and he who gives himself over is given over."

The most terrible thing about sin is just this power to beget sin. It is the awful responsibility of free-will that it can be used in such a way that in the end it is obliterated and a man becomes the slave of sin, self-abandoned to the wrong way. And sin is always a lie, because the sinner thinks that it will make him happy, whereas in the end it ruins life, both for himself and for others, in this world and in the world to come.

AN AGE OF SHAME

Romans 1: 26, 27

> Because of this God abandoned them to dishonourable passions, for their women exchanged the natural relationship, for the relationship which is against nature; and so did the men, for they gave up the natural relationship with women, and were inflamed with their desire for each other, and men were guilty of shameful conduct with men. So within themselves they received their due and necessary rewards for their error.

ROMANS 1: 26–32 might seem the work of some almost hysterical moralist who was exaggerating the contemporary situation and painting it in colours of rhetorical hyperbole. It describes a situation of degeneracy of morals almost without parallel in human history. But Paul said nothing that the Greek and Roman writers of the age did not themselves say.

(i) It was an age when things seemed, as it were, out of control. Virgil wrote: " Right and wrong are confounded; so many wars the world over, so many forms of wrong; no worthy honour is left to the plough; the husbandmen are marched away and the fields grow dirty; the hook has its curve straightened into the sword-blade. In the East, Euphrates is stirring up the war, in the West, Germany; nay, close-neighbouring cities break their mutual league and draw the sword, and the war god's unnatural fury rages over the whole world; even as when in the circus the chariots burst from their floodgates, they dash into the course, and, pulling desperately at the reins, the driver lets the horses drive him, and the car is deaf to the curb."

It was a world where violence had run amok. When Tacitus came to write the history of this period, he wrote: " I am entering upon the history of a period, rich in disasters, gloomy with wars, rent with seditions, savage in its very hours of peace. . . . All was one delirium of hate and terror; slaves were bribed to betray their masters, freedmen their patrons. He who had no foe was destroyed by his friend." Suetonius, writing of the reign of Tiberius, said: " No day passed but someone was executed." It was an age of sheer, utter terror. " Rome," said Livy, the historian, " could neither bear its ills nor the remedies that might have cured them." Propertius, the poet, wrote: " I see Rome, proud Rome, perishing, the victim of her own prosperity." It was an age of moral suicide. Juvenal, the satirist, wrote: " The earth no longer brings forth any but bad men and cowards. Hence God, whoever he is, looks down, laughs at them and hates them."

To the thinking man it was an age when things seemed out of control, and when, in the background, a man could hear the mocking laughter of the gods. As Seneca said, it was an age " stricken with the agitation of a soul no longer master of itself."

(ii) It was an age of unparalleled luxury. In the public baths of Rome the hot and cold water ran from silver taps. Caligula had even sprinkled the floor of the circus arena with gold dust instead of sawdust. Juvenal said bitterly: " A luxury more ruthless than war broods over Rome. . . . No guilt or deed of lust is wanting since Roman poverty disappeared." " Money, the nurse of debauchery . . . and enervating riches sapped the sinews of the age with foul luxury." Seneca spoke of " money, the ruin of the true honour of things," and said, " we ask not what a thing truly is but what it costs." It was an age so weary of ordinary things that it was avid for new sensations. Lucretius speaks of " that bitterness which flows from the very fountain of pleasure." Crime became the only antidote to boredom, until, as Tacitus said, " the greater the infamy, the wilder the delight."

(iii) It was an age of unparalleled immorality. There had not been one single case of divorce in the first 520 years of the history of the Roman republic. The first Roman recorded as having divorced his wife was Spurius Carvilius Ruga in 234 B.C. But now, as Seneca said, " women were married to be divorced and divorced to be married." Roman high-born matrons dated the years by the names of their husbands, and not by the names of the consuls. Juvenal could not believe that it was possible to have the rare good fortune to find a matron with unsullied chastity. Clement of Alexandria speaks of the typical Roman society lady as " girt like Venus with a golden girdle of vice." Juvenal writes: " Is one husband enough for Iberina? Sooner will you prevail upon her to be content with one eye." He cites the case of a woman who had eight husbands in five years. He cites the incredible case of Agrippina, the empress herself, the wife of Claudius, who at night used to leave the royal palace and go down to serve in a brothel for the sake of sheer lust. " They show a dauntless spirit in those things they basely dare." There is nothing that Paul said about the heathen world that the heathen moralists had not themselves already said. And vice did not stop with the crude and natural vices. Society from top to bottom was riddled with unnatural vice. Fourteen out of the first fifteen Roman Emperors were homosexuals.

So far from exaggerating the picture Paul drew it with restraint—and it was there that he was eager to preach the gospel, and it was there that he was not ashamed of the gospel of Christ. The world needed the power that would work salvation, and Paul knew that nowhere else than in Christ did that power exist.

THE LIFE WHICH HAS LEFT GOD OUT
OF THE RECKONING

Romans 1: 28–32

Just as they have given themselves over to a kind of knowledge that rejects the idea of God, so God has given them over to the kind of mind that all reject. The result is that they do things which it is not fitting for any man to do. They are replete with all evil, villainy, the lust to get, viciousness. They are full of envy, murder, strife, deceit, the spirit which puts the worst construction on everything. They are whisperers, slanderers, haters of God. They are insolent men, arrogant, braggarts, inventors of evil things, disobedient to their parents, senseless breakers of agreements, without natural affections, pitless. They are the kind of men who are well aware that those who do such things deserve death, and yet they not only do them themselves, but also heartily approve of those who do them.

THERE is hardly any passage which so clearly shows what happens to a man when he leaves God out of the reckoning. It is not so much that God sends a judgment on a man, as that a man brings a judgment on himself when he gives no place to God in his scheme of things. When a man banishes God from his life he becomes a certain kind of man, and in this passage is one of the most terrible descriptions in literature of the kind of man he becomes. Let us look at the catalogue of dreadful things which enter into the godless life.

Such men do things which are not fitting for any man to do. The Stoics had a phrase. They talked of *ta kathēkonta*, by which they meant *the things it befits a man to do*. Certain things are essentially and inherently part of manhood, and certain things are not. As Shakespeare has it in *Macbeth*:

> " I dare do all that may become a man;
>   Who dares do more is none."

The man who banishes God not only loses godliness; he loses manhood too.

Then comes the long list of terrible things. Let us take them one by one.

Evil (*adikia*). *Adikia* is the precise opposite of *diaiosunē*, which means *justice*; and the Greeks defined *justice* as *giving to God and to men their due*. The *evil* man is the man who robs both man and God of their rights. He has so erected an altar to himself in the centre of things that he worships himself to the exclusion of God and man.

Villainy (*ponēria*). In Greek this word means more than *badness*. There is a kind of badness which, in the main, hurts only the person concerned. It is not essentially an outgoing badness. When it hurts others, as all badness must, the hurt is not deliberate. It may be thoughtlessly cruel, but it is not callously cruel. But the Greeks defined *ponēria* as *the desire of doing harm*. It is the active, deliberate will to corrupt and to inflict injury. When the Greeks described a woman as *ponēra* they meant that she deliberately seduced the innocent from their innocence. In Greek one of the commonest titles of Satan is *ho ponēros*, *the evil one*, the one who deliberately attacks and aims to destroy the goodness of men. *Ponēros* describes the man who is not only bad but wants to make everyone as bad as himself. *Ponēria* is destructive badness.

The lust to get (*pleonexia*). The Greek word is built up of two words which mean *to have more*. The Greeks themselves defined *pleonexia* as *the accursed love of having*. It is an aggressive vice. It has been described as the spirit which will pursue its own interests with complete disregard for the rights of others, and even for the considerations of common humanity. Its keynote is *rapacity*. Theodoret, the Christian writer, describes it as the spirit that aims at more, the spirit which grasps at things which it has no right to take. It may operate in every sphere of life. If it operates in the material sphere, it means grasping at money and goods, regardless of honour and honesty. If it operates in the ethical sphere, it means the ambition which tramples on others to gain something which is not properly meant for it. If it operates in the moral sphere, it means the unbridled lust which takes its pleasure where it has no right to take. *Pleonexia* is the desire which knows no law.

Viciousness (*kakia*). *Kakia* is the most general Greek word for badness. It describes the case of a man who is destitute of every quality which would make him good. For instance, a *kakos kritēs* is a judge destitute of the legal knowledge and the moral sense and uprightness of character which are necessary to make a good judge. It is described by Theodoret as " the *turn* of the soul to the worse." The word he uses for turn is *ropē* which means *the turn of the balance*. A man who is *kakos* is a man the swing of whose life is towards the worse. *Kakia* has been described as the essential viciousness which includes all vice and as the forerunner of all other sins. It is the degeneracy out of which all sins grow and in which all sins flourish.

Envy (*phthonos*). There is a good and a bad envy. There is the envy which reveals to a man his own weakness and inadequacy, and which makes him eager to copy some great example. And there is the envy which is essentially a grudging thing. It looks at a fine person, and is not so much moved to aspire to that fineness, as to resent it. It is the most warped and twisted of human emotions.

Murder (*phonos*). It has always to be remembered that Jesus immeasurably widened the scope of this word. He insisted that not only the deed of violence but the spirit of anger and hatred must be eliminated. He insisted that it is not enough only to keep from angry and savage action. It is enough only when even the desire and the anger are banished from the heart. We may never have struck a man in our lives, but who can say he never wanted to strike anyone? As Aquinas said long ago, " Man regardeth the deed, but God seeth the intention."

Strife (*eris*). Its meaning is the *contention* which is born of envy, ambition, the desire for prestige, and place and prominence. It comes from the heart in which there is jealousy. If a man is cleansed of jealousy, he has gone far to being cleansed of all that arouses contention and strife. It is a God-given gift to be able to take as much pleasure in the successes of others as in one's own.

Deceit (*dolos*). We best get the meaning of this from the corresponding verb (*doloun*). *Doloun* has two characteristic usages. It is used of debasing precious metals and of adulterating wines. *Dolos* is *deceit*; it describes the quality of the man who has a tortuous and a twisted mind, who cannot act in a straightforward way, who stoops to devious and underhand methods to get his own way, who never does anything except with some kind of ulterior motive. It describes the crafty cunning of the plotting intriguer who is found in every community and every society.

The spirit which puts the worst construction on everything (*kakoētheia*). *Kakoētheia* means literally *evil-naturedness*. At its widest it means *malignity*. Aristotle defined it in a narrower sense which it has always retained. He said it was " the spirit which always supposes the worst about other people." Pliny called it " malignity of interpretation." Jeremy Taylor said that it is " a baseness of nature by which we take things by the wrong handle, and expound things always in the worst sense." It may well be that this is the commonest of all sins. If there are two possible constructions to be put upon the action of any man, human nature will choose the worse. It is terrifying to think how many reputations have been murdered in gossip over the teacups, with people maliciously putting a wrong interpretation upon a completely innocent action. When we are tempted so to do, we ought to remember that God hears and remembers every word we speak.

Whisperers and slanderers (*Psithuristēs* and *katalalos*). These two words describe people with slanderous tongues; but there is a difference between them. *Katalalos*, slanderer, describes the man who trumpets his slanders abroad; he quite openly makes his accusations and tells his tales—*Psithuristēs* describes the man who whispers his malicious stories in the listener's ear, who takes a man apart into a corner and whispers a character-destroying story. Both are bad, but the whisperer is the worse. A man can at least defend himself against an open slander, but he is helpless against the secret whisperer who delights in destroying reputations.

Haters of God (*theostugeis*). This describes the man who

hates God because he knows that he is defying him. God is the barrier between him and his pleasures; he is the chain which keeps him from doing exactly as he likes. He would gladly eliminate God if he could, for to him a godless world would be one where he would have, not liberty, but licence.

Insolent men (*hubristēs*). *Hubris* was to the Greek the vice which supremely courted destruction at the hand of the gods. It has two main lines of thought in it. (i) It describes the spirit of the man who is so proud that he defies God. It is the insolent pride that goes before a fall. It is the forgetting that man is a creature. It is the spirit of the man who is so confident in his wealth, his power and his strength that he thinks that he can live life alone. (ii) It describes the man who is wantonly and sadistically cruel and insulting. Aristotle describes it as the spirit which harms and grieves someone else, not for the sake of revenge and not for any advantage that may be gained from it, but simply for the sheer pleasure of hurting. There are people who get pleasure from seeing someone wince at a cruel saying. There are people who take a devilish delight in inflicting mental and physical pain on others. That is *hubris*; it is the sadism which finds delight in hurting others simply for the sake of hurting them.

Arrogant men (*huperēphanos*). This is the word which is three times used in scripture when it is said that God resists the *proud*. (*James* 4: 6; *1 Peter* 5: 5; *Proverbs* 3: 34.) Theophylact called it " the summit of all sins." Theophrastus was a Greek writer who wrote a series of famous character sketches, and he defined *huperēphania* as " a certain contempt for everyone except oneself." He picks out the things in everyday life which are signs of this arrogance. The arrogant man, when he is asked to accept some office, refuses on the ground that he has not time to spare from his own business; he never looks at people on the street unless it pleases him to do so; he invites a man to a meal and then does not appear himself, but sends his servant to attend to his guest. His whole life is surrounded with an atmosphere of contempt and he delights to make others feel small.

Braggarts (alazōn). Alazōn is a word with an interesting history. It literally means *one who wanders about.* It then became the stock word for wandering quacks who boast of cures that they have worked, and for cheapjacks who boast that their wares have an excellence which they are far from possessing. The Greeks defined *alazoneia* as the spirit which pretends to have what it has not. Xenophon said that the name belongs to those who pretend to be richer and braver than they are, and who promise to do what they are really unable to do in order to make some profit or gain. Again Theophrastus has a character study of such a man—*the pretentious man, the snob.* He is the kind of man who boasts of trade deals which exist only in his imagination, of connections with influential people which do not exist at all, of gifts to charities and public services which he never gave or rendered. He says about the house he lives in that it is really too small for him, and that he must buy a bigger one. The braggart is out to impress others—and the world is still full of his like.

Inventors of evil (epheuretēs kakōn). The phrase describes the man who, so to speak, is not content with the usual, ordinary ways of sinning, but who seeks out new and recondite vices because he has grown blasé and seeks a new thrill in some new sin.

Disobedient to their parents (goneusin apeitheis). Both Jews and Romans set obedience to parents very high in the scale of virtues. It was one of the Ten Commandments that parents should be honoured. In the early days of the Roman Republic, the *patria potestas,* the father's power, was so absolute that he had the power of life and death over his family. The reason for including this sin here is that, once the bonds of the family are loosened, wholesale degeneracy must necessarily follow.

Senseless (asunetos). This word describes the man who is a fool, who cannot learn the lesson of experience, who will not use the mind and brain that God has given to him.

Breakers of agreements (asunthetos). This word would come with particular force to a Roman audience. In the great days of Rome, Roman honesty was a wonderful thing. A man's word was as good as his bond. That was in fact one of the great differences between the Roman and the Greek. The Greek was a born pilferer. The Greeks used to say that if a governor or official was entrusted with one talent—£240—even if there were ten clerks and accountants to check up on him, he was certain to succeed in embezzling some of it; while the Roman, whether as a magistrate in office or a general on a campaign, could deal with thousands of talents on his bare word alone, and never a penny went astray. By using this word, Paul was recalling the Romans not only to the Christian ethic, but to their own standards of honour in their greatest days.

Without natural affections (*astorgos*). *Storgē* was the special Greek word for family love. It was quite true that this was an age in which family love was dying. Never was the life of the child so precarious as at this time. Children were considered a misfortune. When a child was born, it was taken and laid at the father's feet. If the father lifted it up that meant that he acknowledged it. If he turned away and left it, the child was literally thrown out. There was never a night when there were not thirty or forty abandoned children left in the Roman forum. Even Seneca, great soul as he was, could write: " We kill a mad dog; we slaughter a fierce ox; we plunge the knife into sickly cattle lest they taint the herd; *children who are born weakly and deformed we drown.*" The natural bonds of human affection had been destroyed.

Pitiless (*aneleēmōn*). There never was a time when human life was so cheap. A slave could be killed or tortured by his master, for he was only a thing and the law gave his master unlimited power over him. In a wealthy household a slave was bringing in a tray of crystal glasses. He stumbled and a glass fell and broke. There and then his master had him flung into the fish pond in the middle of the courtyard where the savage lampreys devoured his living flesh. It was an age pitiless in its very pleasures, for it was the great age of the gladiatorial games where people found their delight in seeing men kill each other. It was an age when the quality of mercy was gone.

Paul says one last thing about these people who have

banished God from life. It usually happens that, even if a man is
a sinner, he knows it, and, even if he allows something in himself,
he knows that it is to be condemned in others. But in those days
men had reached such a level that they sinned themselves and
encouraged others to do so. George Bernard Shaw once said,
" No nation has ever survived the loss of its gods." Here Paul
has given us a terrible picture of what happens when men
deliberately banish God from the reckoning, and, in due time,
Rome perished. Disaster and degeneracy went hand in hand.

THE RESPONSIBILITY OF PRIVILEGE

Romans 2: 1–11

So, then, O man, everyone of you who judges others, you yourself
have no defence. While you judge others, you condemn yourself,
for you who set yourself up as a judge do exactly the same things.
We know that God's judgment is directed against all who do such
things, and that it is based on reality. Are you counting on this, O
man, you who set yourself up as a judge upon people who do such
things and who do them yourself—that you will escape the
condemnation of God? Or, are you treating with contempt the
wealth of his kindness and forbearance and patience, not realizing
that God's kindness is meant to lead you to repentance? In your
obtuseness, and in your impenitent heart, you are storing up for
yourself wrath in the day of wrath, the day when there will be
revealed the righteous judgment of God, who will settle accounts
with each man according to his deeds. To those who sought glory
and honour and immortality in steadfast good work, he will assign
eternal life. To those who were dominated by ambition, who were
disobedient to truth and obedient to evil, there will be wrath and
anger, tribulation and affliction. These things will come upon
every soul of man who does the bad thing, upon the soul of the
Jew first and then of the Greek. But glory and honour and peace
will come to everyone who does the good thing, to the Jew first
and then to the Greek, for there is no favouritism with God.

IN this passage Paul is directly addressing the Jews. The
connection of thought is this. In the foregoing passage Paul had

painted a grim and terrible picture of the heathen world, a world which was under the condemnation of God. With every word of that condemnation the Jew thoroughly agreed. But he never for a moment dreamed that he was under a like condemnation. He thought that he occupied a privileged position. God might be the judge of the heathen, but he was the special protector of the Jews. Here Paul is pointing out forcibly to the Jew that he is just as much a sinner as the Gentile is and that when he is condemning the Gentile he is condemning himself. He will be judged, not on his racial heritage, but by the kind of life that he lives.

The Jews always considered themselves in a specially privileged position with God. " God," they said, " loves Israel alone of all the nations of the earth." " God will judge the Gentiles with one measure and the Jews with another." " All Israelites will have part in the world to come." " Abraham sits beside the gates of hell and does not permit any wicked Israelite to go through." When Justin Martyr was arguing with the Jew about the position of the Jews in the *Dialogue with Trypho*, the Jew said, " They who are the seed of Abraham according to the flesh shall in any case, even if they be sinners and unbelieving and disobedient towards God, share in the eternal Kingdom." The writer of the *Book of Wisdom* comparing God's attitude to Jews and Gentiles said: " These as a father, admonishing them, thou didst prove; but those as a stern king, condemning them, thou didst search out " (*Wisdom* 11: 9). " While therefore thou dost chasten us, thou scourgest our enemies a thousand times more " (*Wisdom* 12: 22). The Jew believed that everyone was destined for judgment except himself. It would not be any special goodness which kept him immune from the wrath of God, but simply the fact that he was a Jew.

To meet this situation Paul reminded the Jews of four things.

(i) He told them bluntly that they were trading on the mercy of God. In verse 4 he uses three great words. He asks them: " Are you treating with contempt the wealth of his *kindness*, and *forbearance* and *patience*? " Let us look at these three great words.

(a) *Kindness* (*chrēstotēs*). Of this Trench says: " It is a beautiful word, as it is the expression of a beautiful idea." There are two words for *good* in Greek; there is *agathos* and there is *chrēstos*. The difference between them is this. The goodness of a man who is *agathos* may well issue in rebuke and discipline and punishment; but the goodness of a man who is *chrēstos* is always essentially kind. Jesus was *agathos* when he drove the moneychangers and the sellers of doves from the Temple in the white heat of his anger. He was *chrēstos* when he treated with loving gentleness the sinning woman who anointed his feet and the woman taken in adultery. So Paul says, in effect, " You Jews are simply trying to take advantage of the great kindness of God."

(b) *Forbearance* (*anochē*). *Anochē* is the word for a *truce*. True, it means a cessation of hostility, but it is a cessation that has a limit. Paul, in effect, is saying to the Jews, " You think that you are safe because God's judgment has not yet descended upon you. But what God is giving you is not *carte blanche* to sin; he is giving you the opportunity to repent and to amend your ways." A man cannot sin forever with impunity.

(c) *Patience* (*makrothumia*). *Makrothumia* is characteristically a word which expresses *patience with people*. Chrysostom defined it as the characteristic of the man who has it in his power to avenge himself and deliberately does not use it. Paul is, in effect, saying to the Jews: " Do not think that the fact that God does not punish you is a sign that he cannot punish you. The fact that his punishment does not immediately follow sin is not a proof of his powerlessness; it is a proof of his patience. You owe your lives to the patience of God."

One great commentator has said that almost everyone has " a vague and undefined hope of impunity," a kind of feeling that " this cannot happen to me." The Jews went further than that; " they openly claimed exemption from the judgment of God." They traded on his mercy, and there are many who to this day seek to do the same.

(ii) Paul told the Jews that they were taking the mercy of God as an invitation to sin rather than as an incentive to repentance. It was Heine who made the famous, cynical statement. He was obviously not worrying about the world to come. He was asked why he was so confident, and his answer was, " God will forgive." He was asked why he was so sure of that, and his reply was, " *C'est son métier* " " It is his trade." Let us think of it in human terms. There are two attitudes to human forgiveness. Suppose a young person does something which is a shame, a sorrow and a heartbreak to his parents, and suppose that in love he is freely forgiven, and the thing is never held against him. He can do one of two things. He can either go and do the same thing again, trading on the fact that he will be forgiven once more; or he can be so moved to wondering gratitude by the free forgiveness that he has received, that he spends his whole life in trying to be worthy of it. It is one of the most shameful things in the world to use love's forgiveness as an excuse to go on sinning. That is what the Jews were doing. That is what so many people still do. The mercy and love of God are not meant to make us feel that we can sin and get away with it; they are meant so to break our hearts that we will seek never to sin again.

(iii) Paul insists that in God's economy there is no most favoured nation clause. There may be nations which are picked out for a special task and for a special responsibility, but none which is picked out for special privilege and special consideration. It may be true, as Milton said, that " When God has some great work he gives it to his Englishmen," but it is a great *work* that is in question, not a great *privilege*. The whole of Jewish religion was based on the conviction that the Jews held a special position of privilege and favour in the eyes of God. We may feel that that is a position which nowadays we are far past. But is it? Is there no such thing nowadays as a colour bar? Is there no such thing as a conscious feeling of superiority to what Kipling called " lesser breeds without the law "? This is not to say that all nations are the same in talent. But it is to say that those nations who have advanced further ought not to look with contempt on the others, but are, rather, under the responsibility to help them move forward.

(iv) Of all passages of Paul this deserves to be studied most carefully in order to arrive at a correct idea of Paulinism. It is often argued that his position was that all that matters is faith. A religion which stresses the importance of works is often contemptuously waved aside as being quite out of touch with the New Testament. Nothing could be further from the truth. " God," said Paul, " will settle with each man according to his deeds." To Paul a faith which did not issue in deeds was a travesty of faith; in fact it was not faith at all. He would have said that the only way in which you can see a man's faith at all is by his deeds. One of the most dangerous of all religious tendencies is to talk as if faith and works were entirely different and separate things. There can be no such thing as faith which does not issue in works, nor can there be works which are not the product of faith. Works and faith are inextricably bound up together. How, in the last analysis, can God judge a man other than by his deeds? We cannot comfortably say, " I have faith," and leave it at that. Our faith must issue in deeds, for it is by our deeds we are accepted or condemned.

THE UNWRITTEN LAW

Romans 2: 12–16

As many as sinned without the law shall also perish without the law; and as many as sinned in the law shall be judged by the law; for it is not the hearers of the law who are righteous in the sight of God, but it is the doers of the law who will be accounted righteous, in that day when God judges the hidden things of men according to my gospel through Jesus Christ. For whenever the Gentiles, who do not possess the law, do by nature the deeds of the law, they, although they do not possess the law, are a law to themselves. They show the work of the law written on their hearts, while their consciences bear them witness, and while their thoughts within accuse or excuse them.

IN the translation we have slightly changed the order of the verses. In the sense of the passage verse 16 follows verse 13, and verses 14 and 15 are a long parenthesis. It is to be remembered that Paul was not writing this letter sitting at a desk and thinking out every word and every construction. He was striding up and down the room dictating it to his secretary, Tertius (*Romans* 16: 22), who struggled to get it down. That explains the long parenthesis, but it is easier to get the correct meaning in English if we go straight from verse 13 to verse 16, and add verses 14 and 15 afterwards.

In this passage Paul turns to the Gentiles. He has dealt with the Jews and with their claims to special privilege. But one advantage the Jew did have, and that was the Law. A Gentile might well retaliate by saying, " It is only right that God should condemn the Jews, who had the Law and who ought to have known better; but we will surely escape judgment because we had no opportunity to know the Law and did not know any better." In answer Paul lays down two great principles.

(i) A man will be judged by what he had the opportunity to know. If he knew the Law, he will be judged as one who knew the Law. If he did not know the Law, he will be judged as one who did not know the Law. God is fair. And here is the answer to those who ask what is to happen to the people who lived in the world before Jesus came and who had no opportunity to hear the Christian message. A man will be judged by his fidelity to the highest that it was possible for him to know.

(ii) Paul goes on to say that even those who did not know the written Law had an unwritten law within their hearts. We would call it the instinctive knowledge of right and wrong. The Stoics said that in the universe there were certain laws operative which a man broke at his peril—the laws of health, the moral laws which govern life and living. The Stoics called these laws *phusis*, which means *nature*, and urged men to live *kata phusin*, according to nature. It is Paul's argument that in the very nature of man there is an instinctive knowledge of what he ought to do. The Greeks would have agreed with that. Aristotle said: " The cultivated and free-minded man will so behave as being *a law to himself*." Plutarch asks: " Who shall govern the governor? " And he answers: " Law, the king of all mortals and immortals, as Pindar calls it, which is not written on papyrus rolls or wooden tablets, but is his own reason within the soul, which perpetually dwells with him and guards him and never leaves his soul bereft of leadership."

Paul saw the world divided into two classes of people. He saw the Jews with their Law given to them direct from God and written down so that all could read it. he saw the other nations, without this written law, but nonetheless with a God-implanted knowledge of right and wrong within their hearts. Neither could claim exemption from the judgment of God. The Jew could not claim exemption on the ground that he had a special place in God's plan. The Gentile could not claim exemption on the ground that he had never received the written Law. The Jew would be judged as one who had known the Law; the Gentile as one who had a God-given conscience. God will judge a man according to what he knows and has the chance to know.

THE REAL JEW

Romans 2: 17–29

If you are called by the name of Jew, if you take your rest in the Law, if you boast in God and know his will, if you give your approval to the excellent things, if you are instructed in the Law, if you believe yourself to be a leader of the blind, a light in darkness, and educator of the foolish, a teacher of the simple, if you believe yourself to have the very shape of knowledge and of truth in the Law—do you, then, who instruct another, not instruct yourself? Do you, who proclaim to others that stealing is forbidden, steal yourself? Do you, who forbid others to commit adultery, commit adultery yourself? Do you, who shudder at idols, rob temples? Do you, who boast in the Law, dishonour others by transgressing the Law? As it stands written, " Because of your conduct, God's name is ill-spoken of among the Gentiles." Circumcision is indeed an advantage if you do the Law. But if you are a transgressor of the Law your circumcision has become the equivalent of un-circumcision. For if uncircumcision observes the moral requirements of the Law, shall not uncircumcision be reckoned as the equivalent of circumcision, and will natural uncircumcision which keeps the Law, not become the judge of you who are a transgressor of the Law, although you have the letter and the circumcision? For he is not a real Jew who is externally a Jew; nor is the real circumcision the external circumcision in the flesh; but he is a real Jew who is a Jew in inward things; and real circumcision is the circumcision of the heart, in spirit, and not in letter. The praise of such a man comes not from men but from God.

To a Jew a passage like this must have come as a shattering experience. He was certain that God regarded him with special favour, simply and solely because of his national descent from Abraham and because he bore the badge of circumcision in his flesh. But Paul introduces an idea to which he will return again and again. Jewishness, he insists, is not a matter of race at all; it has nothing to do with circumcision. It is a matter of conduct. If that is so, many a so-called Jew who is a pure descendant of Abraham and who bears the mark of circumcision in his body, is no Jew at all; and equally many a Gentile who never heard of Abraham and who would never dream of being circumcised, is a Jew in the real sense of the term. To a Jew this would sound the wildest heresy and leave him angry and aghast.

The last verse of this passage contains a pun which is completely untranslatable. " The praise of such a man comes not from men but from God." The Greek word for praise is *epainos*. When we turn back to the Old Testament (*Genesis* 29: 35; 49: 8), we find that the original and traditional meaning of the word *Judah* is *praise* (*epainos*). Therefore this phrase means two things. (*a*) It means the *praise* of such a man comes not from men but from God. (*b*) It means the Jewishness of such a man comes not from men but from God. The sense of the passage is that God's promises are not to people of a certain race and to people who bear a certain mark on their bodies. They are to people who live a certain kind of life irrespective of their race. To be a real Jew is not a matter of pedigree but of character; and often the man who is not racially a Jew may be a better Jew than the man who is.

In this passage Paul says that there are Jews whose conduct makes the name of God ill-spoken of among the Gentiles. It is a simple fact of history that the Jews were, and often still are, the most unpopular people in the world. Let us see just how the Gentiles did regard the Jews in New Testament times.

They regarded Judaism as a " barbarous superstition " and the Jews as " the most disgusting of races," and as " a most contemptible company of slaves." The origins of Jewish religion were twisted with a malicious ignorance. It was said that Jews had originally been a company of lepers who had been sent by the king of Egypt to work in the sand quarries; and that Moses had rallied this band of leprous slaves and led them through the desert to Palestine. It was said that they worshipped an ass's head, because in the wilderness a herd of wild asses had led them to water when they were perishing with thirst. It was said that they abstained from swine's flesh because the pig is specially liable to a skin disease called the itch, and it was that skin disease that the Jews had suffered from in Egypt.

Certain of the Jewish customs were mocked at by the Gentiles. Their abstinence from swine's flesh provided many a jest. Plutarch thought that the reason for it might well be that the Jews worshipped the pig as a god. Juvenal declares that Jewish clemency has accorded to the pig the privilege of living to a good old age, and that swine's flesh is more valuable to them than the flesh of man. The custom of observing the Sabbath was regarded as pure laziness.

Certain things which the Jews enjoyed infuriated the Gentiles. It was the odd fact that, unpopular as they were, the Jews had nonetheless received extraordinary privileges from the Roman government.

(a) They were allowed to transmit the temple tax every year to Jerusalem. This became so serious in Asia about the year 60 B.C. that the export of currency was forbidden and, according to the historians, no less than twenty tons of contraband gold was seized which the Jews had been about to despatch to Jerusalem.

(b) They were allowed, at least to some extent, to have their own courts and live according to their own laws. There is a decree issued by a governor called Lucius Antonius in Asia about the year 50 B.C. in which he wrote: " Our Jewish citizens came to me and informed me that they had their own private gathering, carried out according to their ancestral laws, and their own private place, where they settle their own affairs and deal with cases between each other. When they asked that this custom should be continued, I gave judgment that they should be allowed to retain this privilege." The Gentiles detested the spectacle of a race of people living as a kind of separate and specially privileged group.

(*c*) The Roman government respected the Jewish observance of the Sabbath. It was laid down that the Jew could not be called to give evidence in a law court on the Sabbath. It was laid down that if special doles were being distributed to the populace and the distribution fell on the Sabbath, the Jews could claim their share on the following day. And—a specially sore point with the Gentiles—the Jews enjoyed *astrateia*, that is, exemption from conscription to the Roman army. This exemption was directly due to the fact that the Jewish strict observance of the Sabbath obviously made it impossible for him to carry out military duties on the Sabbath. It can easily be imagined with what resentment the rest of the world would look on this special exemption from a burdensome duty.

There were two special things of which the Jews were accused.

(*a*) They were accused of *atheism* (*atheotēs*). The ancient world had great difficulty in conceiving of the possibility of a religion without any visible images of worship. Pliny called them, " a race distinguished by their contempt for all deities." Tacitus said, " The Jews conceive of their deity as one, by the mind alone, . . . Hence no images are erected in their cities or even in their temples. This reverence is not paid to kings, nor this honour to the Caesars." Juvenal said, " They venerate nothing but the clouds and the deity of the sky." But the truth is that what really moved the Gentile to such dislike, was not so much the imageless worship of the Jews, as the cold contempt in which they held all other religions. No man whose main attitude to his fellows is contempt can ever be a missionary. This contempt for others was one of the things which Paul was thinking of when he said that the Jews brought the name of God into disrepute.

(b) They were accused of *hatred of their fellow-men* (*misanthrōpia*) and *complete unsociability* (*amixia*). Tacitus said of them: " Among themselves their honesty is inflexible, their compassion quick to move, but to all other persons they show the hatred of antagonism." In Alexandria the story was that the Jews had taken an oath never to show kindness to a Gentile, and that they even offered a Greek in sacrifice to their God every year. Tacitus said that the first thing Gentiles converted to Judiasm were taught to do was " to despise the gods, to repudiate their nationality, and to disparage parents, children and brothers." Juvenal declared that if a Jew was asked the way to any place, he refused to give any information except to another Jew, and that if anyone was looking for a well from which to drink, he would not lead him to it unless he was circumcised. Here we have the same thing again. The basic Jewish attitude to other men was contempt and this must ever invite hatred in answer.

It was all too true that the Jews did bring the name of God into disrepute, because they shut themselves into a rigid little community from which all others were shut out and because they showed to the heathen an attitude of contempt for their worship and complete lack of charity for their needs. Real religion is a thing of the open heart and the open door; Judaism was a thing of the shut heart and the shut door.

GOD'S FIDELITY AND MAN'S INFIDELITY

Romans 3: 1–8

What, then, is the something plus which belongs to a Jew? Or what special advantage belongs to those who have been circumcised? Much in every way. In the first place, there is this advantage—that the Jews have been entrusted with the oracles of God. Yes, you say, but what if some of them were unfaithful to them? Surely you are not going to argue that their infidelity invalidates the fidelity of God? God forbid! Let God be shown to be true, though every man be shown to be a liar, as it stands written: " In order that you may be seen to be in the right in your arguments, and that you may win your case when you enter into judgment." But, you say, if our unrighteousness merely provides proof of God's righteousness, what are we to say? Surely you are not going to try to argue that God is unrighteous to unleash the Wrath upon you? (I am using human arguments:) God forbid! For, if that were so, how shall God judge the world? But, you say, if the fact that I am false merely provides a further opportunity to demonstrate the fact that God is true, to his greater glory, why should I still be condemned as a sinner? Are you going to argue—just as some slanderously allege that we suggest—that we should do evil that good may come of it? Anyone can see that statements like that merit nothing but condemnation.

HERE Paul is arguing in the closest and the most difficult way. It will make it easier to understand if we remember that he is carrying on an argument with an imaginary objector. The argument stated in full would run something like this.

The objector: The result of all that you have been saying is that there is no difference between Gentile and Jew and that they are in exactly the same position. Do you really mean that?

Paul: By no means.

The objector: What, then, is the difference?

Paul: For one thing, the Jew possesses what the Gentile never so directly possessed—the commandments of God.

The objector: Granted! But what if some of the Jews disobeyed these commandments and were unfaithful to God and came under his condemnation? You have just said that God gave the Jews a special position and a special promise. Now you go on to say that at least some of them are under the condemnation of God. Does that mean that God has broken his promise and shown himself to be unjust and unreliable?

Paul: Far from it! What it does show is that there is no favouritism with God and that he punishes sin wherever he sees it. The very fact that he condemns the unfaithful Jews is the best possible proof of his absolute justice. He might have been expected to overlook the sins of this special people of his but he does not.

The objector: Very well then! All you have done is to succeed in showing that my disobedience has given God an opportunity to demonstrate his righteousness. My infidelity has given God a marvellous opportunity to demonstrate his fidelity. My sin is, therefore, an excellent thing! It has given God a chance to show how good he is! I may have done evil, but good has come of it! You can't surely condemn a man for giving God a chance to show his justice!

Paul: An argument like that is beneath contempt! You have only to state it to see how intolerable it is!

When we disentangle this passage in this way, we see that there are in it certain basic thoughts of Paul in regard to the Jews.

(i) To the end of the day he believed the Jews to be in a special position in regard to God. That, in fact, is what they believed themselves. The difference was that Paul believed that their special position was one of special *responsibility;* the Jew believed it to be one of special *privilege.* What did Paul say that the Jew had been specially entrusted with? *The oracles of God.* What does he mean by that? The word he uses is *logia*, the regular word in the Greek Old Testament for a special statement or pronouncement of God. Here it means *The Ten Commandments.* God entrusted the Jews with *commandments*, not privileges. He said to them, " You are a special people; therefore you must live a special life." He did *not* say, " You are a special people; therefore you can do what you like." He did say, " You are a special people; *therefore you must do what I like.*" When Lord Dunsany came in safety through the 1914-18 war he tells us that he said to himself, " In some strange way I am still alive. I wonder what God means me to do with a life so specially spared?" That thought never struck the Jews. They never could grasp the fact that God's special choice was for special duty.

(ii) All through his writings there are three basic facts in Paul's mind about the Jews. They occur in embryo here; and they are in fact the three thoughts that it takes this whole letter to work out. We must note that he does not place all the Jews under the one condemnation. He puts it in this way: " What if *some of them* were unfaithful? "

(*a*) He was quite sure that God was justified in condemning the Jews. They had their special place and their special promises; and that very fact made their condemnation all the greater. Responsibility is always the obverse of privilege. The more opportunity a man has to do right, the greater his condemnation if he does wrong.

(*b*) *But* not all of them were unfaithful. Paul never forgot the faithful remnant; and he was quite sure that that faithful remnant—however small it was in numbers—was the true Jewish race. The others had lost their privileges and were under condemnation. They were no longer Jews at all. The remnant was the real nation.

(*c*) Paul was always sure that God's rejection of Israel *was not final*. Because of this rejection, a door was opened to the Gentiles; and, *in the end*, the Gentiles would bring the Jews back within the fold, and Gentile and Jew would be one in Christ. The tragedy of the Jew was that the great task of world evangelization that he might have had, and was designed to have, was refused by him. It was therefore given to the Gentiles, and God's plan was, as it were, reversed, and it was not, as it should have been, the Jew who evangelized the Gentile, but the Gentile who evangelized the Jew—a process which is still going on.

Further, this passage contains two great universal human truths.

(i) The root of all sin is disobedience. The root of the Jew's sin was disobedience to the known law of God. As Milton wrote, it was " man's first disobedience " which was responsible for paradise lost. When pride sets up the will of man against the will of God, there is sin. If there were no disobedience, there would be no sin.

(ii) Once a man has sinned, he displays an amazing ingenuity in justifying his sin. Here we come across an argument that reappears again and again in religious thought, the argument that sin gives God a chance to show at once his justice and his mercy and is therefore a good thing. It is a twisted argument. One might as well argue—it would, in fact, be the same argument—that it is a good thing to break a person's heart, because it gives him a chance to show how much he loves you. When a man sins, the need is not for ingenuity to justify his sin, but for humility to confess it in penitence and in shame.

THE CHRISTLESS WORLD

Romans 3: 9–18

> What then? Are we Jews out ahead? By no means. For we have already charged all Jews and Greeks with being under the power of sin, as it stands written: " There is none righteous, no not one. There is no man of understanding. There is none who seeks the Lord. All have swerved out of the way, and all together have gone bad. There is none whose acts are good, not one single one. Their throat is an open tomb. They practise fraud with their tongues. The poison of asps is under their lips. Their mouths are laden with curses and bitterness. Their feet are swift to shed blood. Destruction and wretchedness are in their ways, and they have not known the way of peace. There is no fear of God before their eyes."

IN the last passage Paul had insisted that, in spite of everything, the Jew had a special position in the economy of God. Not unnaturally the Jewish objector then asks if that means that the Jews are out ahead of other peoples. Paul's answer is that Jew and Gentile alike, so long as they are without Christ, are under the dominion of sin. The Greek phrase that he uses for under sin is very suggestive, *hupo hamartian*. In this sense *hupo* means *in the power of, under the authority of*. In *Matthew* 8: 9 the centurion says: " I have soldiers *hupo emauton, under me*."

That is, I have soldiers *under my command*. A schoolboy is *hupo paidagōgon, under the direction* of the slave who is in control of him. A slave is *hupo zugon, under the yoke* of his master. In the Christless state a man is under the control of sin, and helpless to escape from it.

There is one other interesting word in this passage. It is the word in verse 12 which we have translated. " They have gone bad." The word is *achreioō*, which literally means *to render useless*. One of its uses is of milk that has gone sour. Human nature without Christ is a soured and useless thing.

We see Paul doing here what Jewish Rabbis customarily did. In verses 10–18 he has strung together a collection of Old Testament texts. He is not quoting accurately, because he is quoting from memory, but he includes quotations from *Psalm* 14: 1–3; *Psalm* 5: 9; *Psalm* 140: 3; *Psalm* 10: 7; *Isaiah* 59: 7, 8; *Psalm* 36: 1. It was a very common method of Rabbinic preaching to string texts together like this. It was called *charaz*, which literally means *stringing pearls*.

It is a terrible description of human nature in its Christless state. Vaughan has pointed out that these Old Testament quotations describe three things. (i) A *character* whose characteristics are ignorance, indifference, crookedness and unprofitableness. (ii) A *tongue* whose notes are destructive, deceitful, malignant. (iii) A *conduct* whose marks are oppression, injuriousness, implacability. These things are the result of disregard of God.

No one saw so clearly the evil of human nature as Paul did; but it must always be noted that the evil of human nature was to him, not a call to hopelessness, but a challenge to hope. When we say that Paul believed in original sin and the depravity of human nature, we must never take that to mean that he despaired of human nature or looked on it with cynical contempt. Once, when William Jay of Bath was an old man, he said: " My memory is failing, but there are two things that I never forget—that I am a great sinner and that Jesus Christ is a great Saviour."

Paul never underrated the sin of man and he never underrated the redeeming power of Jesus Christ. Once, when he was a young man, William Roby, the great Lancashire Independent, was preaching at Malvern. His lack of success drove him to despair, and he wished to leave the work. Then came a seasonable reproof from a certain Mr Moody, who asked him, " Are they, then, too bad to be saved? " The challenge sent William Roby back to his work. Paul believed men without Christ to be bad, but he never believed them too bad to be saved. He was confident that what Christ had done for him Christ could do for any man.

THE ONLY WAY TO BE RIGHT WITH GOD

Romans 3: 19–26

> We know that whatever the law says, it says to those who are within the law, and the function of the law is that every mouth should be silenced and that the whole world should be known to be liable to the judgment of God, because no one will ever get into a right relationship with God by doing the works which the law lays down. What does come through the law is a full awareness of sin. But now a way to a right relationship to God lies open before us quite apart from the law, and it is a way attested by the law and the prophets. For a right relationship to God comes through faith in Jesus Christ to all who believe. For there is no distinction, for all have sinned and all fall short of the glory of God, but they are put into a right relationship with God, freely, by his grace, through the deliverance which is wrought by Jesus Christ. God put him forward as one who can win for us forgiveness of our sins through faith in his blood. He did so in order to demonstrate his righteousness because, in the forbearance of God, there had been a passing over of the sins which happened in previous times; and he did so to demonstrate his righteousness in this present age, so that he himself should be just and that he should accept as just the man who believes in Jesus.

HERE again is a passage which is not easy to understand, but which is full of riches when its true meaning is grasped. Let us see if we can penetrate to the basic truth behind it.

The supreme problem of life is, How can a man get into a

right relationship with God? How can he feel at peace with
God? How can he escape the feeling of estrangement and fear
in the presence of God? The religion of Judaism answered: " A
man can attain to a right relationship with God by keeping
meticulously all that the law lays down." But to say that is
simply to say that there is no possibility of any man ever
attaining to a right relationship with God, for no man ever
can keep every commandment of the law.

> " Not the labours of my hands
> Can fulfil thy law's demands."

What then is the use of the law? It is that it makes a man aware
of sin. It is only when a man knows the law and tries to satisfy
it that he realizes he can never satisfy it. The law is designed to
show a man his own weakness and his own sinfulness. Is a man
then shut out from God? Far from it, because the way to God is
not the way of law, but the way of grace; not the way of works,
but the way of faith.

To show what he means Paul uses three metaphors.

(i) He uses a metaphor from the *law courts* which we call
justification. This metaphor thinks of man on trial before God.
The Greek word which is translated *to justify* is *diakioun*. All
Greek verbs which end in *-oun* mean, not to *make* someone
something, but to *treat*, to *reckon*, to *account* him as something.
If an innocent man appears before a judge then to treat him as
innocent is to *acquit* him. But the point about a man's
relationship to God is that he is utterly guilty, and yet God, in
his amazing mercy, treats him, reckons him, accounts him as if
he were innocent. That is what justification means.

When Paul says that " God justifies the ungodly," he means
that God treats the ungodly as if he had been a good man. That
is what shocked the Jews to the core of their being. To them to
treat the bad man as if he was good was the sign of a wicked
judge. " He who justifies the wicked is an abomination to the
Lord " (*Proverbs* 17: 15). " I will not acquit the wicked "
(*Exodus* 23: 7). But Paul says that is precisely what God does.

How can I know that God is like that? I know *because Jesus said so*. He came to tell us that God loves us, bad as we are. He came to tell us that, although we are sinners, we are still dear to God. When we discover that and believe it, *it changes our whole relationship to God*. We are conscious of our sin, but we are no longer in terror and no longer estranged. Penitent and brokenhearted we come to God, like a sorry child coming to his mother, and we know that the God we come to is love.

That is what *justification by faith in Jesus Christ* means. It means that we are in a right relationship with God because we believe with all our hearts that what Jesus told us about God is true. We are no longer terrorized strangers from an angry God. We are children, erring children, trusting in their Father's love for forgiveness. *And we could never have found that right relationship with God, if Jesus had not come to live and to die to tell us how wonderfully he loves us*.

(ii) Paul uses a metaphor from *sacrifice*. He says of Jesus that God put him forward as one who can win forgiveness for our sins.

The Greek word that Paul uses to describe Jesus is *hilastērion*. This comes from a verb which means *to propitiate*. It is a verb which has to do with sacrifice. Under the old system, when a man broke the law, he brought to God a sacrifice. His aim was that the sacrifice should turn aside the punishment that should fall upon him. To put it in another way—a man sinned; that sin put him at once in a wrong relationship with God; to get back into the right relationship he offered his sacrifice.

But it was human experience that an animal sacrifice failed entirely to do that. " Thou hast no delight in sacrifice; were I to give a burnt offering, thou wouldst not be pleased " (*Psalm* 51: 16). " With what shall I come before the Lord, and bow myself before God on high? Shall I come before him with burnt offerings, with calves a year old? Will the Lord be pleased with thousands of rams, with ten thousands of rivers of oil? Shall I give my first-born for my transgression, the fruit of my body for the sin of my soul? " (*Micah* 6: 6, 7.) Instinctively men felt that, once they had sinned, the paraphernalia of earthly sacrifice could not put matters right.

So Paul says, " Jesus Christ, by his life of obedience and his death of love, made the one sacrifice to God which really and truly atones for sin." He insists that what happened on the Cross opens the door back to a right relationship with God, a door which every other sacrifice is powerless to open.

(iii) Paul uses a metaphor from *slavery*. He speaks of the *deliverance* wrought through Jesus Christ. The word is *apolutrōsis*. It means a ransoming, a redeeming, a liberating. It means that man was in the power of sin, and that Jesus Christ alone could free him from it.

Finally, Paul says of God that he did all this because he is just, and accepts as just all who believe in Jesus. Paul never said a more startling thing than this. Bengel called it " the supreme paradox of the gospel." Think what it means. It means that God is just and accepts the sinner as a just man. The natural thing to say would be, " God is just, and, therefore, condemns the sinner as a criminal." But here we have the great paradox—God is just, and somehow, in that incredible, miraculous grace that Jesus came to bring to men, he accepts the sinner, not as a criminal, but as a son whom he still loves.

What is the essence of all this? Where is the difference between it and the old way of the law? The basic difference is this—the way of obedience to the law is concerned with what a man can do for himself; the way of grace is concerned with what God can do, and has done, for him. Paul is insisting that nothing we can ever do can win for us the forgiveness of God; only what God has done for us can win that; therefore the way to a right relationship with God lies, not in a frenzied, desperate, doomed attempt to win acquittal by our performance; it lies in the humble, penitent acceptance of the love and the grace which God offers us in Jesus Christ.

THE END OF THE WAY OF HUMAN ACHIEVEMENT

Romans 3: 27–31

Where, then, is there any ground for boasting? It is completely shut out. Through what kind of law? Through the law of works? No, but through the law of faith. So, then, we reckon that a man enters into a right relationship with God by faith quite apart from works of the law. Or, is God the God of the Jews only? Is he not the God of the Gentiles? Yes, he is the God of the Gentiles too. If, indeed, God is one, he is the God who will bring those who are of the circumcision into a right relationship with himself by faith, and those who never knew the circumcision through faith. Do we then through faith completely cancel out all law? God forbid! Rather, we confirm the law.

PAUL deals with three points here.

(i) If the way to God is the way of faith and of acceptance, then all boasting in human achievement is gone. There was a certain kind of Judaism which kept a kind of profit and loss account with God. In the end a man often came to a frame of mind in which he rather held that God was in his debt. Paul's position was that every man is a sinner and God's debtor, that no man could ever put himself back into a right relationship with God through his own efforts and that grounds for self-satisfaction and boasting in one's own achievement no longer exist.

(ii) But, a Jew might answer, that might be well enough for a Gentile who never knew the law, but what about Jews who do know it? Paul's answer was to turn them to the sentence which is the basis of the Jewish creed, the sentence with which every synagogue service always began and still begins. " Hear, O Israel, the Lord our God is one God " (*Deuteronomy* 6: 4). There is not one God for the Gentiles and another for the Jews. God is *one*. The way to him is the same for Gentile and Jew. It is not the way of human achievement; it is the way of trusting and accepting faith.

(iii) But, says the Jew, does this mean an end of all law? We might have expected Paul to say, " Yes." In point of fact he says, " No." He says that, in fact, it strengthens the law. He means this. Up to this time the Jew had tried to be a good man and keep the commandments because he was afraid of God, and was terrified of the punishment that breaches of the law would bring. That day has for ever gone. But what has taken its place is *the love of God*. Now a man must try to be good and keep God's law, not because he fears God's punishment, but because he feels that he must strive to deserve that amazing love. He strives for goodness, not because he is afraid of God, but because he loves him. He knows now that sin is not so much breaking God's law as it is breaking God's heart, and, therefore, it is doubly terrible.

Take a human analogy. Many a man is tempted to do a wrong thing, and does not do it. It is not so much that he fears the law. He would not greatly care if he were fined, or even imprisoned. What keeps him right is the simple fact that he could not meet the sorrow that would be seen in the eyes of the one who loves him if he made shipwreck of his life. It is not the law of fear but the law of love which keeps him right. It must be that way with us and God. We are rid forever of the terror of God, but that is no reason for doing as we like. We can never again do as we like for we are now for ever constrained to goodness by the law of love; and that law is far stronger than ever the law of fear can be.

THE FAITH WHICH TAKES GOD AT HIS WORD

Romans 4: 1–8

What, then, shall we say that Abraham, our forefather from whom we take our human descent, found? If Abraham entered into a right relationship with God by means of work, he has some ground for boasting—but not in regard to God. For what does scripture say? " Abraham trusted in God and it was accounted to him for righteousness." The man who works does not receive his

pay as a favour; he receives it as a debt due to him. But, as for the
man who does not depend on work, but who trusts in the God
who treats the ungodly as he would treat a good man, his faith is
accounted as righteousness. Just so, David speaks of the counting
happy of the man to whom God accounts righteousness apart
from works—" Happy they whose transgressions are forgiven
and whose sins are covered! Happy the man to whom God does
not account sin! "

PAUL moves on to speak of Abraham for three reasons.

(i) The Jews regarded Abraham as the great founder of the
race and the pattern of all that a man should be. Very naturally
they ask, " If all that you say is true, what was the special thing
that was given to Abraham when God picked him out to be the
ancestor of his special people? What makes him different from
other people? " That is the question which Paul is going on to
answer.

(ii) Paul has just been seeking to prove that what makes a
man right with God is not the performance of the works that
the law lays down, but the simple trust of complete yieldedness
which takes God at his word and believes that he still loves us
even when we have done nothing to deserve that love. The
immediate reaction of the Jews was, " This is something entirely new and a contradiction of all that we have been taught
to believe. This doctrine is completely incredible." Paul's answer is, " So far from being new, this doctrine is as old as the
Jewish faith. So far from being an heretical novelty, it is the
very basis of Jewish religion." That is what he is going on to
prove.

(iii) Paul begins to speak about Abraham because he was a
wise teacher who knew the human mind and the way it works.
He has been talking about *faith*. Now faith is an abstract idea.
The ordinary human mind finds abstract ideas very hard to
grasp. The wise teacher knows that every idea must become a
person, for the only way in which an ordinary person can grasp
an abstract idea is to see it in action, embodied in a person. So
Paul, in effect, says, " I have been talking about faith. If you
want to see what faith is, look at Abraham."

When Paul began to speak about Abraham, he was on ground that every Jew knew and understood. In their thoughts Abraham held a unique position. He was the founder of the nation. He was the man to whom God had first spoken. He was the man who had in a unique way had been chosen by God and who had heard and obeyed him. The Rabbis had their own discussions about Abraham. To Paul the essence of his greatness was this. God had come to Abraham and bidden him leave home and friends and kindred and livelihood, and had said to him, " If you make this great venture of faith, you will become the father of a great nation." Thereupon Abraham had taken God at his word. He had not argued; he had not hesitated; he went out not knowing where he was to go (*Hebrews* 11: 8). It was not the fact that Abraham had meticulously performed the demands of the law that put him into his special relationship with God, it was his complete trust in God and his complete willingness to abandon his life to him. That for Paul was faith, and it was Abraham's faith which made God regard him as a good man.

Some few, some very few, of the more advanced Rabbis believed that. There was a rabbinic commentary which said, " Abraham, our father, inherited this world and the world to come solely by the merit of faith whereby he believed in the Lord; for it is said, ' And he believed in the Lord, and he accounted it to him for righteousness.' "

But the great majority of the Rabbis turned the Abraham story to suit their own beliefs. They held that because he was the only righteous man of his generation, *therefore* he was chosen to be the ancestor of God's special people. The immediate answer is, " But how could Abraham keep the law when he lived hundreds of years before it was given? " The Rabbis advanced the odd theory that he kept it by *intuition* or *anticipation*. " At that time," says the Apocalypse of Baruch (57: 2), " the unwritten law was named among them, and the works of the commandment were then fulfilled." " He kept the law of the Most High," says Ecclesiasticus (44: 20, 21), " and was taken into covenant with God. . . . Therefore God assured

him by an oath that the nations should be blessed in his seed."
The Rabbis were so in love with their theory of works that they
insisted that it was because of his works that Abraham was
chosen, although it meant that they had to argue that he knew
the law by anticipation, since it had not yet come.

Here, again, we have the root cleavage between Jewish
legalism and Christian faith. The basic thought of the Jews was
that a man must *earn* God's favour. The basic thought of
Christianity is that all a man can do is to take God at his word
and stake everything on the faith that his promises are true.
Paul's argument was—and he was unanswerably right—that
Abraham entered into a right relationship with God, not
because he did all kinds of legal works, but because he cast
himself, just as he was, on God's promise.

> " If our love were but more simple,
>   We should take him at his word;
> And our lives would be all sunshine,
>   In the sweetness of our Lord.

It is the supreme discovery of the Christian life that we do not
need to torture ourselves with a losing battle to earn God's love
but rather need to accept in perfect trust the love which God
offers to us. True, after that, any man of honour is under the
life-long obligation to show himself worthy of that love. But he
is no longer a criminal seeking to obey an impossible law; he is
a lover offering his all to one who loved him when he did not
deserve it.

Sir James Barrie once told a story about Robert Louis
Stevenson. " When Stevenson went to Samoa he built a small
hut, and afterwards went into a large house. The first night he
went into the large house he was feeling very tired and
sorrowful that he had not had the forethought to ask his servant
to bring him coffee and cigarettes. Just as he was thinking that,
the door opened, and the native boy came in with a tray
carrying cigarettes and coffee. And Mr Stevenson said to him,
in the native language, ' Great is your forethought '; and the
boy corrected him, and said, ' Great is the love.' " The service

was rendered, not because of the coercion of servitude, but because of the compulsion of love. That also is the motive of Christian goodness.

THE FATHER OF THE FAITHFUL

Romans 4: 9–12

Did, then, this pronouncing of blessedness come to Abraham when he was circumcised? Or when he was uncircumcised? We are just saying, " His faith was accounted to Abraham for righteousness." Under what circumstances was it then accounted? Was it while he was circumcised? Or was it while he was uncircumcised? It was not while he was circumcised, but while he was uncircumcised. And he received the sign of circumcision as a seal of that relationship to God whose source was faith while he was still uncircumcised. This happened that he might be the father of all who believe while they are uncircumcised, so that the accounting of righteousness may come to them too; and that he might also be the father of those who are circumcised, and by that I mean, not those who are circumcised only, but who walk in the steps of that faith which our father Abraham showed when he was still uncircumcised.

To understand this passage we must understand the importance that the Jew attached to circumcision. To the Jew a man who was not circumcised was quite literally not a Jew, no matter what his parentage was. The Jewish circumcision prayer runs: " Blessed is he who sanctified his beloved from the womb, and put his ordinance upon his flesh, and sealed his offspring with the sign of the holy covenant." The rabbinic ordinance lays it down: " Ye shall not eat of the Passover unless the seal of Abraham be in your flesh." If a Gentile accepted the Jewish faith, he could not enter fully into it without three things— baptism, sacrifice and circumcision.

The Jewish objector, whom Paul is answering all the time, is still fighting a rear-guard action. " Suppose I admit," he says, " all that you say about Abraham and about the fact that it was his complete trust that gained him an entry into a right relationship with God, you will still have to agree that he was circumcised." Paul has an unanswerable argument. The story of Abraham's call, and of God's blessing on him, is in *Genesis* 15: 6; the story of Abraham's circumcision is in *Genesis* 17: 10ff. He was not, in fact, circumcised until fourteen years after he had answered God's call and entered into the unique relationship with God. Circumcision was not the gateway to his right relationship with God; it was only the sign and the seal that he had already entered into it. His being accounted righteous had nothing to do with circumcision and everything to do with his act of faith. From this unanswerable fact Paul makes two great deductions.

(i) Abraham is not the father of those who have been circumcised; he is the father of those who make the same act of faith in God as he made. He is the father of every man in every age who takes God at his word as he did. This means that the real Jew is the man who trusts God as Abraham did, no matter what his race is. All the great promises of God are made not to the Jewish nation, but to the man who is Abraham's descendant because he trusts God as he did. Jew has ceased to be a word which describes a nationality and has come to describe a way of life and a reaction to God. The descendants of Abraham are not the members of any particular nation, but those in every nation who belong to the family of God.

(ii) The converse is also true. A man may be a Jew of pure lineage and may be circumcised; and yet in the real sense may be no descendant of Abraham. He has no right to call Abraham his father or to claim the promises of God, unless he makes that venture of faith that Abraham made.

In one short paragraph Paul has shattered all Jewish thought. The Jew always believed that just because he was a Jew he automatically enjoyed the privilege of God's blessings and immunity from his punishment. The proof that he was a Jew was circumcision. So literally did some of the Rabbis take this that they actually said that, if a Jew was so bad that he had to be condemned by God, there was an angel whose task it was to make him uncircumcised again before he entered into punishment.

Paul has laid down the great principle that the way to God is not through membership of any nation, not through any ordinance which makes a mark upon a man's body; but by the faith which takes God at his word and makes everything dependent, not on man's achievement, but solely upon God's grace.

ALL IS OF GRACE

Romans 4: 13–17

It was not through law that there came to Abraham or to his seed the promise that he would inherit the earth, but it came through that right relationship with God which has its origin in faith. If they who are vassals of the law are heirs, then faith is drained of its meaning, and the promise is rendered inoperative; for the law produces wrath, but where law does not exist, neither can transgression exist. So, then, the whole process depends on faith, in order that it may be a matter of grace, so that the promise should be guaranteed to all Abraham's descendants, not only to those who belong to the tradition of the law, but also to those who are of Abraham's family in virtue of faith. Abraham who is the father of us all—as it stands written, " I have appointed you a father of many nations "—in the sight of that God in whom he believed, that God who calls the dead into life, and who calls into being even things which do not exist.

To Abraham God made a very great and wonderful promise. He promised that he would become a great nation, and that in him all families of the earth would be blessed (*Genesis* 12: 2, 3). In truth, the earth would be given to him as his inheritance. Now that promise came to Abraham because of the faith that he showed towards God. It did not come because he piled up merit by doing works of the law. It was the outgoing of God's generous grace in answer to Abraham's absolute faith. The promise, as Paul saw it, was dependent on two things and two things only—the free grace of God and the perfect faith of Abraham.

The Jews were still asking, " How can a man enter into the right relationship with God so that he too may inherit this great promise? " Their answer was, " He must do so by acquiring merit in the sight of God through doing works which the law prescribes." That is to say, he must do it by his own efforts. Paul saw with absolute clearness that this Jewish attitude *had completely destroyed the promise*. It had done so for this reason—no man can fully keep the law; therefore, if the promise depends on keeping the law, it can never be fulfilled.

Paul saw things in terms of black and white. He saw two mutually exclusive ways of trying to get into a right relationship with God. On the one hand there was dependence on human effort; on the other, dependence on divine grace. On the one hand there was the constant losing battle to obey an impossible law; on the other, there was the faith which simply takes God at his word.

On each side there were three things.

(i) On the one side there is God's *promise*. There are two Greek words which mean *promise*. *Huposchesis* means a promise which is entered into upon conditions. " I promise to do this if you promise to do that." *Epaggelia* means a promise made out of the goodness of someone's heart quite unconditionally. It is *epaggelia* that Paul uses of the promise of God. It is as if he is saying, " God is like a human father; he promises to love his children no matter what they do." True, he will love some of us with a love that makes him glad, and he will love some of us with a love that makes him sad; but in either case it is a love which will never let us go. It is dependent not on our merit but only on God's own generous heart.

(ii) There is *faith*. Faith is the certainty that God is indeed like that. It is staking everything on his love.

(iii) There is *grace*. A gift of grace is always something which is unearned and undeserved. The truth is that man can never earn the love of God. He must always find his glory, not in what he can do for God, but in what God has done for him.

(i) On the other side there is *law*. The trouble about law has
always been that it can diagnose the malady but cannot effect a
cure. Law shows a man where he goes wrong, but does not help
him to avoid going wrong. There is in fact, as Paul will later
stress, a kind of terrible paradox in law. It is human nature that
when a thing is forbidden it has a tendency to become desirable.
" Stolen fruits are sweetest." Law, therefore, can actually move
a man to desire the very thing which it forbids. The essential complement of law is judgment, and, so long as a man lives
in a religion whose dominant thought is law, he cannot see
himself as anything other than a condemned criminal at the
bar of God's justice.

(ii) There is *transgression*. Whenever law is introduced,
transgression follows. No one can break a law which does not
exist; and no one can be condemned for breaking a law of
whose existence he was ignorant. If we introduce law and stop
there, if we make religion solely a matter of obeying law, life
consists of one long series of transgressions waiting to be
punished.

(iii) There is *wrath*. Think of *law*, think of *transgression*, and
inevitably the next thought is *wrath*. Think of God in terms of
law and you cannot do other than think of him in terms of
outraged justice. Think of man in terms of law and you cannot
do other than think of him as destined for the condemnation of
God.

So Paul sets before the Romans two ways. The one is a way
in which a man seeks a right relationship with God through his
own efforts. It is doomed to failure. The other is a way in which
a man enters by faith into a relationship with God, which by
God's grace already exists for him to come into in trust.

BELIEVING IN THE GOD WHO MAKES THE
IMPOSSIBLE POSSIBLE

Romans 4: 18–25

In hope Abraham believed beyond hope that he would become the father of many nations, as the saying had it, " So will be your seed.?' He did not weaken in his faith, although he was well aware that by this time his body had lost its vitality (for he was a hundred years old), and that the womb of Sarah was without life. He did not in unfaith waver at the promise of God, but he was revitalized by his faith, and he gave glory to God, and he was firmly convinced that he who had made the promise was also able to perform it. So this faith was accounted to him as righteousness. It was not onlyfor his sake this " it was accounted to him for righteousness " was written. It was written also for our sakes; for it will be so reckoned to us who believe in him who raised Jesus, our Lord, from the dead, who was delivered up for our sin and raised to bring us into a right relationship with God.

THE last passage ended by saying that Abraham believed in the God who calls the dead into life and who brings into being even thingswhich have no existence at all. This passage turns Paul's thoughts to another outstanding example of Abraham's willingness to take God at his word. The promise that all families of the earth would be blessed in his descendants was given to Abraham when he was an old man. His wife, Sarah, had always been childless; and now, when he was one hundred years old and she was ninety (*Genesis* 17: 17), there came the promise that a son would be born to them. It seemed, on the face of it, beyond all belief and beyond all hope of fulfilment, for he was long past he age of begetting and she long past the age of bearing a son. Yet, once again, Abraham took God at his word and once again it was this faith that was accounted to Abraham for righteousness.

It was this willingness to take God at his word which put Abraham into a right relationship with him. Now the Jewish Rabbis had a saying to which Paul here refers. They said,

" What is written of Abraham is written also of his children."
They meant that any promise that God made to Abraham
extends to his children also. Therefore, if Abraham's willingness
to take God at his word brought him into a right relationship
with God, so it will be with us. It is not works of the law, it is
this trusting faith which establishes the relationship between
God and a man which ought to exist.

The essence of Abraham's faith in this case was that he
believed that God could make the impossible possible. So long
as we believe that everything depends on our efforts, we are
bound to be pessimists, for experience has taught the grim
lesson that our own efforts can achieve very little. When we
realize that it is not our effort but God's grace and power which
matter, then we become optimists, because we are bound to
believe that with God nothing is impossible.

It is told that once Saint Theresa set out to build a convent
with a sum the equivalent of twelve pence as her complete
resources. Someone said to her, " Not even Saint Theresa can
accomplish much with twelve pence." " True," she answered,
" but Saint Theresa and twelve pence *and God* can do anything." A man may well hesitate to attempt a great task by
himself; there is nothing which he need hesitate to attempt with
God. Ann Hunter Small, the great missionary teacher, tells how
her father, himself a missionary, used to say: " Oh! the
wickedness as well as the stupidity of the croakers! " And she
herself had a favourite saying: " A church which is alive dares
to do anything." That daring only becomes possible to a man
and to a church who take God at his word.

AT HOME WITH GOD

Romans 5: 1–5

> Since, then, we have been put into a right relationship with God in
> consequence of faith, let us enjoy peace with him through our
> Lord Jesus Christ. Through him, by faith, we are in possession of
> an introduction to this grace in which we stand; and let us glory in

the hope of the glory of God. Not only that, but let us find a cause of glorying in our troubles; for we know that trouble produces fortitude; and fortitude produces character; and character produces hope; and hope does not prove an illusion, because the love of God has been poured out into our hearts through the Holy Spirit who has been given unto us.

HERE is one of Paul's great lyrical passages in which he almost sings the intimate joy of his confidence in God. Trusting faith has done what the labour to produce the works of the law could never do; it has given a man peace with God. Before Jesus came, no man could ever be really close to God.

Some, indeed, have seen him, not as the supreme good, but as the supreme evil. Swinburne wrote:

> " His hidden face and iron feet,
>   Hath not man known and felt them in their way
>   Threaten and trample all things every day?
>   Hath he not sent us hunger? Who hath cursed
>   Spirit and flesh with longing? Filled with thirst
>   Their lips that cried to him? "

Some have seen him as the complete stranger, the utterly untouchable. In one of H. G. Wells's books there is the story of a man of affairs whose mind was so tensed and strained that he was in serious danger of a complete nervous and mental breakdown. His doctor told him that the only thing that could save him was to find the peace that fellowship with God can give. " What! " he said, " to think of that, up there, having fellowship with me! I would as soon think of cooling my throat with the milky way or shaking hands with the stars! " God, to him, was the completely unfindable. Rosita Forbes, the traveller, tells of finding shelter one night in a Chinese village temple because there was nowhere else to sleep. In the night she woke and the moonlight was slanting in through the window on to the faces of the images of the gods, and on every face there was a snarl and a sneer, as of those who hated men.

It is only when we realize that God is the Father of our Lord Jesus Christ that there comes into life that intimacy with him, that new relationship, which Paul calls justification.

Through Jesus, says Paul, we have an introduction to this grace in which we stand. The word he uses for introduction is *prosagōgē*. It is a word with two great pictures in it.

(i) It is the regular word for introducing or ushering someone into the presence of royalty; and it is the regular word for the approach of the worshipper to God. It is as if Paul was saying, " Jesus ushers us into the very presence of God. He opens the door for us to the presence of the King of Kings; and when that door is opened what we find is *grace*; not condemnation, not judgment, not vegeance, but the sheer, undeserved, incredible kindness of God."

(ii) But *prosagōgē* has another picture in it. In late Greek it is the word for the place where ships come in, a *harbour* or *a haven*. If we take it that way, it means that so long as we tried to depend on our own efforts we were tempest-tossed, like mariners striving with a sea which threatened to overwhelm them completely, but now that we have heard the word of Christ, we have reached at last the haven of God's grace, and we know the calm of depending, not on what we can do for ourselves, but on what God has done for us.

Because of Jesus we have entry to the presence of the King of Kings and entry to the haven of God's grace.

No sooner has Paul said this than the other side of the matter strikes him. All this is true, and it is glory; but the fact remains that in this life the Christians are up against it. It is hard to be a Christian in Rome. Remembering that, Paul produces a great climax. " Trouble," he said, " produces fortitude." The word he uses for trouble is *thlipis*, which literally means *pressure*. All kinds of things may press in upon the Christian—want and straitened circumstances, sorrow, persecution, unpopularity and loneliness. All that pressure, says Paul, produces fortitude. The word he uses for *fortitude* is *hupomonē* which means more than endurance. It means the spirit which can overcome the world; it means the spirit which does not passively endure but which actively overcomes the trials and tribulations of life.

When Beethoven was threatened with deafness, that most terrible of troubles for a musician, he said: " I will take life by the throat." That is *hupomonē*. When Scott was involved in ruin because of the bankruptcy of his publishers, he said: " No man will say ' Poor fellow! ' to me; my own right hand will pay the debt." That is *hupomonē*. Someone once said to a gallant soul who was undergoing a great sorrow: " Sorrow fairly colours life, doesn't it? " Back came the reply: " Yes! And I propose to choose the colour! " That is *hupomonē*. When Henley was lying in Edinburgh Infirmary with one leg amputated, and the prospect that the other must follow, he wrote *Invictus*.

> " Out of the night that covers me,
>   Black as the Pit from pole to pole,
> I thank whatever gods may be
>   For my unconquerable soul.

That is *hupomonē*. *Hupomonē* is not the spirit which lies down and lets the floods go over it; it is the spirit which meets things breastforward and overcomes them.

" Fortitude," Paul goes on, " produces character." The word he uses for *character* is *dokimē*. *Dokimē* is used of metal which has been passed through the fire so that everything base has been purged out of it. It is used of coinage as we use the word *sterling*. When affliction is met with fortitude, out of the battle a man emerges stronger, and purer, and better, and nearer God.

" Character," Paul goes on, " produces hope." Two men can meet the same situation. It can drive one of them to despair, and it can spur the other to triumphant action. To the one it can be the end of hope, to the other it can be a challenge to greatness. " I do not like crises," said Lord Reith, " but I do like the opportunities they provide." The difference corresponds to the difference between the men. If a man has let himself become weak and flabby, if he has allowed circumstances to beat him, if he has allowed himself to whine and grovel under affliction, he has made himself such that when the challenge of the crisis comes he cannot do other than despair. If, on the other hand, a man has insisted on meeting life with head up, if he has always faced and, by facing, conquered things, then when the challenge comes, he meets it with eyes aflame with hope. The character which has endured the test always emerges in hope.

Then Paul makes one last great statement: " The Christian hope never proves an illusion for it is founded on the love of God." Omar Khayyam wrote wistfully of human hopes:

> " The Worldly Hope men set their hearts upon
> Turns Ashes—or it prospers; and anon,
> Like Snow upon the Desert's dusty Face
> Lighting a little Hour or two—is gone.

When a man's hope is in God, it cannot turn to dust and ashes. When a man's hope is in God, it cannot be disappointed. When a man's hope is in the love of God, it can never be an illusion, for God loves us with an everlasting love backed by an everlasting power.

THE FINAL PROOF OF LOVE

Romans 5: 6–11

While we were still helpless, in God's good time, Christ died for the ungodly. A man will hardly die for a just man. It may be that a man would even dare to die for the good cause. But God proves his love to us by the fact that while we were still sinners Christ died for us. Since we have been brought into a right relationship with God at the price of his life's blood, much more through him we shall be saved from the Wrath. For if while we were still at enmity with God, we were reconciled to God through the death of his Son, much more, now that we have been reconciled, we shall go on being saved by his life. Not only that, but we glory in God through our Lord Jesus Christ, through whom we have received this reconciliation.

THE fact that Jesus Christ died for us is the final proof of God's love. It would be difficult enough to get a man to die for a just man; it might be possible for a man to be persuaded to die for some great and good principle; a man might have the greater love that would make him lay down his life for his friend. But the wonder of Jesus Christ is that he died for us when we are sinners and in a state of hostility to God. Love can go no further than that.

Rita Snowdon relates an incident from the life of T. E. Lawrence. In 1915 he was journeying across the desert with some Arabs. Things were desperate. Food was almost done, and water was at its last drop. Their hoods were over their heads to shelter them from the wind which was like a flame and full of the stinging sand of the sandstorm. Suddenly someone said, " Where is Jasmin? " Another said, " Who is Jasmin? " A third answered, " That yellow-faced man from Maan. He killed a Turkish tax-collector and fled to the desert." The first said, " Look, Jasmin's camel has no rider. His rifle is strapped to the saddle, but Jasmin is not there." A second said, " Someone has shot him on the march." A third said, " He is not strong in the head, perhaps he is lost in a mirage; he is not strong in the body, perhaps he has fainted and fallen off his camel." Then the first said, " What does it matter? Jasmin was not worth ten pence." And the Arabs hunched themselves up on their camels and rode on. But Lawrence turned and rode back the way he had come. Alone, in the blazing heat, at the risk of his life, he went back. After an hour and a half's ride he saw something against the sand. It was Jasmin, blind and mad with heat and thirst, being murdered by the desert. Lawrence lifted him up on his camel, gave him some of the last drops of precious water, slowly plodded back to his company. When he came up to them, the Arabs looked in amazement. " Here is Jasmin," they said, " Jasmin, not worth ten pence, saved at his own risk by Lawrence, our lord." That is a parable. It was not good men Christ died to save but sinners, not God's friends but men at enmity with him.

Then Paul goes on a step. Through Jesus our *status* with God was changed. Sinners though we were, we were put into a right relationship with God. *But that is not enough.* Not only our *status* must be changed but our *state.* The saved sinner cannot go on being a sinner; he must become good. Christ's death changed our *status*; his risen life changes our *state.* He is not dead but alive; he is with us always to help us and guide us, to fill us with his strength so as to overcome temptation, to clothe our lives with something of his radiance. Jesus begins by putting sinners into a right relationship with God even when they are still sinners; he goes on, by his grace, to enable them to quit their sin and become good men. there are technical names for these things. The change of our *status* is *justification*; that is where the whole saving process begins. The change of our *state* is *sanctification*; that is where the saving process goes on, and never ends, until we see him face to face and are like him.

There is one thing to note here of quite extraordinary importance. Paul is quite clear that the whole saving process, the coming of Christ and the death of Christ, is the proof of *God's* love. Sometimes the thing is stated as if on the one side there was a gentle and loving Christ, and on the other an angry and vengeful God; and as if Christ had done something which changed God's attitude to men. Nothing could be further from the truth. The whole matter springs from the love of God. Jesus did not come to change God's attitude to men; he came to show what it is and always was. He came to prove unanswerably that God is love.

RUIN AND RESCUE

Romans 5: 12–21

Therefore, just as through one man sin entered into the world, and, through sin, death entered into the world, and so death spread to all men, in that they had sinned; for up to the coming of the law sin was in the world, but sin was not debited against men because the law did not yet exist; but death reigned from the time of Adam to the time of Moses even over those who had not sinned in the way that Adam had, Adam, who was the symbol of the one who was to come. But the gift of free grace was not like the trespass. For if the many died in consequence of the sin of the one, much more the grace of God and his free gift in the grace of the one man Jesus Christ abounded to many. The free gift is not like the effect of the one man who sinned. The sentence which followed the one sin was a sentence of condemnation; but the free gift which followed the many trespasses was a sentence of acquittal. For if, because of the trespass of one, death reigned because of one, much more they who receive the superabundance of grace and of that free gift which establishes a right relationship between man and God, shall reign in life through the one Jesus Christ. So, then, as by one sin it came to all men to fall under sentence, so by one supreme act of righteousness it came to men to enter into that relationship with God which gives them life. Just as through the disobedience of one man the many were constituted sinners, so, through the obedience of one man, the many were constituted righteous. But the law slipped in that trespass might abound; but where sin abounded grace superabounded, so that just as sin reigned in death, grace might reign by putting men into a right relationship with God that they might enter into eternal life because of what Jesus Christ our Lord has done.

No passage of the New Testament has had such an influence on theology as this; and no passage is more difficult for a modern mind to understand. It is difficult because Paul expresses himself in a difficult way. We can see, for instance, that the first sentence never ends, but breaks off in mid-air, while Paul pursues another idea down a sideline. Still more, it is thinking and speaking in terms which were familiar to Jews and perfectly understandable to them, but which are unfamiliar to us.

If we were to put the thought of this passage into one sentence, which, indeed, was the sentence which Paul set out to write at the very beginning, and which got sidetracked, it would be this: " By the sin of Adam all men became sinners and were alienated from God; by the righteousness of Jesus Christ all men became righteous and are restored to a right relationship with God." Paul, in fact, said this very much more clearly in 1 *Corinthians* 15: 21: " As by a man came death, by a man has come also the resurrection of the dead. For as in Adam all die, so also in Christ shall all be made alive."

There are two basic Jewish ideas in the light of which this passage must be read.

(i) There is the idea of *solidarity*. The Jew never really
thought of himself as an individual but always thought as part
of a clan, a family, or a nation apart from which he had no real
existence. To this day it is said that if an Australian aboriginal is
asked his name, he gives the name of his tribe or clan. He does
not think of himself as a person, but as a member of a society.
One of the clearest instances of this kind of thing in recogniz-
able action is the blood feud amongst primitive people. Suppose
a man from one tribe murders a man from another tribe. It
becomes the duty of the first tribe to take vengeance on the
second; it is the tribe that has been hurt, and the tribe which
takes vengeance.

In the Old Testament there is one vivid instance of this. It is
the case of Achan as related in *Joshua* 7. At the siege of
Jericho, Achan kept to himself certain spoils in direct defiance
of the commandment of God that all should be destroyed. The
next item in the campaign was the siege of Ai, which should
have fallen without trouble. The assaults against it, however,
failed disastrously. Why? Because Achan had sinned, and, as a
result, the whole nation was branded as sinner and punished by
God. Achan's sin was not one man's sin but the nation's. The
nation was not a collection of individuals; it was a solid mass.
What the individual did, the nation did. When Achan's sin was
admitted, it was not he alone who was executed but his whole
family. Again, Achan was not a solitary, self-responsible individual; he was one of a solid mass of people from whom he
could not be separated.

That is how Paul sees Adam. Adam was not an individual.
He was one of mankind, and because he was one of mankind,
his sin was the sin of all men.

Paul says that all men sinned in Adam. If we are ever to
understand Paul's thought here, we must be quite sure what he
means, and we must be equally sure that he was serious. All
through the history of Christian thinking there have been efforts
to interpret in different ways this conception of the connection
between Adam's sin and that of mankind.

(a) The passage has been taken to mean that " each man is

his own Adam." This really means that, just as Adam sinned, all men have sinned, but that there is no real connection between the sin of Adam and the sin of mankind, other than that it could be said that Adam's sin is typical of the sin of all mankind.

(b) There is what has been called the legal interpretation. This would hold that Adam was *the representative* of mankind and the human race shares in the deed of its representative. But a representative must be *chosen* by the people he represents; and in no sense can we say that of Adam.

(c) There is the interpretation that what we inherit from Adam is *the tendency* to sin. That is true enough, but that is not what Paul meant. It would not, in fact, suit his argument at all.

(d) The passage ought to be given what is called the realistic interpretation, namely that, because of the solidarity of the human race, all mankind actually sinned in Adam. This idea was not strange to a Jew; it was the actual belief of the Jewish thinkers. The writer of 2 *Esdras* is quite clear about it. " A grain of evil was sown in the heart of Adam from the beginning and how much wickedness has it brought forth unto this time; and how much shall it yet bring forth till the time of the threshing come " (4: 30). " For the first Adam, bearing a wicked heart, transgressed and was overcome; and not only he but all they also who are born of him " (3: 21).

(ii) The second basic idea is intimately connected with this in Paul's argument. *Death is the direct consequence of sin.* It was the Jewish belief that, if Adam had not sinned, man would have been immortal. Sirach (2: 23) writes, " A woman was the beginning of sin and through her all die." The Book of Wisdom has it, " God created man for immortality and made him the image of his own proper nature; but by the envy of the devil death entered into the world." In Jewish thought, sin and death are integrally connected. This is what Paul is getting at in the involved and difficult line of thought in verses 12–14. We may trace his thought there in a series of ideas.

(a) Adam sinned because he broke a direct commandment of God not to eat of the fruit of the forbidden tree—and because he sinned, he died, although he was meant to be immortal.

(b) The law did not come until the time of Moses. Now, if there is no law, there can be no breach of the law; that is to say, there can be no sin. Therefore, the men who lived between Adam and Moses did in fact commit sinful actions, but they could not be counted sinners, for the law did not yet exist.

(c) In spite of the fact that sin could not be reckoned to them, they still died. Death reigned over them, although they could not be accused of breaking a non-existent law.

(d) Why, then, did they die? It was because they had sinned in Adam. Their involvement in his sin caused their deaths, although there was no law for them to break. That, in fact, is Paul's proof that all men did sin in Adam.

So, then, we have extracted the essence of one side of Paul's thought. Because of this idea of the complete solidarity of mankind, all men literally sinned in Adam; and because it is the consequence of sin, death reigned over all men.

But this very same conception, which can be used to produce so desperate a view of the human situation, can be used in reverse to fill it with a blaze of glory. Into this situation comes Jesus. To God Jesus offered perfect goodness. And, just as all men were involved in Adam's sin, all men are involved in Jesus's perfect goodness; and, just as Adam's sin was the cause of death, so Jesus's perfect goodness conquers death and gives men life eternal. Paul's triumphant argument is that, as mankind was solid with Adam and was therefore condemned to death, so mankind is solid with Christ and is therefore acquitted to life. Even although the law has come and made sin much more terrible, the grace of Christ overcomes the condemnation which the law must bring.

That is Paul's argument, and on Jewish grounds it is unassailable. But it has one great flaw, as it has one great truth.

(i) The flaw is this. Suppose we assume the literal truth of the Adam story, *our connection with Adam is purely physical*. We have no choice whatever in the matter, any more than a child chooses his father. On the other hand *our connection with Christ is voluntary*. Union with Christ is something a man can accept or reject. The connection is in reality quite different. That is a serious flaw in Paul's argument.

(ii) The great virtue is this. Paul conserves the truth that mankind was involved in a situation from which there was no escape; sin had man in its power and there was no hope. Into this situation came Jesus Christ, and he brought with him something that broke the old deadlock. By what he did, by what he is, by what he gives, he enabled man to escape from a situation in which he was hopelessly dominated by sin. Whatever else we may say about Paul's argument, it is completely true that man was ruined by sin and rescued by Christ.

DYING TO LIVE

Romans 6: 1–11

> What, then, shall we infer? Are we to persist in sin that grace may abound? God forbid! How shall we who have died to sin still live in it? Can you be unaware that all who have been baptized into Jesus Christ have been baptized into his death? We have therefore been buried with him through baptism until we died, in order that, just as Christ was raised from the dead through the glory of the father, so we, too, may live in newness of life. For, if we have become united to him in the likeness of his death, so also shall we be united to him in the likeness of his resurrection. For this we know, that our old self has been crucified with him, that our sinful body might be rendered inoperative, in order that we should no longer be slaves to sin. For a man who has died stands acquitted from sin. But, if we have died with Christ, we believe that we shall also live with him, for we know that, after Christ was raised from the dead, he dies no more. Death has no more lordship over him. He who died, died once and for all to sin; and he who lives, lives to God. So you, too, must reckon yourselves to be dead to sin, but alive to God in Christ Jesus.

As he has so often done in this letter, Paul is once again carrying on an argument against a kind of imaginary opponent. The argument springs from the great saying at the end of the last chapter: " Where sin abounded, grace superabounded." It runs something like this.

The Objector: You have just said that God's grace is great enough to find forgiveness for every sin.

Paul: That is so.

The Objector: You are, in fact, saying that God's grace is the most wonderful thing in all this world.

Paul: That is so.

The Objector: Well, if that is so, let us go on sinning. The more we sin, the more grace will abound. Sin does not matter, for God will forgive anyway. In fact we can go further than that and say that sin is an excellent thing, because it gives the grace of God a chance to operate. The conclusion of your argument is that sin produces grace; therefore sin is bound to be a good thing if it produces the greatest thing in the world.

Paul's first reaction is to recoil from that argument in sheer horror. " Do you suggest," he demands, " that we should go on sinning in order to give grace more chance to operate? God forbid that we should pursue so incredible a course as that."

Then, having recoiled like that, he goes on to something else. " Have you never thought," he demands, " what happened to you when you were baptized? " Now, when we try to understand what Paul goes on to say, we must remember that baptism in his time was different from what it commonly is today.

(*a*) It was adult baptism. That is not to say that the New Testament is opposed to infant baptism, but infant baptism is the result of the Christian family, and the Christian family could hardly be said to have come into being as early as the time of Paul. A man came to Christ as an individual in the early Church, often leaving his family behind.

(*b*) Baptism in the early Church was intimately connected with confession of faith. A man was baptized when he entered the Church; and he was entering the Church direct from paganism. In baptism a man came to a decision which cut his life in two, a decision which often meant that he had to tear himself up by the roots, a decision which was so definite that it often meant nothing less than beginning life all over again.

(c) Commonly baptism was by total immersion and that practice lent itself to a symbolism to which sprinkling does not so readily lend itself. When a man descended into the water and the water closed over his head, it was like being buried. When he emerged from the water, it was like rising from the grave. Baptism was symbolically like dying and rising again. The man died to one kind of life and rose to another; he died to the old life of sin and rose to the new life of grace.

Again, if we are fully to understand this, we must remember that Paul was using language and pictures that almost anyone of his day and generation would understand. It may seem strange to us, but it was not at all strange to his contemporaries.

The Jews would understand it. When a man entered the Jewish religion from heathenism, it involved three things— sacrifice, circumcision and baptism. The Gentile entered the Jewish faith by baptism. The ritual was as follows. The person to be baptized cut his nails and hair; he undressed completely; the baptismal bath must contain at least forty *seahs*, that is two hogsheads, of water; every part of his body must be touched by the water. As he was in the water, he made confession of his faith before three fathers of baptism and certain exhortations and benedictions were addressed to him. The effect of this baptism was held to be complete regeneration; he was called a little child just born, the child of one day. All his sins were remitted because God could not punish sins committed before he was born. The completeness of the change was seen in the fact that certain Rabbis held that a man's child born after baptism was his first-born, even if he had older children. Theoretically it was held—although the belief was never put into practice—that a man was so completely new that he might marry his own sister or his own mother. He was not only a changed man, he was a different man. Any Jew would fully understand Paul's words about the necessity of a baptized man being completely new.

The Greek would understand. At this time the only real Greek religion was found in the mystery religions. They were wonderful things. They offered men release from the cares and sorrows and fears of this earth; and the release was by union with some god. All the mysteries were passion plays. They were based on the story of some god who suffered and died and rose again. The story was played out as a drama. Before a man could see the drama he had to be initiated. He had to undergo a long course of instruction on the inner meaning of the drama. He had to undergo a course of ascetic discipline. He was carefully prepared. The drama was played out with all the resources of music and lighting, and incense and mystery. As it was played out, the man underwent an emotional experience of identification with the god. Before he entered on this he was initiated. Initiation was always regarded as a death followed by a new birth, by which the man was *renatus in aeternum*, reborn for eternity. One who went through the initiation tells us that he underwent " a voluntary death." We know that in one of the mysteries the man to be initiated was called *moriturus*, the one who is to die, and that he was buried up to the head in a trench. When he had been initiated, he was addressed as a little child and fed with milk, as one newly born. In another of the mysteries the person to be initiated prayed: " Enter thou into my spirit, my thought, my whole life; for thou art I and I am thou." Any Greek who had been through this would have no difficulty in understanding what Paul meant by dying and rising again in baptism, and, in so doing, becoming one with Christ.

We are not for one moment saying that Paul borrowed either his ideas or his words from such Jewish or pagan practices; what we do say is that he was using words and pictures that both Jew and Gentile would recognize and understand.

In this passage lie three great permanent truths.

(i) It is a terrible thing to seek to trade on the mercy of God and to make it an excuse for sinning. Think of it in human terms. How despicable it would be for a son to consider himself free to sin, because he knew that his father would forgive. That would be taking advantage of love to break love's heart.

(ii) The man who enters upon the Christian way is committed to a different kind of life. He has died to one kind of life and been born to another. In modern times we may have tended to stress the fact that acceptance of the Christian way need not make so very much difference in a man's life. Paul would have said that it ought to make all the difference in the world.

(iii) But there is more than a mere ethical change in a man's life when he accepts Christ. There is a real identification with Christ. It is, in fact, the simple truth that the ethical change is not possible without that union. A man is *in Christ*. A great scholar has suggested this analogy for that phrase. We cannot live our physical life unless we are in the air and the air is in us; unless we are in Christ, and Christ is in us, we cannot live the life of God.

THE PRACTICE OF THE FAITH

Romans 6: 12–14

> Let not sin reign in your mortal body to make you obey the body's desires. Do not go on yielding your members to sin as weapons of evil; but yield yourselves once and for all to God, as those who were dead and are now alive, and yield your members to God as weapons of righteousness. For sin will not lord it over you. You are not under law but under grace.

THERE is no more typical transition in Paul than that between this passage and the preceding one. The passage which went before was the writing of a mystic. It spoke of the mystical union between the Christian and Christ which came in baptism. It spoke of the way in which a Christian should live so close to Christ that all his life can be said to be lived in him. And now, after the mystical experience, comes the practical demand. Christianity is not an emotional experience; it is a way of life. The Christian is not meant to luxuriate in an experience however wonderful; he is meant to go out and live a certain kind of life in the teeth of the world's attacks and problems. It is common in the world of religious life to sit in church and feel a wave of feeling sweep over us. It is a not uncommon experience, when we sit alone, to feel Christ very near. But the Christianity which has stopped there, has stopped half-way. That emotion must be translated into action. Christianity can never be only an experience of the inner being; it must be a life in the market-place.

When a man goes out into the world, he is confronted with an awesome situation. As Paul thinks of it, both God and sin are looking for weapons to use. God cannot work without men. If he wants a word spoken, he has to get a man to speak it. If he wants a deed done, he has to get a man to do it. If he wants a person encouraged, he has to get a man to do the lifting up. It is the same with sin; every man has to be given the push into it. Sin is looking for men who will by their words or example seduce others into sinning. It is as if Paul was saying: " In this world there is an eternal battle between sin and God; choose your side." We are faced with the tremendous alternative of making ourselves weapons in the hand of God or weapons in the hand of sin.

A man may well say: " Such a choice is too much for me. I am bound to fail." Paul's answer is: " Don't be discouraged and don't be despairing; sin will not lord it over you." Why? Because we are no longer under law but under grace. Why should that make all the difference? Because we are no longer trying to satisfy the demands of law but are trying to be worthy of the gifts of love. We are no longer regarding God as the stern judge; we are regarding him as the lover of the souls of men. There is no inspiration in all the world like love. Who ever went out from the presence of his loved one without the burning desire to be a better person? The Christian life is no longer a burden to be borne; it is a privilege to be lived up to. As Denney put it: " It is not restraint but inspiration which liberates from sin; not Mount Sinai but Mount Calvary which makes saints." Many a man has been saved from sin, not because of the regulations of the law, but because he could not bear to hurt or grieve or disappoint someone whom he loved and someone who, he knew, loved him. At best, the law restrains a man through fear; but love redeems him by inspiring him to be better than his best. The inspiration of the Christian comes, not from the fear of what God will do to him, but from the inspiration of what God has done for him.

THE EXCLUSIVE POSSESSION

Romans 6: 15–23

> What then? Are we to go on sinning because we are not under the law but under grace? God forbid! Are you not aware that if you yield yourselves to anyone as slaves, in order to obey them, you are the slaves of the person whom you have chosen to obey—in this case, either of sin, which leads to death, or of obedience, which leads to righteousness. But, thank God, you, who used to be slaves of sin, have come to a spontaneous decision to obey the pattern of teaching to which you were committed, and, since you have been liberated from sin, you have become the slaves of righteousness. I speak in human terms, because unaided human nature cannot understand any others. Just as you yielded your members as slaves to uncleanness and lawlessness which issues in still more lawlessness, so now you have yielded your members as slaves to righteousness and have started on the road that leads to holiness. When you were slaves of sin, you were free as regards righteousness; but then what fruit did you have? All you had was things of which you are now heartily ashamed, for the end of these things is death. But now, since you have been liberated from sin, and since you have become the slaves of God, the fruit you enjoy is designed to lead you on the road to holiness and its end is eternal life. For sin's pay is death, but God's free gift is eternal life in Christ Jesus our Lord.

To a certain type of mind the doctrine of free grace is always a temptation to say, " If forgiveness is as easy and as inevitable as all that, if God's one desire is to forgive men and if his grace is wide enough to cover every spot and stain, why worry about sin? Why not do as we like? It will be all the same in the end."

Paul counters this argument by using a vivid picture. He says: " Once you gave yourselves to sin as its slave; when you did that, righteousness had no claim over you. But now you have given yourselves to God as the slave of righteousness; and so sin has no claim over you."

To understand this, we must understand the status of the slave. When we think of a servant, in our sense of the word, we think of a man who gives a certain agreed part of his time to his master and who receives a certain agreed wage for doing so. Within that agreed time he is at the disposal and in the command of his master. But, when that time ends, he is free to do as he likes. During his working hours he belongs to his master, but in his free time he belongs to himself. But, in Paul's time, the status of the slave was quite different. Literally he had no time which belonged to himself; every single moment belonged to his master. He was his master's absolutely exclusive possession. That is the picture that is in Paul's mind. He says: " At one time you were the slave of sin. Sin had exclusive possession of you. At that time you could not talk of anything else but sinning. But now you have taken God as your master and he has exclusive possession of you. Now you cannot even talk about sinning; you must talk about nothing but holiness."

Paul actually apologizes for using this picture. He says: " I am only using a human analogy so that your human minds can understand it." He apologized because he did not like to compare the Christian life to any kind of slavery. But the one thing that this picture does show is that the Christian can have no master but God. He cannot give a part of his life to God, and another part to the world. With God it is all—or nothing. So long as man keeps some part of his life without God, he is not really a Christian. A Christian is a man who has given complete control of his life to Christ, holding nothing back. No man who has done that can ever think of using grace as an excuse for sin.

But Paul has something more to say, " You took a spontaneous decision to obey the pattern of the teaching to which you were committed." In other words, he is saying, " You knew what you were doing, and you did it of your own free will." This is interesting. Remember that this passage has arisen from a discussion of baptism. This therefore means that baptism was instructed baptism. Now we have already seen that baptism in the early Church was adult baptism and confession of faith. It is, then, quite clear that no man was ever allowed into the Christian Church on a moment of emotion. He was instructed; he had to know what he was doing; he was shown what Christ offered and demanded. Then, and then only, could he take the decision to come in.

When a man wishes to become a member of the great Benedictine order of monks he is accepted for a year on probation. During all that time the clothes which he wore in the world hang in his cell. At any time he can put off his monk's habit, put on his worldly clothes, and walk out, and no one will think any the worse of him. Only at the end of the year are his clothes finally taken away. It is with open eyes and a full appreciation of what he is doing that he must enter the order.

It is so with Christianity. Jesus does not want followers who have not stopped to count the cost. He does not want a man to express an impermanent loyalty on the crest of a wave of emotion. The Church has a duty to present the faith in all the riches of its offer and the heights of its demands to those who wish to become its members.

Paul draws a distinction between the old life and the new. The old life was characterized by *uncleanness* and *lawlessness*. The pagan world was an unclean world; it did not know the meaning of chastity. Justin Martyr has a terrible jibe when talking about the exposure of infants. In Rome unwanted children, especially girls, were literally thrown away. Every night numbers of them were left lying in the forum. Some of them were collected by dreadful characters who ran brothels, and brought up to be prostitutes to stock the brothels. So Justin turns on his heathen opponents and tells them that, in their immorality, they had every chance of going into a city brothel, and, all unknown, having intercourse with their own child.

The pagan world was lawless in the sense that men's lusts were their only laws; and that lawlessness produced more lawlessness. That, indeed, is the law of sin. Sin begets sin. The first time we do a wrong thing, we may do it with hesitation and a tremor and a shudder. The second time we do it, it is easier; and if we go on doing it, it becomes effortless; sin loses its terror. The first time we allow ourselves some indulgence, we may be satisfied with very little of it; but the time comes when we need more and more of it to produce the same thrill. Sin leads on to sin; lawlessness produces lawlessness. To start on the path of sin is to go on to more and more.

The new life is different; it is life which is righteous. Now the Greeks defined righteousness as *giving to man and to God their due*. The Christian life is one which gives God his proper place and which respects the rights of human personality. The Christian will never disobey God nor ever use a human being to gratify his desire for pleasure. That life leads to what the Revised Standard Version calls *sanctification*. The word in Greek is *hagiasmos*. All Greek nouns which end in *-asmos* describe, not a completed state, but a *process*. Sanctification is the road to holiness. When a man gives his life to Christ, he does not then become a perfect man; the struggle is by no means over. But Christianity has always regarded the direction in which a man is facing as more important than the particular stage he has reached. Once he is Christ's he has started on the process of sanctification, the road to holiness.

> " Leaving every day behind
>   Something which might hinder;
>   Running swifter every day;
>   Growing purer, kinder."

Robert Louis Stevenson said: " To travel hopefully is a better thing than to arrive." What is true is that it is a great thing to set out to a great goal, even if we never get the whole way.

Paul finishes with a great saying that contains a double metaphor. " Sin's pay is death," he says, " but God's free gift is eternal life." Paul uses two military words. For *pay* he uses *opsōnia*. *Opsōnia* was the soldier's pay, something that he earned with the risk of his body and the sweat of his brow, something that was due to him and could not be taken from him. For gift he uses *charisma*. The *charisma* or, in Latin, the *donativum*, was a totally unearned gift which the army sometimes received. On special occasions, for instance on his birthday, or on his accession to the throne, or the anniversary of it, an emperor handed out a free gift of money to the army. It had not been earned; it was a gift of the emperor's kindness and grace. So Paul says: " If we got the pay we had earned it would be death; but out of his grace God has given us life."

THE NEW ALLEGIANCE

Romans 7: 1–6

> You are bound to know, brothers—for I speak to men who know what law means—that the law has authority over a man only for the duration of his life. Thus, a married woman remains bound by law to her husband as long as he is alive; but, if her husband dies, she is completely discharged from the law concerning her husband. Accordingly, she will be called an adulteress if she marries another man while her husband is still alive; but, if her husband dies, she is free from the law, and she is no longer an adulteress if she marries another man. Just so, my brothers, you have died to the law, through the body of Jesus Christ (for you shared in his death by baptism) in order that you should enter into union with another, I mean, with him who has been raised from the dead, in order that we may bear fruit to God. In the days of our unaided human nature, the passions of our sins, which were set in motion by the law, worked in our members to bear fruit for death. But now we are completely discharged from the law, because we have died to that by which we were held captive, so that we serve, not under the old written law, but in the new life of the spirit.

SELDOM did Paul write so difficult and so complicated a passage as this. C. H. Dodd has said that when we are studying it we should try to forget what Paul says and to find out what he means.

The basic thought of the passage is founded on the legal maxim that death cancels all contracts. Paul begins with an illustration of this truth and wishes to use this picture as a symbol of what happens to the Christian. So long as a woman's

husband is alive, she cannot marry another without becoming
an adulteress. But if her husband dies, the contract is, so to
speak, cancelled, and she is free to marry anyone she likes.

In view of that, Paul could have said that we were married to
sin; that sin was slain by Christ; and that, therefore, we are now
free to be married to God. That is undoubtedly what he set out
to say. But into this picture came the law. Paul could still have
put the thing quite simply. He could have said that we were
married to the law; that the law was killed by the work of
Christ; and that now we are free to be married to God. But,
quite suddenly, he puts it the other way, and, in his suddenly
changed picture, it is *we* who die to the law.

How can that be? By baptism we share in the death of
Christ. That means that, having died, we are discharged from
all obligations to the law and become free to marry again. This
time we marry, not the law, but Christ. When that happens,
Christian obedience becomes, not an externally imposed obedience to some written code of laws, but an inner allegiance of the
spirit to Jesus Christ.

Paul is drawing a contrast between the two states of man—
without Christ and with him. Before we knew Christ we tried to
rule life by obedience to the written code of the law. That was
when we were *in the flesh*. By *the flesh* Paul does not mean
simply the body, because a man retains a physical body to the
end of the day. In man there is something which answers to the
seduction of sin; and it is that part of man which provides a
bridgehead for sin that Paul calls *the flesh*.

The flesh is human nature apart from and unaided by God.
Paul says that, when our human nature·was unaided by God,
the law actually moved our passions to sin. What does he mean
by that? More than once he has the thought that the law
actually produces sin, because the very fact that a thing is
forbidden lends it a certain attraction. When we had nothing
but the law, we were at the mercy of sin.

Then Paul turns to the state of a man with Christ. When a
man rules his life by union with Christ he rules it not by
obedience to a written code of law which may actually awaken

the desire to sin but by an allegiance to Jesus Christ within his spirit and his heart. Not law, but love, is the motive of his life; and the inspiration of love can make him able to do what the restraint of law was powerless to help him do.

THE EXCEEDING SINFULNESS OF SIN

Romans 7: 7–13

What then are we to infer? That the law is sin? God forbid! So far from that, I would never have known what sin meant except through the law. I would never have known desire if the law had not said, " You must not covet." For, when sin had, through the commandment, obtained a foothold, it produced every kind of desire in me; for, without law, sin is lifeless. Once I lived without the law; but, when the commandment came, sin sprang to life, and in that moment I knew that I had incurred the penalty of death. The commandment that was meant for life—I discovered that that very commandment was in me for death. For, when sin obtained a foothold through the commandment, it seduced me, and, through it, killed me. So the law is holy, and the commandment is holy, just and good. Did then that which was good become death to me? God forbid! But the reason was that sin might be revealed as sin by producing death in me, through the very thing which was in itself good, so that, through the commandment, sin might become surpassingly sinful.

HERE begins one of the greatest of all passages in the New Testament; and one of the most moving; because here Paul is giving us his own spiritual autobiography and laying bare his very heart and soul.

Paul deals with the torturing paradox of the law. In itself it is a fine and a splendid thing. It is *holy*. That is to say it is the very voice of God. The root meaning of the word *holy* (*hagios*) is *different*. It describes something which comes from a sphere other than this world. The law is divine and has in it the very voice of God. It is *just*. We have seen that the root Greek idea of justice is that it consists in giving to man, and to God, their due. Therefore the law is that which settles all relationships, human and divine. If a man perfectly kept the law, he would be in a perfect relationship both with God and with his fellow men. The law is *good*. That is to say, it is designed for nothing other than our highest welfare. It is meant to make a man good.

All that is true. And yet the fact remains that this same law is the very thing through which sin gains entry into a man. How does that happen? There are two ways in which the law may be said to be, in one sense, the source of sin.

(i) *It defines sin*. Sin without the law, as Paul said, has no existence. Until a thing is defined as sin by the law, a man cannot know that it is sin. We might find a kind of remote analogy in any game, say tennis. A man might allow the ball to bounce more than once before he returned it over the net; so long as there were no rules he could not be accused of any fault. But then the rules are made, and it is laid down that the ball must be struck over the net after only one bounce and that to allow it to bounce twice is a fault. The rules define what a fault is, and that which was allowable before they were made, now becomes a fault. So the law defines sin.

We may take a better analogy. What is pardonable in a child, or in an uncivilized man from a savage country, may not be allowable in a mature person from a civilized land. The mature, civilized person is aware of laws of conduct which the child and the savage do not know; therefore, what is pardonable in them is fault in him.

The law creates sin in the sense that it defines it. It may for long enough be legal to drive a motor car in either direction along a street; then that street is declared one-way; after that a new breach of the law exists—that of driving in a forbidden direction. The new regulation actually creates a new fault. The law, by making men aware of what it is, creates sin.

(ii) But there is a much more serious sense in which the law produces sin. One of the strange facts of life is the fascination of the forbidden thing. The Jewish rabbis and thinkers saw that human tendency at work in the Garden of Eden. Adam at first lived in innocence; a commandment was given him not to touch the forbidden tree, and given only his good; but the serpent came and subtly turned that prohibition into a temptation. The fact that the tree was forbidden made it desirable; so Adam was seduced into sin by the forbidden fruit; and death was the result.

Philo allegorized the whole story. The *serpent* was pleasure; *Eve* stood for the *senses*; pleasure, as it always does, wanted the forbidden thing and attacked through the senses. *Adam* was the *reason*; and, through the attack of the forbidden thing on the senses, reason was led astray, and death came.

In his *Confessions* there is a famous passage in which Augustine tells of the fascination of the forbidden thing.

> " There was a pear tree near our vineyard, laden with fruit. One stormy night we rascally youths set out to rob it and carry our spoils away. We took off a huge load of pears—not to feast upon ourselves, but to throw them to the pigs, though we ate just enough to have the pleasure of forbidden fruit. They were nice pears, but it was not the pears that my wretched soul coveted, for I had plenty better at home. I picked them simply in order to become a thief. The only feast I got was a feast of iniquity, and that I enjoyed to the full. What was it that I loved in that theft? Was it the pleasure of acting against the law, in order that I, a prisoner under rules, might have a maimed counterfeit of freedom by doing what was forbidden, with a dim similitude of impotence? ... The desire to steal was awakened simply by the prohibition of stealing."

Set a thing in the category of forbidden things or put a place out of bounds, and immediately they become fascinating. In that sense the law produces sin.

Paul has one revealing word which he uses of sin. " Sin," he says, " *seduced* me." There is always deception in sin. Vaughan says that sin's delusion works in three directions. (i) We are deluded regarding the *satisfaction* to be found in sin. No man ever took a forbidden thing without thinking that it would make him happy, and no man ever found that it did. (ii) We are deluded regarding the *excuse* that can be made for it. Every man thinks that he can put up a defence for doing the wrong thing; but no man's defence ever sounded anything else but futile when it was made in the presence of God. (iii) We are deluded regarding the *probability of escaping the consequences of it*. No man sins without the hope that he can get away with it. But it is true that, soon or late, our sin will find us out.

Is, then, the law a bad thing because it actually produces sin? Paul is certain that there is wisdom in the whole sequence. (i) First he is convinced that, whatever the consequence, sin had to be defined as sin. (ii) The process shows the terrible nature of sin, because sin took a thing—the law—which was holy and just as good, and twisted it into something which served the ends of evil. The awfulness of sin is shown by the fact that it could take a fine thing and make it a weapon of evil. That is what sin does. It can take the loveliness of love and turn it into lust. It can take the honourable desire for independence and turn it into the obsession for money and for power. It can take the beauty of friendship and use it as a seduction to the wrong things. That is what Carlyle called " the infinite damnability of sin." The very fact that it took the law and made it a bridgehead to sin shows the supreme sinfulness of sin. The whole terrible process is not accidental; it is all designed to show us how awful a thing sin is, because it can take the loveliest things and defile them with a polluting touch.

THE HUMAN SITUATION

Romans 7: 14–25

> We are aware that the law is spiritual; but I am a creature of flesh and blood under the power of sin. I cannot understand what I do. What I want to do, that I do not do; but what I hate, that I do. If what I do not want to do I in point of fact do, then I acquiesce in the law, and I agree that it is fair. As it is, it is no longer I who do it, but the sin which resides in me—I mean in my human nature. To will the fair thing is within my range, but not to do it. For I do not do the good that I want to do; but the evil that I do not want to do, that is the very thing I do. And if I do that very thing that I do not want to do, it is no longer I who do it, but the sin which resides in me. My experience of the law, then, is that I wish to do

the fine thing and that the evil thing is the only thing that is within my ability. As far as my inner self is concerned, I fully agree with the law of God; but I see another law in my members, continually carrying on a campaign against the law of my mind, and making me a captive by the law of sin which is in my members. O wretched man that I am! Who will deliver me from this fatal body? God will! Thanks be to him through Jesus Christ our Lord. Therefore with my mind I serve the law of God, but with my human nature the law of sin.

PAUL is baring his very soul; and he is telling us of an experience which is of the very essence of the human situation. He knew what was right and wanted to do it; and yet, somehow, he never could. He knew what was wrong and the last thing he wanted was to do it; and yet, somehow, he did. He felt himself to be a split personality. It was as if two men were inside the one skin, pulling in different directions. He was haunted by this feeling of frustration, his ability to see what was good and his inability to do it; his ability to recognize what was wrong and his inability to refrain from doing it.

Paul's contemporaries well knew this feeling, as, indeed, we know it ourselves. Seneca talked of " our helplessness in necessary things." He talked about how men hate their sins and love them at the same time. Ovid, the Roman poet, had penned the famous tag: " I see the better things, and I approve them, but I follow the worse."

No one knew this problem better than the Jews. They had solved it by saying that in every man there were two natures, called the *Yetser hatob* and the *Yetser hara*. It was the Jewish conviction that God had made men like that with a good impulse and an evil impulse inside them.

There were Rabbis who believed that that evil impulse was in the very embryo in the womb, there before a man was even born. It was " a malevolent second personality." It was " man's implacable enemy." It was there waiting, if need be for a lifetime, for a chance to ruin man. But the Jew was equally clear, in theory, that no man need ever succumb to that evil impulse. It was all a matter of choice.

Ben Sirach wrote:

> " God himself created man from the beginning.
> And he left him in the hand of his own counsel.
> If thou so desirest thou shalt keep the commandments,
> And to perform faithfulness is of thine own good pleasure.
> He hath set fire and water before thee,
> Stretch forth thy hand unto whichever thou wilt.
> Before man is life and death,
> And whichever he liketh shall be given unto him. . . .
> He hath commanded no man to do wickedly,
> Neither have he given any man licence to sin."
>   (15: 11–20).

There were certain things which would keep a man from falling to the evil impulse. There was *the law*. They thought of God as saying:

> " I created for you the evil impulse; I created for you the law as an antiseptic."
> " If you occupy yourself with the law you will not fall into the power of the evil impulse."

There was *the will and the mind*.

> " When God created man, he implanted in him his affections and his dispositions; and then, over all, he enthroned the sacred, ruling mind."

When the evil impulse attacked, the Jew held that wisdom and reason could defeat it; to be occupied with the study of the word of the Lord was safety; the law was a prophylactic; at such a time the good impulse could be called up in defence.

Paul knew all that; and knew, too, that, while it was all theoretically true, in practice it was not true. There were things in man's human nature—that is what Paul meant by *this fatal* body—which answered to the seduction of sin. It is part of the human situation that we know the right and yet do the wrong, that we are never as good as we know we ought to be. At one and the same time we are haunted by goodness and haunted by sin.

From one point of view this passage might be called a demonstration of inadequacies.

(i) It demonstrates *the inadequacy of human knowledge*. If to know the right thing was to do it, life would be easy. But knowledge by itself does not make a man good. It is the same in every walk of life. We may know exactly how golf should be played but that is very far from being able to play it; we may know how poetry ought to be written but that is very far from being able to write it. We may know how we ought to behave in any given situation but that is very far from being able so to behave. That is the difference between religion and morality. Morality is knowledge of a code; religion is knowledge of a person; and it is only when we know Christ that we are able to do what we know we ought.

(ii) It demonstrates the inadequacy of *human resolution*. To resolve to do a thing is very far from doing it. There is in human nature an essential weakness of the will. The will comes up against the problems, the difficulties, the opposition—and it fails. Once Peter took a great resolution. " Even if I must die with you," he said, " I will not deny you " (*Matthew* 26: 35); and yet he failed badly when it came to the point. The human will unstrengthened by Christ is bound to crack.

(iii) It demonstrates *the limitations of diagnosis*. Paul knew quite clearly what was wrong; but he was unable to put it right. He was like a doctor who could accurately diagnose a disease but was powerless to prescribe a cure. Jesus is the one person who not only knows what is wrong, but who can also put the wrong to rights. It is not criticism he offers but help.

THE LIBERATION OF OUR HUMAN NATURE

Romans 8: 1–4

There is, therefore, now no condemnation against those who are in Christ Jesus. For the law which comes from the Spirit and leads to life has in Christ Jesus set me free from the law which begets sin and leads to death. As for the impotency of the law, that

weakness of the law which resulted from the effects of our sinful
human nature—God sent his own Son as a sin offering with that
very same human nature which in us had sinned; and thereby,
while he existed in the same human nature as we have, he
condemned sin, so that as a result the righteous demand of the law
might be fulfilled in us, who live our lives not after the principle of
sinful human nature, but after the principle of the Spirit.

THIS is a very difficult passage because it is so highly compressed, and because, all through it, Paul is making allusions to
things which he has already said.

Two words keep occurring again and again in this chapter,
flesh (*sarx*) and *spirit* (*pneuma*). We will not understand the
passage at all unless we understand the way in which Paul is using
these words.

(i) *Sarx* literally means flesh. The most cursory reading of
Paul's letters will show how often he uses the word, and how he
uses it in a sense that is all his own. Broadly speaking, he uses it in
three different ways.

(*a*) He uses it quite literally. He speaks of physical circumcision, literally " in the flesh " (*Romans* 2: 28). (*b*) Over and
over again he uses the phrase *kata sarka*, literally *according to the
flesh*, which most often means *looking at things from the human
point of view*. For instance, he says that Abraham is our forefather
kata sarka, from the human point of view. He says that Jesus is
the son of David *kata sarka* (*Romans* 1: 3), that is to say, on the
human side of his descent. He speaks of the Jews being his
kinsmen *kata sarka* (*Romans* 9: 3), that is to say, speaking of
human relationships. When Paul uses the phrase *kata sarka*, it
always implies that he is looking at things from the human point
of view.

(*c*) But he has a use of this word *sarx* which is all his own.
When he is talking of the Christians, he talks of the days when we
were *in the flesh* (*en sarki*) (*Romans* 7: 5). He speaks of those *who
walk according to the flesh* in contradistinction to those who live
the Christian life (*Romans* 8: 4, 5). He says that those who are *in
the flesh* cannot please God (*Romans* 8: 8). He says that *the mind
of the flesh* is death, and that it is hostile to God (*Romans* 8: 6, 8).

He talks about *living according to the flesh* (*Romans* 8: 12). He says to his Christian friends, " You are not *in the flesh* " (*Romans* 8: 9).

It is quite clear, especially from the last instance, that Paul is not using flesh simply in the sense of the body, as we say *flesh and blood*. How, then, is he using it? He really means human nature in all its weakness and he means human in its vulnerability to sin. He means that part of man which gives sin its bridgehead. He means sinful human nature, apart from Christ, everything that attaches a man to the world instead of to God. *To live according to the flesh* is to live a life dominated by the dictates and desires of sinful human nature instead of a life dominated by the dictates and the love of God. The flesh is the lower side of man's nature.

It is to be carefully noted that when Paul thinks of the kind of life that a man dominated by the *sarx* lives he is *not* by any means thinking exclusively of sexual and bodily sins. When he gives a list of the works of the flesh in *Galatians* 5: 19–21, he includes the bodily and the sexual sins; but he also includes idolatry, hatred, wrath, strife, heresies, envy, murder. The flesh to him was not a physical thing but spiritual. It was human nature in all its sin and weakness; it was all that man is without God and without Christ.

(ii) There is the word *Spirit*; in this single chapter it occurs no fewer than twenty times. This word has a very definite Old Testament background. In Hebrew it is *ruach*, and it has two basic thoughts. (*a*) It is not only the word for *Spirit*; it is also the word for *wind*. It has always the idea of power about it, power as of a mighty rushing wind. (*b*) In the Old Testament, it always has the idea of something that is more than human. *Spirit*, to Paul, represented a power which was divine.

So Paul says in this passage that there was a time when the Christian was at the mercy of his own sinful human nature. In that state the law simply became something that moved him to sin and he went from bad to worse, a defeated and frustrated man. But, when he became a Christian, into his life there came the surging power of the Spirit of God, and, as a result, he entered into victorious living.

In the second part of the passage Paul speaks of the effect of the work of Jesus on us. It is complicated and difficult, but what Paul is getting at is this. Let us remember that he began all this by saying that every man sinned in Adam. We saw how the Jewish conception of solidarity made it possible for him to argue that, quite literally, all men were involved in Adam's sin and in its consequence—death. But there is another side to this picture. Into this world came Jesus; with a completely human nature; and he brought to God a life of perfect obedience, of perfect fulfilment of God's law. Now, because Jesus was fully a man, just as we were one with Adam, we are now one with him; and, just as we were involved in Adam's sin, we are now involved in Jesus's perfection. In him mankind brought to God the perfect obedience, just as in Adam mankind brought to God the fatal disobedience. Men are saved because they were once involved in Adam's sin but are now involved in Jesus's goodness. That is Paul's argument, and, to him and to those who heard it, it was completely convincing, however hard it is for us to grasp it. Because of what Jesus did, there opens out to the Christian a life no longer dominated by the flesh but by that Spirit of God, which fills a man with a power not his own. The penalty of the past is removed and strength for his future is assured.

THE TWO PRINCIPLES OF LIFE

Romans 8: 5–11

Those who live according to the dictates of sinful human nature are absorbed in worldly human things. Those who live according to the dictates of the Spirit are absorbed in the things of the Spirit. To be absorbed in worldly human things is death; but to be absorbed in the things of the Spirit is life and peace, because absorption in the things which fascinate our sinful human nature is hostility to God, for it does not obey the law of God, nor indeed, can it do so. Those whose life is a purely worldly thing cannot please God; but you are not dominated by the pursuits which fascinate our sinful human nature; you are dominated by the Spirit, if so it be that the Spirit of God dwells in you. If anyone

does not possess the Spirit of Christ he does not belong to Christ.
But if Christ is in you, even if because of sin your body is mortal,
your Spirit has life through righteousness. If the Spirit of him who
raised Jesus from the dead dwells in you he will make even your
mortal bodies alive through his Spirit indwelling in you.

PAUL is drawing a contrast between two kinds of life.

(i) There is the life which is dominated by sinful human
nature; whose focus and centre is self; whose only law is its own
desires; which takes what it likes where it likes. In different
people that life will be differently described. It may be passion-
controlled, or lust-controlled, or pride-controlled, or ambition-
controlled. Its characteristic is its absorption in the things that
human nature without Christ sets its heart upon.

(ii) There is the life that is dominated by the Spirit of God.
As a man lives in the air, he lives in Christ, never separated
from him. As he breathes in the air and the air fills him, so
Christ fills him. He has no mind of his own; Christ is his mind.
He has no desires of his own; the will of Christ is his only law.
He is Spirit-controlled, Christ-controlled, God-focused.

These two lives are going in diametrically opposite directions. The life that is dominated by the desires and activities of
sinful human nature is on the way to death. In the most literal
sense, there is no future in it—because it is getting further and
further away from God. To allow the things of the world
completely to dominate life is self extinction; it is spiritual
suicide. By living it, a man is making himself totally unfit ever
to stand in the presence of God. He is hostile to him, resentful
of his law and his control. God is not his friend but his enemy,
and no man ever won the last battle against him.

The Spirit-controlled life, the Christ-centred life, the God-
focused life is daily coming nearer heaven even when it is still
on earth. It is a life which is such a steady progress to God that
the final transition of death is only a natural and inevitable
stage on the way. It is like Enoch who walked with God and
God took him. As the child said: " Enoch was a man who went
walks with God—and one day he didn't come back."

No sooner has Paul said this than an inevitable objection

strikes him. Someone may object: " You say that the Spirit-controlled man is on the way to life; but in point of fact every man must die. Just what do you mean? " Paul's answer is this. All men die because they are involved in the human situation. Sin came into this world and with sin came death, the consequence of sin. Inevitably, therefore, all men die; but the man who is Spirit-controlled and whose heart is Christ-occupied, dies only to rise again. Paul's basic thought is that the Christian is indissolubly one with Christ. Now Christ died and rose again; and the man who is one with Christ is one with death's conqueror and shares in that victory. The Spirit-controlled, Christ-possessed man is on the way to life; death is but an inevitable interlude that has to be passed through on the way.

ENTRY INTO THE FAMILY OF GOD

Romans 8: 12–17

> So then, brothers, a duty is laid upon us—and that duty is *not* to our own sinful human nature, to live according to the principles of that same nature; for, if you live according to the principles of sinful human nature, you are on the way to death; but if by the spirit you kill the deeds of the body, you will live. For all who are guided by the Spirit of God, these, and only these, are the children of God. For you did not receive a state whose dominating condition is slavery so that you might relapse into fear; but you received a state whose dominating characteristic is adoption, in which we cry, " Abba! Father! " The Spirit itself bears witness with our spirit that we are children of God. If we are children then we are also heirs; and if we are the heirs of God then we are joint-heirs with Christ. If we suffer with him we shall also be glorified with him.

PAUL is introducing us to another of the great metaphors in which he describes the new relationship of the Christian to God. He speaks of the Christian being adopted into the family of God. It is only when we understand how serious and complicated a step Roman adoption was that we really understand the depth of meaning in this passage.

Roman adoption was always rendered more serious and more difficult by the Roman *patria potestas*. This was the father's power over his family; it was the power of absolute disposal and control, and in the early days was actually the power of life and death. In regard to his father, a Roman son never came of age. No matter how old he was, he was still under the *patria potestas*, in the absolute possession and under the absolute control, of his father. Obviously this made adoption into another family a very difficult and serious step. In adoption a person had to pass from one *patria potestas* to another.

There were two steps. The first was known as *mancipatio*, and was carried out by a symbolic sale, in which copper and scales were symbolically used. Three times the symbolism of sale was carried out. Twice the father symbolically sold his son, and twice he bought him back; but the third time he did not buy him back and thus the *patria potestas* was held to be broken. There followed a ceremony called *vindicatio*. The adopting father went to the *praetor*, one of the Roman magistrates, and presented a legal case for the transference of the person to be adopted into his *patria potestas*. When all this was completed, the adoption was complete. Clearly this was a serious and an impressive step.

But it is the consequences of adoption which are most significant for the picture that is in Paul's mind. There were four main ones. (i) The adopted person lost all rights in his old family and gained all the rights of a legitimate son in his new family. In the most binding legal way, he got a new father. (ii) It followed that he became heir to his new father's estate. Even if other sons were afterwards born, it did not affect his rights. He was inalienably co-heir with them. (iii) In law, the old life of the adopted person was completely wiped out; for instance, all debts were cancelled. He was regarded as a new person entering into a new life with which the past had nothing to do. (iv) In the eyes of the law he was absolutely the son of his new father. Roman history provides an outstanding case of how completely this was held to be true. The Emperor Claudius adopted Nero in order that he might succeed him on the throne; they were not in any sense blood relations. Claudius already had a daughter, Octavia. To cement the alliance Nero wished to marry her. Nero and Octavia were in no sense blood relations; yet, in the eyes of the law, they were brother and sister; and before they could marry, the Roman senate had to pass special legislation.

That is what Paul is thinking of. He uses still another picture from Roman adoption. He says that God's spirit witnesses with our spirit that we really are his children. The adoption ceremony was carried out in the presence of seven witnesses. Now, suppose the adopting father died and there was some dispute about the right of the adopted son to inherit, one or more of the seven witnesses stepped forward and swore that the adoption was genuine. Thus the right of the adopted person was guaranteed and he entered into his inheritance. So, Paul is saying, it is the Holy Spirit himself who is the witness to our adoption into the family of God.

We see then that every step of Roman adoption was meaningful in the mind of Paul when he transferred the picture to our adoption into the family of God. Once we were in the absolute control of our own sinful human nature; but God, in his mercy, has brought us into his absolute possession. The old life has no more rights over us; God has an absolute right. The past is cancelled and its debts are wiped out; we begin a new life with God and become heirs of all his riches. If that is so, we become joint heirs with Jesus Christ, God's own Son. That which Christ inherits, we also inherit. If Christ had to suffer, we also inherit that suffering; but if Christ was raised to life and glory, we also inherit that life and glory.

It was Paul's picture that when a man became a Christian he entered into the very family of God. He did nothing to deserve it; God, the great Father, in his amazing love and mercy, has taken the lost, helpless, poverty-stricken, debt-laden sinner and adopted him into his own family, so that the debts are cancelled and the glory inherited.

THE GLORIOUS HOPE

Romans 8: 18–25

> For I am convinced that the sufferings of this present age cannot
> be compared with the glory which is destined to be disclosed to
> us. The created world awaits with eager expectation the day when
> those who are the sons of God will be displayed in all their glory.
> For the created world has been subjected to chaos, not because of
> its own choice, but through him who passed the sentence of such
> subjugation upon it, and yet it still has the hope that the created
> world also will be liberated from this slavery to decay and will be
> brought to the freedom of the glory of the children of God; for we
> know that the whole creation unites together in groans and
> agonies. Not only does the created world do so, but so do we, even
> though we have received the first-fruits of the spirit as a foretaste
> of the coming glory, yes, we too groan within ourselves earnestly
> awaiting the full realization of our adoption into the family of
> God. I mean the redemption of our body. For it is by hope that we
> are saved; but a hope which is already visible is not a hope; for
> who hopes for what he already sees? But if we hope for what we
> do not see, then in patience we eagerly wait for it.

PAUL has just been speaking of the glory of adoption into the
family of God; and then he comes back to the troubled state of
this present world. He draws a great picture. He speaks with a
poet's vision. He sees all nature waiting for the glory that shall
be. At the moment creation is in bondage to decay.

" Change and decay in all around I see."

The world is one where beauty fades and loveliness decays; it is
a dying world; but it is waiting for its liberation from all this
and the coming of the state of glory.

When Paul was painting this picture, he was working with
ideas that any Jew would recognize and understand. He talks of
this present age and of the glory that will be disclosed. Jewish
thought divided time into two sections—this present age and
the age to come. This present age was wholly bad, subject to
sin, and death and decay. Some day there would come The Day

of the Lord. That would be a day of judgment when the world would be shaken to its foundations; but out of it there would come a new world.

The renovation of the world was one of the great Jewish thoughts. The Old Testament speaks of it without elaboration and without detail. " Behold I create new heavens and a new earth " (*Isaiah* 65: 17). But in the days between the Testaments, when the Jews were oppressed and enslaved and persecuted, they dreamed their dreams of that new earth and that renovated world.

> " The vine shall yield its fruit ten thousand fold, and on each vine there shall be a thousand branches; and each branch shall produce a thousand clusters; and each cluster produce a thousand grapes; and each grape a cor of wine. And those who have hungered shall rejoice; moreover, also, they shall behold marvels every day. For winds shall go forth from before me to bring every morning the fragrance of aromatic fruits, and at the close of the day clouds distilling the dews of health" (*The Apocalypse of Baruch* 29: 5).

> " And earth, and all the trees, and the innumerable flocks of sheep shall give their true fruit to mankind, of wine and of sweet honey and of white milk and corn, which to men is the most excellent gift of all" (*Sibylline Oracles* 3: 620–633).

> " Earth, the universal mother, shall give to mortals her best fruit in countless store of corn, wine and oil. Yea, from heaven shall come a sweet draught of luscious honey. The trees shall yield their proper fruits, and rich flocks, and kine, and lambs of sheep and kids of goats. He will cause sweet fountains of white milk to burst forth. And the cities shall be full of good things, and the fields rich; neither shall there be any sword throughout the land or battle-din; nor shall the earth be convulsed any more with deep-drawn groans. No war shall be any more, nor shall there be any more drought throughout the land, no famine, or hail to work havoc on the crops" (*Sibylline Oracles* 3: 744–756).

The dream of the renovated world was dear to the Jews. Paul knew that, and here he, as it were, endows creation with consciousness. He thinks of nature longing for the day when sin's dominion would be broken, death and decay would be gone, and God's glory would come. With a touch of imaginative insight, he says that the state of nature was even worse than the state of men. Man had sinned deliberately; but it was involuntarily that nature was subjected. Unwittingly she was involved in the consequences of the sin of man. " Cursed is the ground because of you," God said to Adam after his sin (*Genesis* 3: 17). So here, with a poet's eye, Paul sees nature waiting for liberation from the death and decay that man's sin had brought into the world.

If that is true of nature, it is still truer of man. So Paul goes on to think of human longing. In the experience of the Holy Spirit men had a foretaste, a first instalment, of the glory that shall be; now they long with all their hearts for the full realization of what adoption into the family of God means. That final adoption will be the redemption of their bodies. In the state of glory Paul did not think of man as a disembodied spirit. Man in this world is a body and a spirit; and in the world of glory the total man will be saved. But his body will no longer be the victim of decay and the instrument of sin; it will be a spiritual body fit for the life of a spiritual man.

Then comes a great saying. " We are saved by hope." The blazing truth that lit life for Paul was that the human situation is not hopeless. Paul was no pessimist. H. G. Wells once said: " Man, who began in a cave behind a windbreak, will end in the disease soaked ruins of a slum." Not so Paul. He saw man's sin and the state of the world; but he also saw God's redeeming power; and the end of it all for him was hope. Because of that, to Paul life was not a despairing waiting for an inevitable end in a world encompassed by sin and death and decay; life was an eager anticipation of a liberation, a renovation and a re-creation wrought by the glory and the power of God.

In verse 19 he uses a wonderful word for *eager expectation*. It is *apokaradokia* and it describes the attitude of a man who scans the horizon with head thrust forward, eagerly searching the distance for the first signs of the dawn break of glory. To Paul life was not a weary, defeated waiting; it was a throbbing, vivid expectation. The Christian is involved in the human situation. Within he must battle with his own evil human nature; without he must live in a world of death and decay. Nonetheless, the Christian does not live only in the world; he also lives in Christ. He does not see only the world; he looks beyond it to God. He does not see only the consequences of man's sin; he sees the power of God's mercy and love. Therefore, the keynote of the Christian life is always hope and never despair. The Christian waits, not for death, but for life.

ALL IS OF GOD

Romans 8: 26–30

> Even so, the Spirit helps us in our weakness; for we do not know what we should pray, if we are to pray as we ought. But the Spirit himself intercedes for us with groanings which baffle speech to utter; but he who searches the hearts knows the mind of the Spirit, because it is by God's will that he intercedes for those whose lives are consecrated to God. We know that God intermingles all things for good for those who love him, for those who are called according to his purpose. For those whom he knew long ago he long ago designed to be conformed to the likeness of his Son, that he might be the first born among many brothers. Those whom he long ago designed for this purpose, he also called; and those whom he called he put into a right relationship with himself; and those whom he put into a right relationship with himself he also glorified.

THE first two verses form one of the most important passages on prayer in the whole New Testament. Paul is saying that, because of our weakness, we do not know what to pray for, but the prayers we ought to offer are offered for us by the Holy Spirit. C. H. Dodd defines prayer in this way—" Prayer is the divine in us appealing to the Divine above us."

There are two very obvious reasons why we cannot pray as we ought. First, we cannot pray aright because we cannot foresee the future. We cannot see a year or even an hour ahead; and we may well pray, therefore, to be saved from things which are for our good and we may well pray for things which would be to our ultimate harm. Second, we cannot pray aright because in any given situation we do not know what is best for us. We are often in the position of a child who wants something which would be bound only to hurt him; and God is often in the position of a parent who has to refuse his child's request or compel him to do something he does not want to do, because he knows what is to the child's good far better than the child himself.

Even the Greeks knew that. Pythagoras forbade his disciples to pray for themselves, because, he said, they could never in their ignorance know what was expedient for them. Xenophon tells us that Socrates taught his disciples simply to pray for good things, and not to attempt to specify them, but to leave God to decide what the good things were. C. H. Dodd puts it in this way. We cannot know our own real need; we cannot with our finite minds grasp God's plan; in the last analysis all that we can bring to God is an inarticulate sigh which the Spirit will translate to God for us.

As Paul saw it, prayer, like everything else, is of God. He knew that by no possible human effort can a man justify himself; and he also knew that by no possible effort of the human intelligence can a man know for what to pray. In the last analysis the perfect prayer is simply, " Father, into Thy hands I commend my spirit. Not my will, but Thine be done."

But Paul goes on from there. He says that those who love God, and who are called according to his purpose, know well that God is intermingling all things for good to them. It is the experience of life for the Christian that all things do work together for good. We do not need to be very old to look back and see that things we thought were disasters worked out to our good; things that we thought were disappointments worked out to greater blessings.

But we have to note that that experience comes only *to those who love God*. The Stoics had a great idea which may well have been in Paul's mind when he wrote this passage. One of their great conceptions was the *logos* of God, which was God's mind or the reason. The Stoic believed that this world was permeated with that *logos*. It was the *logos* which put sense into the world. It was the *logos* which kept the stars in their courses and the planets in their appointed tracks. It was the *logos* which controlled the ordered succession of night and day, and summer and winter and spring and autumn. The *logos* was the reason and the mind of God in the universe, making it an order and not a chaos.

The Stoic went further. He believed that the *logos* not only had an order for the universe, but also a plan and a purpose for the life of every individual man. To put it in another way, the Stoic believed that nothing could happen to a man which did not come from God and which was not part of God's plan for him. Epictetus writes: " Have courage to look up to God and to say, ' Deal with me as thou wilt from now on. I am as one with thee; I am thine; I flinch from nothing so long as thou dost think that it is good. Lead me where thou wilt; put on me what raiment thou wilt. Wouldst thou have me hold office or eschew it, stay or flee, be rich or poor? For this I will defend thee before men.' " The Stoic taught that the duty of every man was *acceptance*. If he accepted the things that God sent him, he knew peace. If he struggled against them, he was uselessly battering his head against the ineluctable purpose of God.

Paul has the very same thought. He says that all things work together for good, but only *to them that love God*. If a man loves and trusts and accepts God, if he is convinced that God is the all-wise and all-loving Father, then he can humbly accept all that he sends to him. A man may go to a physician, and be prescribed a course of treatment which at the time is unpleasant or even painful; but if he trusts the wisdom of the man of skill, he accepts the thing that is laid upon him. It is so with us if we love God. But if a man does not love and trust God, he may well resent what happens to him and may well fight against God's will. It is only to the man who loves and trusts that all things work together for good, for to him they come from a

Father who in perfect wisdom, love and power is working ever for the best.

Paul goes further; he goes on to speak of the spiritual experience of every Christian. The Authorized Version rendering is famous. " For whom he did foreknow he also did predestinate to be conformed to the image of his Son, that he might be the firstborn among many brethren. Moreover, whom he did predestinate, them he also called; and whom he called them he also justified; and whom he justified them he also glorified." This is a passage which has been very seriously misused. If we are ever to understand it we must grasp the basic fact that Paul never meant it to be the expression of theology or philosophy; he meant it to be the almost lyrical expression of Christian experience. If we take it as philosophy and theology and apply the standards of cold logic to it, it must mean that God chose some and did not choose others. But that is not what it means.

Think of the Christian experience. The more a Christian thinks of his experience the more he becomes convinced that he had nothing to do with it and all is of God. Jesus Christ came into this world; he lived; he went to the Cross; he rose again. We did nothing to bring that about; that is God's work. We heard the story of this wondrous love. We did not *make* the story; we only *received* the story. Love woke within our hearts; the conviction of sin came, and with it came the experience of forgiveness and of salvation. We did not achieve that; all is of God. That is what Paul is thinking of here.

The Old Testament has an illuminating use of the word *to know*. " I knew you in the wilderness," said God to Hosea about the people of Israel (*Hosea* 13: 5). " You only have I *known* of all the families of the earth," said God to Amos (*Amos* 3: 2). When the Bible speaks of God *knowing* a man, it means that he has a purpose and a plan and a task for that man. And when we look back upon our Christian experience, all we can say is, " I did not do this; I could never have done this; God did everything." And we know well that this does not take freewill away. God knew Israel, but the day came when Israel refused the destiny God meant her to have. God's unseen guiding is in our lives, but to the end of the day we can refuse it and take our own way.

It is the deep experience of the Christian that all is of God; that he did nothing and that God did everything. That is what Paul means here. He means that from the beginning of time God marked us out for salvation; that in due time his call came to us; but the pride of man's heart can wreck God's plan and the disobedience of man's will can refuse the call.

THE LOVE FROM WHICH NOTHING CAN SEPARATE US

Romans 8: 31–39

What then shall we say to these things? If God is for us, who is against us? The very God who did not spare his own Son but who delivered him up for us all, how shall he not with him also freely give us all things? Who shall impeach the elect of God? It is God who acquits. Who is he who condemns? It is Jesus Christ who died, nay rather, who was raised from the dead, and who is at the right hand of God, who also intercedes for us. Who will separate us from the love of Christ? Shall trial, or distress, or persecution, or famine, or nakedness, or peril, or sword? As it stands written, " For Thy sake we are killed all the day long; we are reckoned as sheep for the slaughter." But in all these things we are more than conquerors through him who loved us. For I am convinced that neither death, nor life, nor angels, nor principalities, nor the present age, nor the age to come, nor powers, nor height, nor depth, nor any other creation will be able to separate us from the love of God which is in Christ Jesus our Lord.

THIS is one of the most lyrical passages Paul ever wrote. In verse 32 there is a wonderful allusion which would stand out to any Jew who knew his Old Testament well. Paul says in effect: " God for us did not spare his own Son; surely that is the final guarantee that he loves us enough to supply all our needs." The words Paul uses of God are the very words God used of

Abraham when Abraham proved his utter loyalty by being willing to sacrifice his son Isaac at God's command. God said to Abraham: " You have not withheld your son, your only son, from me " (*Genesis* 22: 12). Paul seems to say: " Think of the greatest human example in the world of a man's loyalty to God; God's loyalty to you is like that." Just as Abraham was so loyal to God that he was prepared to sacrifice his dearest possession, God is so loyal to men that he is prepared to sacrifice his only Son for them. Surely we can trust a loyalty like that for anything.

It is difficult to know just how to take verses 33–35. There are two ways of taking them and both give excellent sense and precious truth.

(i) We can take them as two statements, followed by two questions which give the inferences to be made from these statements. (*a*) It is God who acquits men—that is the statement. If that be so who can possibly condemn men? If man is acquitted by God, then he is saved from every other condemnation. (*b*) Our belief is in a Christ who died and rose again and who is alive for evermore—that is the statement. If that be so, is there anything in this or any other world that can separate us from our Risen Lord?

If we take it that way two great truths are laid down. (*a*) God has acquitted us; therefore no one can condemn us. (*b*) Christ is risen; therefore nothing can ever separate us from him.

(ii) But there is another way to take it. God has acquitted us. Who then can condemn us? The answer is that the Judge of all men is Jesus Christ. He is the one who has the right to condemn—but so far from condemning, he is at God's right hand interceding for us, and therefore we are safe.

It may be that in verse 34 Paul is doing a very wonderful thing. He is saying four things about Jesus. (*a*) He died. (*b*) He rose again. (*c*) He is at the right hand of God. (*d*) He makes intercession for us there. Now the earliest creed of the Church, which is still the essence of all Christian creeds, ran like this: " He was crucified dead and buried; the third day he rose again from the dead; and sitteth at the right hand of God; *from thence he shall come to judge the quick and the dead.*" Three items in Paul's statement and in the early creed are the same, that Jesus died, rose again, and is at the right hand of God. *But the fourth is different.* In the creed the fourth is that Jesus will come *to be the judge of the quick and the dead.* In Paul the fourth is that Jesus is at God's right hand *to plead our case.* It is as if Paul said: " You think of Jesus as the Judge who is there to condemn; and well he might for he has won the right. But you are wrong; he is not there to be our prosecuting counsel but to be the advocate to plead our cause."

I think that the second way of taking this is right. With one tremendous leap of thought Paul has seen Christ, not as the Judge but as the lover of the souls of men.

Paul goes on with a poet's fervour and a lover's rapture to sing of how nothing can separate us from the love of God in our Risen Lord.

(i) No affliction, no hardship, no peril can separate us. (Verse 35.) The disasters of the world do not separate a man from Christ; they bring him closer yet.

(ii) In verses 38 and 39 Paul makes a list of terrible things.

Neither *life nor death* can separate us from Christ. In life we live with Christ; in death we die with him; and because we die with him, we also rise with him. Death, so far from being a separation, is only a step into his nearer presence; not the end but " the gate on the skyline " leading to the presence of Jesus Christ.

The angelic powers cannot separate us from him. At this particular time the Jews had a highly developed belief in angels. Everything had its angel. There was an angel of the winds, of the clouds, of the snow and hail and hoarfrost, of the thunder and the lightning, of cold and heat, of the seasons. The Rabbis said that there was nothing in the world, not even a blade of grass, that had not got its angel. According to the Rabbis there were three ranks of angels. The first included thrones, cherubim and seraphim. The second included powers, lordships and mights. The third included angels and archangels and princi-palities. More than once Paul speaks of these angels (*Ephesians*

1: 21; 3: 10; 6: 12; *Colossians* 2: 10, 15; 1 *Corinthians* 15: 24). Now the Rabbis—and Paul had once been a Rabbi—believed that they were grudgingly hostile to men. They believed that they had been angry when God created man. It was as if they did not want to share God with anyone and had grudged man his share in him. The Rabbis had a legend that when God appeared on Sinai to give Moses the law he was attended by his hosts of angels, and the angels grudged Israel the law, and assaulted Moses on his way up the mountain and would have stopped him had not God intervened. So Paul, thinking in terms of his own day, says, " Not even the grudging, jealous angels can separate us from the love of God, much as they would like to do so."

No age in time can separate us from Christ. Paul speaks of *things present and things to come*. We know that the Jews divided all time into *this present age* and *the age to come*. Paul is saying: " In this present world nothing can separate us from God in Christ; the day will come when this world will be shattered and the new age will dawn. It does not matter; even then, when this world has passed and the new world come, the bond is still the same."

No malign influences (powers) will separate us from Christ. Paul speaks about *height and depth*. These are astrological terms. The ancient world was haunted by the tyranny of the stars. They believed that a man was born under a certain star and thereby his destiny was settled. There are some who still believe that; but the ancient world was really haunted by this supposed domination of a man's life by the influence of the stars. *Height* (*hupsōma*) was the time when a star was at its zenith and its influence was greatest; *depth* (*hathos*) was the time when a star was at its lowest, waiting to rise and to put its influence on some man. Paul says to these haunted men of his age: " The stars cannot hurt you. In their rising and their setting they are powerless to separate you from God's love."

No other world can separate us from God. The word that Paul uses for *other* (*heteros*) has really the meaning of *different*. He is saying: " Suppose that by some wild flight of imagination there emerged another and a different world, you would still be safe; you would still be enwrapped in the love of God."

Here is a vision to take away all loneliness and all fear. Paul is saying: " You can think of every terrifying thing that this or any other world can produce. Not one of them is able to separate the Christian from the love of God which is in Jesus Christ, Lord of every terror and Master of every world." Of what then shall we be afraid?

THE PROBLEM OF THE JEWS

In chapters 9 to 11 Paul tries to deal with one of the most bewildering problems that the Church has to solve—the problem of the Jews. They were God's chosen people; they had had a unique place in God's purposes; and yet when God's Son had come into the world they had rejected him and crucified him. How is this tragic paradox to be explained? That is the problem with which Paul seeks to deal in these chapters. They are complicated and difficult, and, before we begin to study them in detail, it will be well to set out the broad lines of the solution which Paul presented.

One thing we must note before we begin to disentangle Paul's thought—the chapters were written not in anger but in heartbreak. He could never forget that he was a Jew and he would gladly have laid down his own life if, by so doing, he could have brought his brethren to Jesus Christ.

Paul never denies that the Jews were the chosen people. God adopted them as his own; he gave them the covenants and the service of the Temple and the law; he gave them the presence of his own glory; he gave them the patriarchs. Above all Jesus was a Jew. The special place of the Jews in God's economy of salvation Paul accepts as an axiom and as the starting-point of the whole problem.

The first point which he makes is this—it is true that the Jews as a nation rejected and crucified Jesus, but it is also true, that *not all the Jews rejected him*; some received him and believed in him, for all the early followers of Jesus were Jews. Paul then looks back on history and insists that racial descent from Abraham does not make a Jew. Over and over again in Jewish history there was in God's ways a process of selection—Paul calls it *election*—whereby some of those who were racial descendants of Abraham were chosen and some rejected. In the case of Abraham, Isaac, the son born according to the promise of God, was chosen, but Ishmael, the son born of purely natural desire, was not. In the case of Isaac, his son Jacob was chosen, but Esau, Jacob's twin, was not. This selection had nothing to do with merit; it was the work entirely of God's electing wisdom and power.

Further, the real chosen people never lay in the whole nation; it always lay in *the righteous remnant*, the few who were true to God when all others denied him. It was so in the days of Elijah, when seven thousand remained faithful to God after the rest of the nation had gone after Baal. It was an essential part of the teaching of Isaiah, who said: " Though the number of the children of Israel be as the sand of the sea, *only a remnant of them will be saved* " (*Isaiah* 10: 22; *Romans* 9: 27). Paul's first point is that at no time were the whole people the chosen people. There was always selection, *election*, on the part of God.

Is it fair of God to elect some and to reject others? And, if some men are elected and others are rejected through no virtue or fault of their own, how can you blame them if they reject Christ, and how can you praise them if they accept him? Here Paul uses an argument at which the mind staggers, and from which we quite properly recoil. Bluntly, it is that God can do what he likes and that man has no right whatever to question his decisions, however inscrutable they may be. The clay cannot talk back to the potter. A craftsman may make two vessels, one for an honourable purpose and another for a menial purpose; the vessels have nothing whatever to do with it. That, said Paul, is what God has a right to do with men. He quotes the instance of Pharaoh (*Romans* 9: 17) and says that he was brought on to the stage of history simply to be the instrument through which God's avenging power was demonstrated. In any event, the people of Israel had been forewarned of the election of the Gentiles and of their own rejection, for, did not the prophet Hosea write: " Those who were not my people I will call ' my people ', and her who was not beloved I will call ' my beloved ' " (*Hosea* 1: 10; *Romans* 9: 25).

However, this rejection of Israel was not callous and haphazard. The door was shut to the Jews that it might be opened to the Gentiles. God hardened the hearts of the Jews and blinded their eyes with the ultimate purpose of opening a way for the Gentiles into the faith. Here is a strange and terrible argument. Stripped of all its non-essentials, it is that God can do what he likes with any man or nation, and that he deliberately darkened the minds and shut the eyes of the Jews in order that the Gentiles might come in.

What was the fundamental mistake of the Jews? This may seem a curious question to ask in view of what we have just said. But, paradoxically, Paul holds that though the rejection of the Jews was the work of God, it need never have happened. He cannot get rid of the eternal paradox—nor does he desire to—that at one and the same time all is of God and man has free will. The fundamental mistake of the Jews was that they tried to get into a right relationship with God through their own efforts. They tried to earn salvation; whereas the Gentiles simply accepted the offer of God in perfect trust. The Jews should have known that the only way to God was the way of faith and that human achievement led nowhere. Did not Isaiah say: " No one who believes in him will be put to shame "? (*Isaiah* 28: 16; *Romans* 10: 11.) Did not Joel say: " Everyone who calls upon the name of the Lord will be saved "? (*Joel* 2: 32; Romans 10: 13.) True, no man can have faith until he hears the offer of God; but to the Jews that offer was made. They clung to the way of human achievement through obedience to the law; they staked everything on works; but they should have known that the way to God was the way of faith, for the prophets had told them so.

Once again it is to be stressed that all this was God's arrangement; and that it was so arranged to allow the Gentiles to come in. Paul therefore turns to the Gentiles. He orders them to have no pride. They are in the position of wild olive shoots which have been grafted into a garden olive tree. They did not achieve their own salvation any more than the Jews did; in point of fact they are dependent on the Jews; they are only engrafted branches; the root and the stem are still the chosen people. The fact of their own election and the fact of the rejection of the Jews are not to produce pride in Gentile hearts. If that happens, rejection can and will happen to them.

Is this the end? Far from it. It is God's purpose that the Jews will be moved to envy at the relationship of the Gentiles to him and that they will ask to be admitted to it themselves. Did not Moses say: " I make you jealous of those who are not a nation; with a foolish nation I will make you angry "? (*Deuteronomy* 32: 21; *Romans* 10: 19.) In the end the Gentiles will be the very instrument by which the Jews will be saved. " And so all Israel will be saved " (*Romans* 11: 26).

So Paul comes to the end of the argument. We may summarily set out its steps.

(i) Israel is the chosen people.

(ii) To be a member of Israel means more than racial descent. There has always been election within the nation; and the best of the nation has always been the remnant who were faithful.

(iii) This selection by God is not unfair, for he has the right to do what he likes.

(iv) God did harden the hearts of the Jews, but only to open the door to the Gentiles.

(v) Israel's mistake was dependence on human achievement founded on the law; the necessary approach to God is that of the totally trusting heart.

(vi) The Gentiles must have no pride for they are only wild olives grafted into the true olive stock. They must remember that.

(vii) This is not the end; the Jews will be so moved to wondering envy at the privilege that the Gentiles have received that in the end they will be brought in by them.

(viii) So in the very end all, Jew and Gentile, will be saved.

The glory is in the end of Paul's argument. He began by saying that some were elected to reception and some to rejection. In the end he comes to say that it is God's will that all men should be saved.

THE TRAGIC FAILURE

Romans 9: 1–6

I tell you the truth as one who is united to Christ is bound to do. I do not lie. My conscience bears witness with me in the Holy Spirit when I say that my grief is great and there is unceasing anguish in my heart. I could pray that I myself might be accursed so that I was completely separated from Christ for the sake of my brothers, my kinsmen as far as human relationship goes. For my kinsmen are the Israelites, and theirs is the special sonship of God, and the glory and the covenants and the giving of the law and the worship of the Temple and the promises. To them the fathers belong. And from them, on his human side, came the Anointed One of God. Blessed for ever be the God who is over all! Amen.

PAUL begins his attempt to explain the Jewish rejection of Jesus Christ. He begins, not in anger, but in sorrow. Here is no tempest of anger and no outbreak of enraged condemnation; here is the poignant sorrow of the broken heart. Paul was like the God whom he loved and served—he hated the sin, but he loved the sinner. No man will ever even begin to try to save men unless he first loves them. Paul sees the Jews, not as people to be lashed with anger, but as people to be yearned over with longing love.

Willingly Paul would have laid down his life if he could have won the Jews for Christ. It may be that his thoughts were going back to one of the greatest episodes in Jewish history. When Moses went up the mountain to receive the law from the hands of God, the people who had been left below sinned by making the golden calf and worshipping it. God was wroth with them; and then Moses prayed the great prayer: " Yet now, if thou wilt forgive their sin—and if not, blot me, I pray thee, out of thy book which thou hast written " (*Exodus* 32: 32).

Paul says that for the sake of his brethren he would consent to be accursed if it would do any good. The word he uses is *anathema* and it is a terrible word. A thing which was anathema was *under the ban*; it was devoted to God for utter destruction. When a heathen city was taken, everything in it was devoted to utter destruction, for it was polluted (*Deuteronomy* 3: 6; 2: 34; *Joshua* 6: 17; 7: 1–26). If a man tried to lure Israel away from the worship of the true God, he was pitilessly condemned to utter destruction (*Deuteronomy* 13: 8–11). The dearest thing in all Paul's life was the fact that nothing could separate him from the love of God in Christ Jesus; but, if it would do anything to save his brethren, he would even accept banishment from God.

Here again is the great truth that the man who would save the sinner must love him. When a son or a daughter has done something wrong and incurred punishment, many a father and a mother would gladly bear that punishment if only they could. As Myers makes Paul say in his poem *Saint Paul*:

> " Then with a thrill the intolerable craving,
>   Shivers throughout me like a trumpet call;
> O to save these, to perish for their saving—
>   Die for their life, be offered for them all."

That is what God felt; that is what Paul felt; and that is what we must feel.

Paul did not for a moment deny the place of the Jews in the economy of God. He enumerates their privileges.

(i) In a special sense they were children of God, specially chosen, specially adopted into the family of God. " You are the sons of the Lord your God " (*Deuteronomy* 14: 1). " Is not he your father, who created you? " (*Deuteronomy* 32: 6). " Israel is my firstborn son " (*Exodus* 4: 22). " When Israel was a child, I loved him, and out of Egypt called my son " (*Hosea* 11: 1). The Bible is full of this idea of the special sonship of Israel and of Israel's refusal to accept it in the fullest sense.

Boreham somewhere tells how he was visiting in a friend's house when he was a boy. There was one room into which it was forbidden to go. One day he was opposite the room when the door opened and inside he saw a boy of his own age, but in a dreadful state of animal idiocy. He saw the boy's mother go to his side. She must have seen young Boreham in all his health and sanity and then looked at her own son; and the comparison must have pierced her heart. He saw her kneel by the idiot boy's bedside and heard her cry out in a kind of anguish: " I've fed you and clothed you and loved you—and you've never known me." That was what God might have said to Israel—only in this case it was worse, for Israel's rejection was deliberate and open-eyed. It is a terrible thing to break the heart of God.

(ii) Israel had the glory. The *shekinah* or *kaboth* occurs again and again in Israel's history. It was the divine splendour of light which descended when God was visiting his people (*Exodus* 16: 10; 24: 16, 17; 29: 43; 33: 18–22). Israel had seen the glory of God and yet had rejected him. To us it has been given to see the glory of God's love and mercy in the face of Jesus Christ; it is a terrible thing if we then choose the ways of earth.

(iii) Israel had the covenants. A covenant is a relationship entered into between two people, a bargain for mutual profit, an engagement for mutual friendship. Again and again God had approached the people of Israel and entered into a special relationship with them. He did so with Abraham, with Isaac, with Jacob and upon Mount Sinai when he gave the law.

Irenaeus distinguishes four great occasions when God entered into agreement with men. The first was the covenant with Noah after the flood, and the sign was the rainbow in the heavens which stood for God's promise that the floods would not come again. The second was the covenant with Abraham and its sign was the sign of circumcision. The third was the covenant with the nation entered into on Mount Sinai and its basis was the law. The fourth is the new covenant in Jesus Christ.

It is an amazing thing to think of God approaching men and entering into a pledged relationship with them. It is the simple truth that God has never left men alone. He did not make one approach and then abandon them. He has made approach after approach; and he still makes approach after approach to the individual human soul. He stands at the door and knocks; and it is the awful responsibility of human will that man can refuse to open.

(iv) They had the law. Israel could never plead ignorance of God's will; God had told them what he desired them to do. If they sinned, they sinned in knowledge and not in ignorance, and the sin of knowledge is the sin against the light which is worst of all.

(v) They had the worship of the Temple. Worship is in essence the approach of the soul to God; and God in the Temple worship had given to the Jews a special road of approach to himself. If the door to God was shut, they had shut it on themselves.

(vi) They had the promises. Israel could never say that it did not know its destiny. God had told them of the task and the privilege which were in store for them in his purpose. They knew that they were destined for great things in the economy of God.

(vii) They had the fathers. They had a tradition and a history; and it is a poor man who can dare to be false to his traditions and to shame the heritage into which he has entered.

(viii) Then comes the culmination. From them there came the Anointed One of God. All else had been a preparation for this; and yet when he came they rejected him. The biggest grief a man can have is to give his child every chance of success, to sacrifice and save and toil to give him the opportunity, and then to find that the child, through his disobedience or rebelliousness or self-indulgence, has failed to grasp it. Therein lies tragedy, for therein is the waste of love's labour and the defeat of love's dream. The tragedy of Israel was that God had prepared her for the day of the coming of his Son—and all the preparation was frustrated. It was not that God's law had been broken; it was that God's love had been spurned. It is not the anger, but the broken heart of God, which lies behind Paul's words.

THE CHOICE OF GOD

Romans 9: 7–13

But it is not as though the word of God had been completely frustrated. For not all who belong to the race of Israel are really Israel; nor are all really children because they can claim physical descent from Abraham. On the contrary, it is written: " In *Isaac* will your descendants be called." That is to say, it is not the children who can claim merely physical descent who are really the children of God. No! It is the children of the promise who are reckoned as the true descendants of Abraham, for the word of the promise runs like this: " I will come at this time and Sarah will have a son." Not only this, but when Rebecca, too, was brought to bed with child by one, I mean Isaac, our father—and note that the children were not yet born, and had done nothing either good or bad, so that God's purpose in choice should stand, not in consequence of any deeds, but simply because he called them—it was said to her: " The elder will be the servant of the younger." As it stands written: " Jacob I have loved, but Esau I have hated."

IF the Jews have rejected and crucified Jesus, the Son of God, is that to say that God's purposes were frustrated and his plan defeated? Paul produces a strange argument to prove that it is not so. In point of fact not all the Jews did reject Jesus; some of them accepted him, for, of course, all the early followers were Jews, as was Paul himself. Now, he says, if we go back through the history of Israel, we will see again and again a process of selection at work. Again and again we see that it was not *all* Jews who were within the design of God. Some were and some were not. The line of the nation through which God worked, and in which he carried out his plan, was not at any time composed of *all* those who could claim physical descent from Abraham. At the back of the whole plan there is not merely physical descent; there is the selection, the election of God.

To prove his case, Paul cites two instances from Jewish history and buttresses them with proof texts. Abraham had two sons. There was Ishmael, who was the son of the bondwoman

Hagar, and there was Isaac, who was the son of his wife Sarah. Both were true blood descendants of Abraham. It was late in life when Sarah had a son, so late that it was, humanly speaking, an impossibility. As he grew up, there came a day when Ishmael mocked at Isaac. Sarah resented it, and demanded that Hagar and Ishmael should be ejected and that Isaac alone should inherit. Abraham was very unwilling to eject them, but God told him to do so, for it was in Isaac that his descendants would preserve his name (*Genesis* 21: 12). Now Ishmael had been the son of natural human desire; but Isaac had been the son of God's promise (*Genesis* 18: 10–14). It was to the child of the promise that the real descent was given. Here is the first proof that not all physical descendants of Abraham are to be ranked as the chosen ones. Within the nation, God's selection and election have gone on.

Paul proceeds to cite another instance. When Rebecca, the wife of Isaac, was with child, she was told by God that in her womb there were two children who would be the fathers of two nations; but that in the days to come the elder would serve and be subject to the younger (*Genesis* 25: 23). So the twins Esau and Jacob were born. Esau was the elder twin, and yet the choice of God fell on Jacob, and it was through the line of Jacob that God's will was to be done. To clinch the argument Paul cites *Malachi* 1: 2, 3, where God is represented as saying to the prophet: " I have loved Jacob but I have hated Esau."

Paul argues that there is more to Jewishness than descent from Abraham, that the chosen people were not simply the entire sum of all the physical descendants of Abraham, that within that family there was a process of election all through history. A Jew would thoroughly understand and accept the argument so far. The Arabs were the descendants of Ishmael who was a flesh and blood son of Abraham, but the Jews would never have dreamed of saying that the Arabs belonged to the chosen people. The Edomites were the descendants of Esau—that in fact is what Malachi means—and Esau was a true son of Isaac, even the twin brother of Jacob, but no Jew would ever have said that the Edomites had any share in the chosen people.

From the Jewish point of view Paul has made his point; there *was* election within the family of Abraham's physical descendants.

He makes the further point that that selection had nothing to do with deeds and merit. The proof is that Jacob was chosen and Esau was rejected, *before either of them was born*. The choice was made while they were still their mother's womb.

Our minds stagger at this argument. It presents us with the picture of a God who apparently quite arbitrarily chooses one and rejects the other. To us it is not a valid argument, because it makes God responsible for an action which does not seem to be ethically justified. But the fact remains that it would strike home to a Jew. And even to us, at the heart of this argument one great truth remains. Everything is of God; behind everything is his action; even the things which seem arbitrary and haphazard go back to him. Nothing in this world moves with aimless feet.

THE SOVEREIGN WILL OF GOD

Romans 9: 14–18

> What shall we then say? Are you going to say that there is injustice with God? God forbid! For, he says to Moses: " I will have mercy on whomsoever I will have mercy and I will have pity on whomsoever I will have pity." So then the whole matter depends not on man's will and not on man's effort, but entirely on the mercy of God. For scripture says to Pharaoh: " For this one thing I assigned you a part in the drama of history—that I might demonstrate my power by what happens to you, and that my name might be broadcast throughout all the world." So then he has mercy on whom he will, but he hardens whom he will.

PAUL now begins to meet the very arguments and objections which rise in our own minds. He has stated that in all Israel's history the process of selection and election has gone on; he has stressed the fact that this election was based not on any merit of the person elected but on nothing else than the will of God himself. The objector asks: " Is that fair? Is it just of God to pursue a policy of quite arbitrary selection altogether? " Paul's answer is that God can do what he chooses to do. In the terrible days of the Roman Empire, when no man's life was safe and any one might die at the whim of an irresponsible and suspicious Emperor, Galba said, when he became Emperor, that now " he could do what he liked and do it to anyone." To be honest, that is what Paul is saying about God in this passage.

Again he cites two instances to prove his point and buttresses them with scripture quotations. The first is from *Exodus* 33: 19. Moses is beseeching some real proof that God is really with the people of Israel. God's answer is that he will have mercy on those on whom he chooses to have mercy. His attitude of loving mercy to the nation depends on himself alone. The other instance is from Israel's battle for release from Egypt and the power of Pharaoh. When Moses first went to ask for that release, he warned Pharaoh that God had simply brought him on to the stage of history to demonstrate the divine power and to serve to all men as an example of what happens to the man who opposes it (*Exodus* 9–16).

Once again our mind staggers at this argument. It is, of course, not true to say that God can do anything. He cannot do anything which contradicts his own nature. He cannot be responsible for any act which is unjust and which, in fact, breaks his own laws. We find it hard, and even impossible, to conceive of a God who irresponsibly gives mercy to one and not to another, and who raises up a king to be a mere puppet or lay figure through which his own avenging power may be demonstrated. But the argument would be valid and convincing to a Jew, because again it, in essence, means that God is behind everything.

When we get to the foot of this argument, it does conserve one great truth. It is impossible to think of the relationship between God and man in terms of *justice*. Man has no claim on God whatever. The created has no claim on the Creator. Whenever justice enters into it, the answer is that from God man deserves nothing and can claim nothing. In God's dealings with men, the essential things are his will and his mercy.

THE POTTER AND THE CLAY

Romans 9: 19–29

But, then, you may ask, " If this is so how can God go on blaming men if they do not take his way? Who can withstand God's purpose? " Fellow! Who are you to be arguing with God? Surely the thing that is moulded into shape cannot say to the man who moulds it, " Why did you make me like this? " Has not the potter complete authority over the clay, to make from the same lump one vessel for an honourable use and another for a menial service? What if God, although it was his will to demonstrate his wrath and to make known his power, did nonetheless treat with long patience the objects of his wrath, although they were ripe and ready for destruction? Yes, and what if he did it because it is his will to make known the wealth of his glory to the objects of his mercy, which he had prepared beforehand for glory—I mean us whom he called not only from among the Jews but also from among the Gentiles? Just as he says in Hosea: " A people which was not mine I will call my people; and her who was not beloved I will call beloved." And as he says in that same place where it was said to them: " You are not my people; there they shall be called the sons of the living God." And Isaiah cries about Israel: " Even though the number of the sons of Israel shall be as the sand of the sea, only the remnant will be saved, for the Lord will carry out his sentence on earth completely and summarily." And even as Isaiah foretold: " Unless the Lord of Hosts had left us some descendants, we would have become as Sodom, and we would have been like Gomorrah."

IN the previous passage Paul had been showing that all through the history of Israel there had been going on a process of election and selection by God. A very natural objection arises—if at the back of the whole process there is the selection and rejection of God, how can God possibly blame the men who have rejected him? Surely the fault is not theirs at all, but God's. Paul's answer is blunt almost to the point of crudity. He says that no man has any right to argue with God. When a potter makes a vessel, it cannot talk back to him; he has absolute power over it; out of the one lump of clay he can make one vessel for an honourable purpose and another for a menial purpose, and the clay has nothing to do with it and has no right whatever to protest. In point of fact Paul took this picture from Jeremiah (*Jeremiah* 18: 1–6). There are two things to be said about it.

(i) It is a bad analogy. One great New Testament commentator has said that this is one of the very few passages which we wish Paul had not written. There is a difference between a human being and a lump of clay. A human being is a person and a lump of clay is a thing. Maybe you can do what you like with a *thing*, but you cannot do what you like with a *person*. Clay does not desire to answer back; does not desire to question; cannot think and feel; cannot be bewildered and tortured. If someone has inexplicably suffered some tremendous sorrow, it will not help much to tell him that he has no right to complain, because God can do what he likes. That is the mark of a tyrant and not of a loving Father. It is the basic fact of the gospel that God does *not* treat men as a potter treats a lump of clay; he treats them as a loving father treats his child.

(ii) But when we have said that we must remember one thing—it was out of anguish of heart that Paul wrote this passage. He was faced with the bewildering fact that God's own people, his own kinsmen, had rejected and crucified God's own Son. It was not that Paul *wished* to say this; he was *driven* to say it. The only possible explanation he could see was that, for his own purposes, God had somehow blinded his people.

In any event, Paul does not leave the argument there. He goes on to say that this rejection by the Jews had happened in order that the door might be opened to the Gentiles. His argument is not good. It is one thing to say that God *used* an evil situation to bring good out of it; it is quite another thing to say that he *created* it to produce good in the end. Paul is saying that God deliberately darkened the minds and blinded the eyes and hardened the hearts of the mass of the Jewish people in order that the way might open for the Gentiles to come in. We must remember that this is not the argument of a theologian sitting quietly in a study thinking things out; it is the argument of a man whose heart was in despair to find some reason for a completely incomprehensible situation. In the end the only answer Paul can find is that God did it.

Now Paul was arguing with Jews, and he knew that the only way he could buttress his argument was with quotations from their own scriptures. So he goes on to cite texts to prove that this rejection of the Jews and acceptance of the Gentiles had actually been foretold in the prophets. Hosea had said that God would make a people his people who were not his people (*Hosea* 2: 23). He said that a people who were not God's people would be called the sons of God (*Hosea* 1: 10). He showed how Isaiah had foreseen a situation when Israel would have been obliterated had not a remnant been left (*Isaiah* 10: 22, 23; 37: 32). It is his argument that Israel could have foreseen her doom had she only understood.

It is easy in this passage to criticize him, but the one thing that must be remembered is that Paul, in his despairing anguish for his own people, clung to the fact that somehow everything was God's work. For him there was nothing left to say but that.

THE JEWISH MISTAKE

Romans 9: 30–33

What shall we then say? The Gentiles who were not looking for a right relationship with God received such a relationship, but it was a relationship which was the result of faith, while Israel which was looking for a law which would produce a right relationship with God never succeeded in finding such a law. Why? Because they tried to get into a right relationship with God, not by trusting God, but by depending on their own human achievements. They stumbled over the stone which makes men stumble, even as it stands written: " I have set in Zion a stone which makes men stumble, and a rock which makes them trip. And he who believes in him will not be put to shame."

HERE Paul draws a contrast between two ways of feeling towards God. There was the Jewish way. The aim of the Jew was to set himself right with God and he regarded a right relationship with God as something which could be earned. There is another way to put that which will show really what it means. Fundamentally, the Jewish idea was that a man, by strict obedience to the law, could pile up a credit balance. The result would be that God was in his debt and owed him salvation. But it was obviously a losing battle, because man's imperfection could never satisfy God's perfection; nothing that man could do could even begin to repay what God has done for him.

That is precisely what Paul found. As he said, the Jew spent his life searching for a law, obedience to which would put him right with God, and he never found it because there was no such law to be found. The Gentile had never engaged upon this search; but when he suddenly was confronted with the incredible love of God in Jesus Christ, he simply cast himself upon that love in total trust. It was as if the Gentile saw the Cross and said, " If God loves me like that I can trust him with my life and with my soul."

The Jew sought to put God in his debt; the Gentile was content to be in God's debt. The Jew believed he could win salvation by doing things for God; the Gentile was lost in amazement at what God had done for him. The Jew sought to find the way to God by works; the Gentile came by the way of trust.

> " Not the labours of my hands
> Can fulfil thy law's demands;
> Could my zeal no respite know,
> Could my tears for ever flow,
> All for sin could not atone:
> Thou must save, and thou alone."

Paul would have said " Amen " to that.

The stone is one of the characteristic references of the early Christian writers. In the Old Testament there is a series of rather mysterious references to *the stone*. In *Isaiah* 8: 14 it is said that God shall be for *a stone of offence* and a rock of stumbling to the houses of Israel. In *Isaiah* 28: 16 God says that he will lay in Zion for a foundation *a stone, a precious corner stone*, a sure foundation. In *Daniel* 2: 34, 35, 44, 45, there is a reference to a mysterious *stone*. In *Psalm* 118: 22 the Psalmist writes: " The *stone* which the builders rejected is become the head of the corner."

When the Christians began to search the Old Testament for forecasts of Christ they came across these references to this wonderful stone; and they identified Jesus with it. Their warrant was that the gospel story shows Jesus himself making that identification and taking the verse in *Psalm* 118: 22 and applying it to himself (*Matthew* 21: 42). The Christians thought of the stone which was the sure foundation, the stone which was the corner stone binding the whole building together, the stone which had been rejected and had then become the chief of all the stones, as pictures of Christ himself.

The actual quotation which Paul uses here is a combination of *Isaiah* 8: 14 and 28: 16. The Christians, including Paul, took it to mean this—God had intended his Son to be the foundation of every man's life, but when he came the Jews rejected him, and because they rejected him that gift of God which had been meant for their salvation became the reason for their condemnation. This picture of the stone fascinated the Christians. We get it again and again in the New Testament (*Acts* 4: 11; *Ephesians* 2: 20; 1 *Peter* 2: 4–6).

The eternal truth behind this thought is this. Jesus was sent into this world to be the Saviour of men; but he is also the touch-stone by which all men are judged. If a man's heart goes out in love and submission to him, Jesus is for him salvation. If a man's heart is entirely unmoved or angrily rebellious, Jesus is for him condemnation. Jesus came into the world for our salvation, but by his attitude to him a man can either gain salvation or merit condemnation.

THE MISTAKEN ZEAL

Romans 10: 1–13

Brothers, the desire of my heart for the Jews and my prayer to God for them is that they may be saved. I do say this for them—that they do have a zeal for God, but it is not a zeal which is based on a real knowledge. For they do not realize that a man can only achieve the status of righteousness by God's gift, and they seek to establish their own status, and so they have not submitted themselves to that power of God which alone can make them righteous in his sight. For Christ is the end of the whole system of law, for he came to bring everyone who believes and trusts into a right relationship with God. Moses writes that the man who works at the righteousness which comes from the law shall live by it. But the righteousness which stems from faith speaks like this—" Do not say in your heart, ' Who shall go up into heaven? ' (that is, to bring Christ down), or, ' Who shall go down into the deep abyss? ' (that is, to bring Christ again from among the dead)." But what does it say? " The word is near you. It is in your mouth and in your heart." And that word is the message of faith which we proclaim. This word of faith is our message, that, if you acknowledge with your mouth that *Jesus is Lord*, and if you believe in your heart that God raised him from the dead, you will be saved. For belief with the heart is the way to a right relationship with God, and confession with the mouth is the way to salvation, For scripture says, " Every one who believes in him will not be put to shame," for there is no distinction between Jew and Greek; for the same Lord is Lord over all, and he has ample resources for all who call upon him. For " every one who calls on the name of the Lord will be saved."

PAUL has been saying some hard things about the Jews. He has been telling them truths which were difficult for them to hear and bear. The whole passage from *Romans* 9 to 11 is a condemnation of the Jewish attitude to religion. Yet from beginning to end there is no anger in it; there is nothing but wistful longing and heartfelt yearning. It is Paul's one desire that the Jews may be saved.

If ever we are to bring men to the Christian faith, our attitude must be the same. Great preachers have known this. " Don't scold," said one. " Always remember to keep your voice down," said another. A great present-day preacher called preaching " pleading with men." Jesus wept over Jerusalem. There is a preaching which blasts the sinner with tempestuously angry words; but always Paul speaks the truth in love.

Paul was entirely ready to admit that the Jews were zealous for God; but he also saw that their zeal was a misdirected thing. Jewish religion was based on meticulous obedience to the law. Now it is clear that that obedience could be given only by a man who was desperately in earnest about his religion. It was not an easy thing; it must often have been made extremely inconvenient; and it must often have made life very uncomfortable.

Take the Sabbath law. It was laid down exactly how far a man could walk on the Sabbath. It was laid down that he must lift no burden which weighed more than two dried figs. It was laid down that no food must be cooked on the Sabbath. It was laid down that, in the event of sickness, measures might be taken to keep the patient from becoming worse, but not to make him better. To this day there are strict orthodox Jews in this country who will not poke or mend a fire on the Sabbath or switch on a light. If a fire has to be poked a Gentile is employed to do it. If a Jew is wealthy enough he will sometimes instal a time switch to switch on the lights at dusk on Sabbath without his doing so himself.

This is not something to smile at, but to admire. The way of the law was not easy. No one would undertake it at all unless he was supremely in earnest. Zealous the Jews were and are. Paul had no difficulty in granting that, but the zeal was misdirected and misapplied.

In the Fourth Book of *Maccabees* there is an amazing incident. Eleazar the priest was brought before Antiochus Epiphanes whose aim was to stamp out Jewish religion. Antiochus ordered him to eat pork. The old man refused. " No, not if you pluck out my eyes, and consume my bowels in the fire. We, O Antiochus," he said, " who live under a divine law, consider no compulsion to be so forcible as obedience to our law." If he had to die, his fathers would receive him " holy and pure." He was ordered to be beaten.

" His flesh was torn off by the whips, and he streamed down with blood, and his flanks were laid open by wounds." He fell and a soldier kicked him. In the end the soldiers so pitied him that they brought him dressed meat, which was not pork, and told him to eat it and say that he had eaten pork. He refused. He was in the end killed. " I am dying by fiery torments for thy law's sake," he prayed to God. " He resisted," says the writer, " even to the agonies of death, for the law's sake."

And what was all this about? *It was about eating pork.* It seems incredible that a man should die like that for a law like that. But the Jews did so die. Truly they had a zeal for the law. No man can say that they were not desperately in earnest about their service to God.

The whole Jewish approach was that by this kind of obedience to the law a man earned credit with God. Nothing shows better the Jewish attitude than the three classes into which they divided mankind. There were those who were good, whose balance was on the right side; there were those who were bad, whose balance was on the debit side; there were those who were in between, who, by doing one more good work, could become good. It was all a matter of law and achievement. To this Paul answers: " Christ is the end of the law." What he meant was: " Christ is the end of legalism." The relationship between God and man is no longer the relationship between a creditor and a debtor, between an earner and an assessor, between a judge and a man standing at the bar of judgment. Because of Jesus Christ, man is no longer faced with the task of satisfying God's justice; he need only accept his love. He has no longer to win God's favour; he need simply take the grace and love and mercy which he freely offers.

To make his point Paul uses two Old Testament quotations. First, he quotes *Leviticus* 18: 5 where it says that, if a man meticulously obeys the commandments of the law, he will find life. That is true—*but no one ever has*. Then he quotes *Deuteronomy* 30: 12, 13. Moses is saying that God's law is not inaccessible and impossible; it is there in a man's mouth and life and heart. Paul allegorizes that passage. It was not our effort which brought Christ into the world or raised him from the dead. It is not our

effort which wins us goodness. The thing is done for us, and we
have only to accept.

Verses 9 and 10 are of prime importance. They give us the
basis of the first Christian creed.

(i) A man must say *Jesus Christ is Lord*. The word for Lord is
kurios. This is the key word of early Christianity. It has four
stages of meaning. (*a*) It is the normal title of respect like the
English *sir*, the French *monsieur*, the German *herr*. (*b*) It is the
normal title of the Roman Emperors. (*c*) It is the normal title of
the Greek gods, prefaced before the god's name. *Kurios Serapis*
is Lord Serapis. (*d*) In the Greek translation of the Hebrew
scriptures it is the regular translation of the divine name, Jahveh
or Jehovah. So, then, if a man called Jesus *kurios* he was ranking
him with the Emperor and with God; he was giving him the
supreme place in his life; he was pledging him implicit obedience
and reverent worship. To call Jesus *kurios* was to count him
unique. First, then, a man to be a Christian must have a sense of
the utter *uniqueness* of Jesus Christ.

(ii) A man must believe that Jesus is risen from the dead. The
resurrection was an essential of Christian belief. The Christian
must believe not only that Jesus *lived*, but also that he *lives*. He
must not only know *about Christ*: he must *know* him. He is not
studying an historical personage, however great; he is living with
a real presence. He must know not only Christ *the martyr*: he
must know Christ the *victor*, too.

(iii) But a man must not only believe in his heart; he must
confess with his lips. Christianity is belief plus confession; it
involves witness before men. Not only God, but also our fellow
men, must know what side we are on.

A Jew would find it hard to believe that the way to God was not
through the law; this way of trust and of acceptance was
shatteringly and incredibly new to him. Further, he would have
real difficulty in believing that the way to God was open to
everybody. The Gentiles did not seem to him to be in the same
position as the Jews at all. So Paul concludes his argument by
citing two Old Testament texts to prove his case. First, he cites
Isaiah 28: 16: " Every one who *believes* in him will not be put to

shame." There is nothing about law there; it is all based on faith. Second, he cites *Joel* 2: 32: " *All* who call upon the name of the Lord shall be delivered." There is no limitation there; the promise is to *everyone*; therefore, there is no difference between Jew and Greek.

In essence this passage is an appeal to the Jews to abandon the way of legalism and accept the way of grace. It is an appeal to them to see that their zeal is misplaced. It is an appeal to listen to the prophets who long ago declared that faith is the only way to God, and that that way is open to every man.

THE DESTRUCTION OF EXCUSES

Romans 10: 14–21

How are they to call on him on whom they have not believed? How are they to believe in him of whom they have not heard? How are they to hear without someone to proclaim the good news to them? How are they to proclaim the good news unless they are sent to do so? But this is the very thing that has happened, as it stands written: " How beautiful are the feet of those who bring the good news of good things."

But all have not obeyed the good news. That is quite true, because Isaiah says: " Lord, who has believed what they heard from us? " So, then, faith comes from hearing, and hearing comes from the word which comes from Christ and which tells of him. But, suppose I still say: " Can it be that they have not heard? " Indeed they have. " Their voice is gone out to all the earth, and their words to the boundaries of the inhabited world." Well, then, suppose I say: " Did Israel not understand? " First, Moses says: " I will make you jealous of a nation which is no nation. I will make you angry with a nation that has no understanding." Then Isaiah says, greatly daring: " I was found by those who did not seek me. I appeared plainly to those who did not enquire after me." And he says to Israel: " All the day I have stretched out my hands to a people who are disobedient and contrary."

IT is agreed by all commentators that this is one of the most difficult and obscure passages in the letter to the Romans. It seems to us that what we have here is not so much a finished passage as summary notes. There is a kind of telegraphic quality about the writing. It may well be that what we have here is the notes of some address which Paul was in the habit of making to the Jews to convince them of their error.

Basically the scheme is this—in the previous passage Paul has been saying that the way to God is not that of works and of legalism, but of faith and trust. The objection is: But what if the Jews never heard of that? It is with that objection Paul deals; and, as he deals with it in its various forms, on each occasion he clinches his answer with a text from scripture.

Let us take the objections and the answering scripture texts one by one.

(i) The first objection is: " You cannot call on God unless you believe in him. You cannot believe in him unless you hear about him. You cannot hear about him unless there is someone to proclaim the good news. There can be no one to proclaim the good news unless God commissions someone to do so." Paul deals with that objection by quoting *Isaiah* 52: 7. There the prophet points out how welcome those are who bring the good news of good things. So Paul's first answer is: " You cannot say there was no messenger; Isaiah describes these very messengers; and Isaiah lived long ago."

(ii) The second objection is: " But, in point of fact, Israel did *not* obey the good news, even if your argument is true. What have you to say to that? " Paul's answer is: " Israel's disbelief was only to be expected, for, long ago, Isaiah was moved to say in despair: ' Lord, who has believed what we have heard? ' " (*Isaiah* 53: 1.) It is true that Israel did not acept the good news from God, and in their refusal they were simply running true to form; history was repeating itself.

(iii) The third objection is a restatement of the first: " But, what if I insist that they never got the chance to hear? " This time Paul quotes *Psalm* 19: 4: " Their voice goes out through all the earth, and their words to the end of the world." His answer is: " You cannot say that Israel never got the chance to hear; for scripture plainly says that God's message has gone out to *all* the world."

(iv) The fourth objection is: " But what if Israel did not understand? " Apparently the meaning is: " What if the message was so difficult to grasp that even when Israel did hear it they were unable to grasp its significance? " Here is where the passage becomes really difficult. But Paul's answer is: " *Israel* may have failed to understand; but the *Gentiles* did not. They grasped the meaning of this offer all right, when it came to them unexpectedly and unsought." To prove this point Paul quotes two passages. One is from *Deuteronomy* 32: 21 where God says that, because of Israel's disobedience and rebellion, he will transfer his favour to another people, and they will be forced to become jealous of a nation which has no nation. The second passage is from *Isaiah* 65: 1 where God says that, in a strange way, he has been found by a people who were not looking for him at all.

Finally, Paul insists that, all through history, God has been stretching out hands of appeal to Israel, and Israel has always been disobedient and perverse.

A passage like this may seem strange to us and unconvincing; and it may seem that some at least of the texts Paul quotes have been wrenched out of their context and made to mean what they were never intended to mean. Nevertheless there is in this passage something of permanent value. Beneath it there runs the conviction that there are certain kinds of ignorance which are inexcusable.

(i) There is the ignorance which comes from neglect of knowledge. There is a legal maxim which says that genuine ignorance may be a defence, but neglect of knowledge never is. A man cannot be blamed for not knowing what he never had a chance to know; but he can be blamed for neglecting to know that which was always open to him. For instance, if a man signs a contract without having read the conditions, he cannot complain if afterwards he finds out that the conditions are very different from what he thought they were. If we fail to equip ourselves for a task when every chance is given to us to equip ourselves adequately for it, we must stand condemned. A man is responsible for failing to know what he might have known.

(ii) There is the ignorance which comes from wilful blindness. Men have an infinite and fatal capacity for shutting their minds to what they do not wish to see, and stopping their ears to what they do not wish to hear. A man may be well aware that some habit, some indulgence, some way of life, some friendship, some association must have disastrous results; but he may simply refuse to look at the facts. To turn a blind eye may be in some few cases a virtue; in most cases it is folly.

(iii) There is the ignorance which is in essence a lie. The things about which we are in doubt are far fewer than we would like to think. There are in reality very few times when we can honestly say: " I never knew that things would turn out like this." God gave us conscience and the guidance of his Holy Spirit; and often we plead ignorance, when, if we were honest, we would have to admit that in our heart of hearts we knew the truth.

One thing remains to be said of this passage. In the argument so far as it has gone there is a paradox. All through this section Paul has been driving home the personal responsibility of the Jews. They ought to have known better; they had every chance to know better; but they rejected the appeal of God. Now he began the argument by saying that everything was of God and that men had no more to do with it than the clay had to do with the work of the potter. He has set two things side by side; everything is of God, and everything is of human choice. Paul makes no attempt to resolve this dilemma; and the fact is that there is no resolution of it. It is a dilemma of human experience. We know that God is behind everything; and yet, at the same time, we know that we have free will and can accept or reject God's offer. It is the paradox of the human situation that God is in control and yet the human will is free.

THE CALLUS ON THE HEART

Romans 11: 1–12

So then, I ask, " Has God repudiated his people? " God forbid! I, too, am an Israelite, a descendant of Abraham, a member of the tribe of Benjamin. God has not repudiated his people whom long ago he marked out for his purposes. Do you not know what scripture says in the passage about Elijah? You remember how he talked to God in complaint against Israel: " Lord, they have killed your prophets; they have torn down your altars; and I alone am left and they are seeking my life." But what was the answer that came to him? " I have kept for myself seven thousand men, who have not bowed the knee to Baal." So, then, at this present time too, there is a remnant chosen by his grace. And if they were chosen by grace, their relationship to God is no longer dependent on works, for, if that were so, grace is no longer grace. What then? Israel has not obtained that for which she is searching; but the chosen remnant has obtained it, while the rest have been made so dull and insensitive in heart that they cannot see. As it stands written: " God gave them a spirit of lethargy—eyes not to see, ears not to hear—down to this day." And David says: " Let their table become a snare, and a trap, and a thing to trip them up, and a retribution for them, and let their backs be bent for ever." So, I say, " Have they stumbled that their fall might be complete? " God forbid! So far from that, salvation has become a gift for the Gentiles because of their fall, so as to move them to jealousy of the Gentiles. If their fall has brought wealth to the world, if their failure has brought wealth to the Gentiles, how much more shall the whole world be enriched, when they come in, and the whole process of salvation is completed?

THERE was a question now to be asked which any Jew was bound to ask. Does all this mean that God has repudiated his people? That is a question that Paul's heart cannot bear. After all, he himself is a member of that people. So he falls back on an idea which runs through much of the Old Testament. In the days of Elijah, Elijah was in despair (1 *Kings* 19: 10–18). He had come to the conclusion that he alone was left to be true to God. But God told him that, in fact, there were still seven thousand in Israel who had not bowed the knee to Baal. So into Jewish thought came the idea of *The Remnant*.

The prophets began to see that there never was a time, and never would be, when the whole nation was true to God; nevertheless, always within the nation a remnant was left who had never forsaken their loyalty or compromised their faith. Prophet after prophet came to see this. Amos (9: 8–10) thought of God sifting men as corn is in a sieve until only the good are left. Micah (2: 12; 5: 3) had a vision of God gathering the remnant of Israel. Zephaniah (3: 12, 13) had the same idea. Jeremiah foresaw the remnant being gathered from all the countries throughout which they had been scattered (*Jeremiah* 23: 3). Ezekiel, the individualist, was convinced that a man could not be saved by either a national or an inherited righteousness; the righteous would deliver their own souls by their righteousness (*Ezekiel* 14: 14, 20, 22). Above all, this idea dominated the thought of Isaiah. He called his son *Shear-Jashub*, which means *The Salvation of the Remnant*. Again and again he returns to this idea of the faithful remnant who will be saved by God (*Isaiah* 7: 3; 8: 2, 18; 9: 12; 6: 9–13).

There is a tremendous truth beginning to dawn here. As one great scholar put it: " No Church or nation is saved *en masse*." The idea of a *Chosen People* will not hold water for this basic reason. The relationship with God is an individual relationship. A man must give his own heart and surrender his own life to God. God does not call men in crowds; he has " His own secret stairway into every heart." A man is not saved because he is a member of a nation or of a family, or because he has inherited righteousness and salvation from his ancestors; he is saved because he has made a personal decision for God. It is not now the whole nation who are lumped together as the Chosen People. It is those individual men and women who have given their hearts to God, of whom the remnant is composed.

Paul's argument is that the Jewish nation has not been rejected; but it is not the nation as a whole, but the faithful remnant within it who are the true Jews.

What of the others? It is here that Paul has a terrible thought. He has the idea of God sending a kind of torpor upon them, a drowsy sleep in which they cannot and will not hear. He puts together the thought of a series of Old Testament passages to prove this (*Deuteronomy* 29: 4; *Isaiah* 6: 9, 10: 29: 10). He quotes *Psalm* 69: 22, 23. " Let their table become a snare." The idea is that men are sitting feasting comfortably at their banquet; and their very sense of safety has become their ruin. They are so secure in their fancied safety that the enemy can come upon them all unaware. That is what the Jews were like. They were so secure, so self-satisfied, so at ease in their confidence of being the Chosen People, that that very idea had become the thing that ruined them.

The day will come when they cannot see at all, and when they will grope with bent backs like men stumbling blindly in the dark. In verse 7 the Authorized Version says, " they have been blinded." More correctly, it should be, " they have been hardened." The verb is *pōroun*. The noun *pōrōsis* will give us the meaning better. It is a medical word, and it means a *callus*. It was specially used for the callus which forms round the fracture when a bone is broken, the hard bone formation which helps to mend the break. When a callus grows on any part of the body that part loses feeling. It becomes insensitive. The minds of the mass of the people have become insensitive; they can no longer hear and feel the appeal of God.

It can happen to any man. If a man takes his own way long enough, he will in the end become insensitive to the appeal of God. If he goes on sinning, he will in the end become insensitive to the horror of sin and the fascination of goodness. If a man lives long enough in ugly conditions he will in the end become insensitive to them. As Burns wrote:

> " I waive the quantum of the sin,
>   The hazard of concealing;
> But och! it hardens a' within,
>   And petrifies the feeling! "

Just as a callus can grow on the hand, a callus can grow on the heart. That is what had happened to the mass of Israel. God save us from that!

But Paul has more to say. That is tragedy, but out of it God has brought good, because that very insensitiveness of Israel opened the way to the Gentiles to come in. Because Israel did not want the message of the good news, it went out to people who were ready to welcome it. Israel's refusal has enriched the world.

Then Paul touches on the dream which is behind it all. If the refusal of Israel has enriched the world by opening a door to the Gentiles, what will the riches be like at the end of the day, when God's plan is fully completed and Israel comes in, too?

So, in the end, after tragedy comes the hope. Israel became insensitive, the nation with the callus on her heart; the Gentiles came by faith and trust into the love of God; but a day will come when the love of God will act like a solvent, even on the callus of the heart, and both Gentile and Jew will be gathered in. It is Paul's conviction that nothing in the end can defeat the love of God.

THE WILD OLIVE—PRIVILEGE AND WARNING

Romans 11: 13–24

Now I speak to you Gentiles. You well know that in so far as I am the apostle to the Gentiles, I magnify my office, for somehow I want to find a way to move my own flesh and blood to envy of the Gentiles, so that I may save some of them; for, if the fact that they are cast away has resulted in the reconciliation of the world to God, what will their reception mean? It can only be like life from the dead! If the first part of the dough is consecrated to God, so is the whole lump; if the root is consecrated to God, so are the branches. If some of the branches have been cut off, and if you like a wild olive have been grafted in among them, and if you have become a sharer in the rich root of the olive, do not allow yourself to look down boastfully upon the branches. If you are tempted to act like that, remember you do not bear the root but the root bears you. You will say: " Branches have been broken off that I may be grafted in." Well said! They were broken off because of their lack of faith; and you stand because of faith. Do not become proudly contemptuous, but keep yourself in godly fear; for if God did not spare the branches, which were natural branches, neither will he spare you. See, then, the kindness *and* the severity of God. On those who fell there comes the severity; on you there comes the kindness of God, if only you remain in that kindness. If you do not, you, too, will be cut away. But they, if they do not continue in their lack of faith, will be grafted in; for God is able to graft them in again. For, if you were cut from the olive, which is by nature a wild olive, and, if, contrary to nature, you were engrafted into the garden olive, how much more will the natural branches be engrafted into the olive to which they really belong?

IT is to the Jews that Paul has been talking up to this time, and now he turns to the Gentiles. He is the apostle to the Gentiles, but he cannot ever forget his own people. In fact he goes the length of saying that one of his main objects is to move the Jews to envy when they see what Christianity has done for the Gentiles. One of the surest ways to make a man desire Christianity is to make him see in actual life what it can do.

There was a soldier who was wounded in battle. The padre crept out and did what he could for him. He stayed with him when the remainder of the troops retreated. In the heat of the day he gave him water from his own waterbottle, while he himself remained parched with thirst. In the night, when the chill frost came down, he covered the wounded man with his own coat, and finally wrapped him up in even more of his clothes to save him from the cold. In the end the wounded man looked up at the padre. " Padre," he said, " you're a Christian? " " I try to be," said the padre. " Then," said the wounded man, " if Christianity makes a man do for another man what you have done for me, tell me about it, because I want it." Christianity in action moved him to envy a faith which could produce a life like that.

It was Paul's hope and prayer and ambition that some day the Jews would see what Christianity had done for the Gentiles and be moved to desire it.

To Paul it would be paradise if the Jews came in. If the rejection of the Jews had done so much, if, through it, the Gentile world had been reconciled to God, what superlative glory must come when the Jews came in. If the tragedy of rejection has had results so wonderful, what will the happy ending be like, when the tragedy of rejection has changed to the glory of reception? Paul can only say that it will be like life from the dead.

Then Paul uses two pictures to show that the Jews can never be finally rejected. All food, before it was eaten, had to be offered to God. So the law laid it down (*Numbers* 15: 19, 20) that, if dough was being prepared, the first part of it must be offered to God; when that was done, the whole lump of dough became sacred. It was not necessary, as it were, to offer every separate mouthful to God. The offering of the first part sanctified the whole. It was a common thing to plant sacred trees in places sacred to the gods. When the sapling was planted, it was dedicated to God; and thereafter every branch that came from it was sacred to God.

What Paul deduces from that is this—the patriarchs were sacred to God; they had in a special way heard God's voice and obeyed God's word; in a special way they had been chosen and consecrated by God. From them the whole nation sprang; and just as the first consecrated handful of dough made the whole lump sacred and the dedication of the sapling made the whole tree sacred, so the special consecration of its founders made the whole nation sacred in a special way to God. There is truth here. The remnant in Israel did not make themselves what they were; they inherited faith from their forefathers before them. Every one of us lives to some extent on the spiritual capital of the past. None of us is self-made. We are what godly parents and ancestors have made us; and, even if we strayed far away and shamed our heritage, we cannot totally part ourselves from the goodness and fidelity that made us what we are.

Paul goes on to use a long allegory. More than once the prophets had pictured the nation of Israel as the olive tree of God. That was natural, because the olive tree was the commonest and most useful tree in the Mediterranean world. " The Lord once called you a green olive tree, fair with goodly fruit " (*Jeremiah* 11: 16). " His shoots shall spread out; his beauty shall be like the olive " (*Hosea* 14: 6). So Paul thinks of the Gentiles as branches of wild olive engrafted into the garden olive tree which was Israel. From the point of view of horticulture Paul's picture is impossible. In horticulture it is the good olive that is grafted into the stock of the wild olive so that a fruit-bearing olive may result. The process that Paul pictures was never used in actual practice, because it would have served no useful purpose. But the point Paul wishes to make is quite clear. The Gentiles had been out in the deserts and the wildernesses and among the wild briars; and now, by the act of God's grace, they are engrafted into the richness and fertility of the garden olive tree.

Out of this picture Paul has two words to speak.

(i) The first is *a word of warning*. It would have been easy for the Gentiles to develop an attitude of contempt. Had not the Jews been rejected that they might enter in? In a world where the Jews were universally hated such an attitude would have been all too easy. Paul's warning is still necessary. In effect, he says *there would have been no such thing as Christianity unless there had been Judaism first*. It will be a bad day when the Christian Church forgets its debt to the root from which it sprang. It has a debt to Judaism which it can never pay by any other means than by bringing Christianity to the Jews. So Paul warns the Gentiles against contempt. Grimly, he says that if the true branches were lopped off because of their unbelief, still more can that happen to the branches which were only grafted on.

(ii) The second is *a word of hope*. The Gentiles have experienced God's kindness; and the Jews his severity. If the Gentiles remain in faith they will remain in that kindness; but, if the Jews come out of their unbelief and enter into belief, once again they, too, will be engrafted in; for, says Paul, if it was possible for a wild olive to be engrafted into the garden olive tree, how much more is it possible that the olive tree's own natural branches can be grafted in again? Once again Paul is dreaming of the day when the Jews will come in.

Much in this passage is hard to understand. It thinks in pictures which are out of our world altogether; but one thing is crystal clear—the connection between Judaism and Christianity, between the old and the new. Here is the answer to those who wish to discard the Old Testament as merely a Jewish book which is irrelevant for Christianity. He is a foolish man who kicks away the ladder which raised him to the height which he has reached. It would be a foolish branch which cut itself off from its stem. The Jewish faith is the root from which Christianity grew. The consummation will come only when the wild olive and the garden olive are one, and when there are no branches at all left unengrafted on the parent stem.

THAT ALL MAY BE OF MERCY

Romans 11: 25–32

Brothers, I do want you to grasp this secret which only those who know God can understand, because I do not want you to become conceited about your own wisdom. I want you to understand that it is only a partial hardening which has happened to Israel, and it will last only until the full number of the Gentiles shall have come in. And then, in the end, all Israel will be saved, as it stands written: " A Saviour will come forth from Zion; and he will remove all kinds of wickedness from Jacob. This is the fulfilment of my covenant with them when I take away their sins." As far as the good news goes, they are enemies of God—but it is for your sake. But as far as God's choice goes, they are beloved of God, for their fathers' sakes, for the free gifts and the calling of God can never be gone back upon. Once you disobeyed God, but now you have found his mercy because of their disobedience; just so, they have now disobeyed, so that they now may enter into the same mercy as you have now found. For God has shut up all men to disobedience, that he may have mercy upon all.

PAUL is coming to the end of his argument. He has faced a bewildering, and, for a Jew, a heartbreaking situation. Somehow he has had to find an explanation of the fact that God's people rejected his Son when he came into the world. Paul never shut his eyes to that tragic fact, but he found a way in which the whole tragic situation could be fitted into the plan of God. It is true that the Jews rejected Christ; but, as Paul saw it, that rejection happened in order that Christ might be offered to the Gentiles. To maintain the sovereignty of God's purpose, Paul even went the length of saying that it was he himself who hardened the hearts of the Jews in order to open a way to the Gentiles; but, even then, however contradictory it might sound, he still insisted on the personal responsibility of the Jews for their failure to accept God's offer. Paul held fast at one and the same time to divine sovereignty and human responsibility. But now comes the note of hope. His argument is a little complicated, and it will make it easier if we try to separate the various strands in it.

(i) Paul was sure that this hardening of the hearts of the Jews was neither total nor permanent. It was to serve a purpose, and when that purpose had been achieved, it would be taken away.

(ii) Paul sets out the paradox of the Jewish place in the plan of God. In order that the Gentiles might come in and that the universal purpose of the gospel might be fulfilled, the Jews had arrived at a situation where they were the enemies of God. The word that Paul uses is *echthroi*. It is difficult to translate, because it has both an active and a passive meaning. It can mean either *hating* or *hated*. It may well be that in this passage it has to be read in the two meanings at the one time. The Jews were hostile to God and had refused his offer, and therefore they were under his displeasure. That was the present fact about the Jews. But there was another fact about them. Nothing could alter the fact that they were God's chosen people and had a special place in his plan. No matter what they did, God could never go back upon his word. His promise had been made to the fathers, and it must be fulfilled. It was therefore clear to Paul, and he quotes *Isaiah* 59: 20, 21 to prove it, that God's rejection of the Jews could not be permanent; they, too, in the end must come in.

(iii) Then Paul has a strange thought. " God," he says, " shut up all men to disobedience that he may have mercy upon all." The one thing Paul cannot conceive of is that any man of any nation could merit his own salvation. Now, if the Jews had observed complete obedience to God's will, they might well have reckoned that they had earned the salvation of God as a right. So Paul is saying that God involved the Jews in disobedience in order that when his salvation did come to them it might be unmistakably an act of his mercy and due in no way to their merit. Neither Jew nor Gentile could ever be saved apart from the mercy of God.

In many ways Paul's argument may seem strange to us and the " proofs " he brings forward unconvincing. Our minds and hearts may even shudder at some of the things he says. But the argument is not irrelevant, for the tremendous thing at the back of it is *a philosophy of history*. To Paul, *God was in control.* Nothing moved with aimless feet. Not even the most heartbreaking event was outside the purpose of God. Events could never run amok. The purposes of God could never be frustrated.

It is told that once a child stood at the window on a night when the gale was terrifying in its savage velocity. " God," she said, " must have lost grip of his winds tonight." To Paul, that was precisely what never happened. Nothing was ever out of God's control; everything was serving his purpose.

To that Paul would have added another tremendous conviction. He would have insisted that in it and through it all, *God's purpose was a purpose of salvation and not of destruction*. It may well be that Paul would even have gone the length of saying that God's arranging of things was designed to save men *even against their will*. In the last analysis it was not the wrath of God which was pursuing men, but the love of God which was tracking them down.

The situation of Israel was exactly that which Francis Thompson so movingly portrayed in *The Hound of Heaven*.

> " I fled him down the nights and down the days;
>   I fled him down the arches of the years;
> I fled him down the labyrinthine ways
>   Of my own mind; and in the mist of tears
> I hid from him, and under running laughter.

.   .   .   .   .   .

> But with unhurrying chase,
>   And unperturbed pace,
> Deliberate speed, majestic instancy,
>   They beat—and a Voice beat
>   More instant than the feet—
> ' All things betray thee, who betrayest me.' "

Then comes the time when the fugitive is beaten.

> " Naked I wait thy love's uplifted stroke!
>   My harness piece by piece thou hast hewn from me,
>   And smitten to my knee,
>   I am defenceless utterly."

Then comes the end:

> " Halts by me that footfall;
>   Is my gloom, after all,
> Shade of his hand, outstretched caressingly?
>   ' Ah, fondest, blindest, weakest,
>   I am he whom thou seekest!
> Thou dravest love from thee, who dravest me! ' "

That was exactly Israel's situation. They fought their long battle against God; they are still fighting it. But God's pursuing love is ever after them. Whatever else *Romans* 9 to 11 may sometimes read like, it is in the last analysis the story of the still uncompleted pursuit of love.

THE CRY OF THE ADORING HEART

Romans 11: 33–36

O the depth of the riches and the wisdom and the knowledge of God! How his decisions are beyond the mind of man to trace! How mysterious are his ways! For who has known the mind of the Lord? Or, who has become his counsellor? Who has first given anything to him, so that he is due any repayment from God? For all things come from him, and exist through him, and end in him. To him be glory for ever! Amen.

PAUL never wrote a more characteristic passage than this. Here theology turns to poetry. Here the seeking of the mind turns to the adoration of the heart. In the end all must pass out in a mystery that man cannot now understand but at whose heart is love. If a man can say that all things come from God, that all things have their being through him, and that all things end in him, what more is left to say? There is a certain paradox in the human situation. God gave man a mind, and it is man's duty to use that mind to think to the very limit of human thought. But it is also true that there are times when that limit is reached and all that is left is to accept and to adore.

> " How could I praise,
>   If such as I might understand? "

Paul had battled with a heartbreaking problem with every resource which his great mind possessed. He does not say that he has solved it, as one might neatly solve a geometrical problem; but he does say that, having done his best, he is content to leave it to the love and power of God. At many times in life there is nothing left but to say: " I cannot grasp thy mind, but with my whole heart I trust thy love. Thy will be done! "

THE TRUE WORSHIP AND THE ESSENTIAL CHANGE

Romans 12: 1, 2

> Brothers, I call upon you, by the mercies of God, to present your bodies to him, a living, consecrated sacrifice, well-pleasing to God—for that is the only kind of worship which is truly spiritual. And do not shape your lives to meet the fleeting fashions of this world; but be transformed from it, by the renewal of your mind, until the very essence of your being is altered, so that, in your own life, you may prove that the will of God is good and well-pleasing and perfect.

HERE we have Paul following the pattern he always followed when he wrote to his friends. He always ends his letters with practical advice. The sweep of his mind may search through the infinities, but he never gets lost in them; he always finishes with his feet firmly planted upon the earth. He can, and does, wrestle with the deepest problems which theology has to offer, but he always ends with the ethical demands which govern every man.

" Present your bodies to God," he says. There is no more characteristically Christian demand. We have already seen that that is what a Greek would never say. To the Greek, what mattered was the spirit; the body was only a prison-house, something to be despised and even to be ashamed of. No real Christian ever believed that. The Christian believes that his body belongs to God just as much as his soul does, and that he can serve him just as well with his body as with his mind or his spirit.

The body is the temple of the Holy Spirit and the instrument through which the Holy Spirit works. After all, the great fact of the incarnation basically means that God did not grudge to take a human body upon himself, to live in it and to work through it. Take the case of a church or a cathedral. It is built for the offering of worship to God. But it has to be designed by the mind of some architect; it has to be built by the hands of craftsmen and of labouring men; only then does it become a shrine where men meet to worship. It is a product of the mind and the body and the spirit of man.

" So," Paul says, " take your body; take all the tasks that you have to do every day; take the ordinary work of the shop, the factory, the shipyard, the mine; and offer all that as an act of worship to God." The word in verse 1 which we along with the Revised Standard Version have translated *worship*, has an interesting history. It is *latreia*, the noun of the verb *latreuein*. Originally *latreuein* meant *to work for hire or pay*. It was the word used of the labouring man who gave his strength to an employer in return for the pay the employer would give him. It denotes, not slavery, but the voluntary undertaking of work. It then came to mean quite generally *to serve*; but it also came to mean *that to which a man gives his whole life*. For instance, a man could be said *latreuein kallei*, which means *to give his life to the service of beauty.* In that sense, it came very near meaning *to dedicate one's life to.* Finally, it came to be the word distinctively used of *the service of the gods.* In the Bible it never means human service; it is always used of service to and worship of God.

Here we have a most significant thing. True worship is the offering to God of one's body, and all that one does every day with it. Real worship is not the offering to God of a liturgy, however noble, and a ritual, however magnificent. *Real worship is the offering of everyday life to him,* not something transacted in a church, but something which sees the whole world as the temple of the living God. As Whittier wrote:

> " For he whom Jesus loved hath truly spoken:
> The holier worship which he deigns to bless,
> Restores the lost, and binds the spirit broken,
> And feeds the widow and the fatherless."

A man may say, " I am going to church to worship God," but he should also be able to say, " I am going to the factory, the shop, the office, the school, the garage, the locomotive shed, the mine, the shipyard, the field, the byre, the garden, to worship God."

This, Paul goes on, demands a radical change. We must not be conformed to the world, but transformed from it. To express this idea he uses two almost untranslatable Greek words— words which we have taken almost sentences to express. The word he uses to be conformed to the world is *suschēmatizesthai*; its root is *schēma*, which means *the outward form* that varies from year to year and from day to day. A man's *schēma* is not the same when he is seventeen as it is when he is seventy; it is not the same when he goes out to work as when he is dressed for dinner. It is continuously altering. So Paul says, " Don't try to match your life to all the fashions of this world; don't be like a chameleon which takes its colour from its surroundings."

The word he uses for being *transformed* from the world is *metamorphousthai.* Its root is *morphē*, which means the *essen-*

tial unchanging shape or element of anything. A man has not the same *schēma* at seventeen and seventy, but he has the same *morphē*; a man in dungarees has not the same *schēma* as a man in evening dress, but he has the same *morphē*; his outward form changes, but inwardly he is the same person. So, Paul says, to worship and serve God, we must undergo a change, not of our outward form, but of our inward personality. What is that change? Paul would say that left to ourselves we live a life *kata sarka*, dominated by human nature at its lowest; in Christ we live a life *kata Christon* or *kata pneuma*, dominated by Christ or by the Spirit. The essential man has been changed; now he lives, not a self-centred, but a Christ-centred life.

This must happen, Paul says, by the renewal of your mind. The word he uses for *renewal* is *anakainōsis*. In Greek there are two words for new—*neos* and *kainos*. *Neos* means new *in point of time*; *kainos* means new *in point of character and nature*. A newly manufactured pencil is *neos*; but a man who was once a sinner and is now on the way to being a saint is *kainos*. When Christ comes into a man's life he is a *new* man; his mind is different, for the mind of Christ is in him.

When Christ becomes the centre of life then we can present real worship, which is the offering of every moment and every action to God.

EACH FOR ALL AND ALL FOR EACH

Romans 12: 3–8

For, through the grace that has been given to me, I say to everyone among you, not to have a mind proud beyond that which a mind should be, but to have a mind directed towards wisdom, as God has given the measure of faith to each one of you. For just as we have many members in one body, but all the members do not have the same function, so, although we are many, we are one body in Christ, and we are all members of each other. Since, then, we have different gifts, according to the grace that has been given to us, let us use them in mutual service. If we

have received the gift of prophecy, let us prophesy according to
the proportion of faith that we have received. If we have received
the gift of practical service, let us use it in service. If our gift is in
teaching, let us use it in teaching. If it lies in exhortation, let us use
it in exhortation. If we are called upon to share, let us do it with
simple kindliness. If we are called upon to supply leadership, let us
do so with zeal. If the occasion arises when we must show mercy,
let us do so with gracious cheerfulness.

ONE of Paul's favourite thoughts is of the Christian Church as
a body (cp. 1 *Corinthians* 12: 12–27). The members of the body
neither argue with each other nor envy each other nor dispute
about their relative importance. Each part of the body carries
out its own function, however prominent or however humbly
unseen that function may be. It was Paul's conviction that the
Christian Church should be like that. Each member has a task
to do; and it is only when each contributes the help of his own
task that the body of the Church functions as it ought.

Beneath this passage lie very important rules for life.

(i) First of all, it urges us to know ourselves. One of the first
basic commandments of the Greek wise men was: " Man, know
thyself." We do not get very far in this world until we know
what we can and what we cannot do. An honest assessment of
our own capabilities, without conceit and without false
modesty, is one of the first essentials of a useful life.

(ii) Second, it urges us to accept ourselves and to use the gift
God has given us. We are not to envy someone else's gift and
regret that some other gift has not been given to us. We are to
accept ourselves as we are, and use the gift we have. The result
may be that we have to accept the fact that service for us means
some humble sphere and some almost unseen part.

It was one of the great basic beliefs of the Stoics that there
was a spark of God in every living creature. The Sceptics
laughed at this doctrine. " God in worms? " demanded the
Sceptic. " God in dungbeetles? " Whereat the Stoic replied:
" Why not? Cannot an earthworm serve God? Do you suppose
that it is only a general who is a good soldier? Cannot the
lowest private or camp attendant fight his best and give his life

for the cause? Happy are you if you are serving God, and carrying out the great purpose as truly as an earthworm."

The efficiency of the life of the universe depends on the humblest creatures. Paul is here saying that a man must accept himself; and, even if he finds that the contribution he has to offer will be unseen, without praise and without prominence, he must make it, certain that it is essential and that without it the world and the Church can never be what they are meant to be.

(iii) Third, Paul is really saying that whatever gift a man has comes from God. He calls gifts *charismata*. In the New Testament a *charisma* is something given to a man by God which the man himself could not have acquired or attained.

In point of fact, life is like that. A man might practise for a lifetime and yet never play the violin like Yehudi Menuhin. He has more than practice; he has the something plus, the *charisma* which is a gift of God. A man might toil for a lifetime and still be handless in the use of tools and wood and metals; another can fashion wood and mould metal with a special skill, and tools become part of himself; he has the something plus, the *charisma* which is a gift of God. One man might practise speaking for ever and a day, and still never acquire that magic something which moves an audience or a congregation; another steps on to a platform or climbs into a pulpit, and the audience are in the hollow of his hand; he has that something plus, that *charisma* which is a gift of God. A man might toil for a lifetime and never acquire the gift of putting his thoughts on paper in a vivid and intelligible way; another without effort sees his thoughts grow on the sheet of paper in front of him; the second man has the something plus, the *charisma*, which is the gift of God.

Every man has his own *charisma*. It may be for writing sermons, building houses, sowing seeds, fashioning wood, manipulating figures, playing the piano, singing songs, teaching children, playing football or golf. It is a something plus given him by God.

(iv) Fourth, whatever gift a man has, he must use it and the motive of use must be, not his personal prestige, but the conviction that it is at one and the same time his duty and his privilege to make his own contribution to the common good.

Let us look now at the gifts Paul singles out here for special mention.

(i) There is the gift of *prophecy*. It is only rarely that prophecy in the New Testament has to do with foretelling the future; it usually has to do with *forthtelling* the word of God. The prophet is the man who can announce the Christian message with the authority of one who knows. To announce Christ to others a man must first know him himself. " What this parish needs," said Carlyle's father, " is a man who knows Christ other than at second-hand."

(ii) There is the gift of *practical service* (*diakonia*). It is surely significant that practical service came to Paul's mind so high on the list. It may be that a man will never have the privilege of standing forth in public and proclaiming Christ; but there is no man who cannot every day show the love of Christ in deeds of service to his fellow men.

(iii) There is *teaching*. The message of Christ needs not only to be proclaimed; it needs also to be *explained*. It may well be that one of the great failures of the Church at this present time is just in this realm. Exhortation and invitation without a background of teaching are empty things.

(iv) There is *exhortation*. Exhortation should have one dominating note, and that should be *encouragement*. There is a naval regulation which says that no officer shall speak discouragingly to any other officer about any undertaking in which he may be engaged. There is a kind of exhortation which is daunting. Real exhortation aims not so much at dangling a man over the flames of hell as spurring him on to the joy of life in Christ.

(v) There is *sharing*. Sharing is to be carried out with *simple kindliness*. The word that Paul uses is *haplotes*, and it is difficult to translate, because it has in it the meaning both of simplicity and of generosity. One great commentary quotes a passage from *The Testament of Issachar* which perfectly illustrates its meaning. " And my father blessed me, seeing that I walked in simplicity (*haplotēs*). And I was not inquisitive in my actions, nor wicked and envious towards my neighbour. I did not speak evil of anyone or attack a man's life, but I walked with a single eye (literally, with *haplotēs* of my eyes). To every poor and every afflicted man I provided the good things of earth in simplicity (*haplotēs*) of heart. The simple (*haplous*) man does not desire gold, doth not ravish his neighbour, doth not care for all kinds of dainty meats, doth not wish for diversity of clothing, doth not promise himself length of days, but receiveth only the will of God. He walketh in uprightness of life and beholdeth all things in simplicity (*haplotēs*)." There is a giving which pries into the circumstances of another as it gives, which gives a moral lecture along with the gift, which gives not so much to relieve the need of the other as to pander to its own vanity and self-satisfaction, which gives with a grim sense of duty instead of a radiant sense of joy, which gives always with some ulterior motive and never for the sheer joy of giving. Christian sharing is with *haplotēs*, the simple kindliness which delights in the sheer pleasure of giving for giving's sake.

(vi) There is *being called to occupy a leading place*. Paul says that if we are so called we must do it with zeal. One of the most difficult problems of the Church today is the getting of leaders in all departments of its work. There are fewer and fewer people with a sense of service and of responsibility, willing to give up their leisure and their pleasure to undertake leadership. In many cases unfitness and unworthiness is pleaded when the real reason is disinclination and laziness. If such leadership is taken up, Paul says that it is to be taken up with *zeal*. There are two ways in which an elder may deliver a communion card— through the letter-box or at the fireside. There are two ways in which a teacher may prepare a lesson—with heart and mind or in the most perfunctory way. A man may dully and drably go through some task in the Church, or he may do it with the joy and thrill of zeal. The Church today needs leaders with zeal in their hearts.

(vii) There is *the time when mercy has to be shown*. It has to be shown with gracious kindliness, Paul says. It is possible to forgive in such a way that the very forgiveness is an insult. It is possible to forgive and at the same time to demonstrate an attitude of criticism and contempt. If ever we have to forgive a sinner, we must remember that we are fellow sinners. " There but for the grace of God, go I," said George Whitefield as he saw the criminal walk to the gallows. There is a way of forgiving a man which pushes him further into the gutter; and there is a way of forgiving him which lifts him out of the mire. Real forgiveness is always based on love and never on superiority.

THE CHRISTIAN LIFE IN EVERYDAY ACTION

Romans 12: 9–13

> Your love must be completely sincere.
> Hate that which is evil and cling to that which is good.
> Be affectionate to one another in brotherly love.
> Give to each other priority in honour.
> Do not be sluggish in zeal.
> Keep your spirit at boiling point.
> Seize your opportunities.
> Rejoice in hope.
> Meet tribulation with triumphant fortitude.
> Be persevering in prayer.
> Share what you have to help the needs of God's dedicated people.
> Be eager in giving hospitality.

PAUL presents his people with ten telegraphic rules for ordinary, everyday life. Let us look at them one by one.

(i) Love must be completely sincere. There must be no hypocrisy, no play-acting, no ulterior motive. There is such a thing as cupboard love, which gives affection with one eye on the gain which may result. There is such a thing as a selfish love, whose aim is to get far more than it is to give. Christian love is cleansed of self; it is a pure outgoing of the heart to others.

(ii) We must hate that which is evil and cling to that which is good. It has been said that our one security against sin lies in our being shocked by it. It was Carlyle who said that what we need is to see the infinite beauty of holiness and the infinite damnability of sin. The words Paul uses are strong. It has been said that no virtue is safe which is not passionate. He must *hate* evil and *love* good. Regarding one thing we must be clear—what many people hate is not *evil*, but *the consequences of evil*. No man is really a good man when he is good simply because he fears the consequences of being bad. As Burns had it:

> " The fear o' Hell's a hangman's whip
> To haud the wretch in order;
> But where ye feel your honour grip,
> Let that ay be your border."

Not to fear the consequences of dishonour, but to love honour passionately is the way to real goodness.

(iii) We must be affectionate to one another in brotherly love. The word Paul uses for affectionate is *philostorgos*, and *storgē* is the Greek for *family love*. We must love each other, because we are members of one family. We are not strangers to each other within the Christian Church; much less are we isolated units; we are brothers and sisters, because we have the one father, God.

(iv) We must give each other priority in honour. More than half the trouble that arises in Churches concerns rights and privileges and prestige. Someone has not been given his or her place; someone has been neglected or unthanked. The mark of the truly Christian man has always been humility. One of the humblest of men was that great saint and scholar Principal Cairns. Someone recollects an incident which showed Cairns as he was. He was a member of a platform party at a great gathering. As he appeared there was a tremendous burst of applause. Cairns stood back to let the man next him pass, and began to applaud himself; he never dreamed that the applause was for him. It is not easy to give each other priority in honour. There is enough of the natural man in most of us to like to get our rights; but the Christian man has no rights—he has only duties.

(v) We must not be sluggish in zeal. There is a certain intensity in the Christian life; there is no room for lethargy in it. The Christian cannot take things in an easy-going way, for the world is always a battleground between good and evil, the time is short, and life is a preparation for eternity. The Christian may burn out, but he must not rust out.

(vi) We must keep our spirit at boiling point. The one man whom the Risen Christ could not stand was the man who was neither hot nor cold (*Revelation* 3: 15, 16). Today people are apt to look askance upon enthusiasm; the modern battle-cry is " I couldn't care less." But the Christian is a man desperately in earnest; he is aflame for Christ.

(vii) Paul's seventh injunction may be one of two things. The ancient manuscripts vary between two readings. Some read, " Serve the Lord," and some read, " Serve the time," that is, " Grasp your opportunities." The reason for the double reading is this. All the ancient scribes used contractions in their writing. In particular the commoner words were always abbreviated. One of the commonest ways of abbreviating was to miss out the vowels—as shorthand does—and to place a stroke along the top of the remaining letters. Now the word for *Lord* is *kurios* and the word for *time* is *kairos*, and the abbreviation for both of these words is *krs*. In a section so filled with practical advice it is more likely that Paul was saying to his people, " Seize your opportunities as they come." Life presents us with all kinds of opportunities—the opportunity to learn something new or to cut out something wrong; the opportunity to speak a word of encouragement or of warning; the opportunity to help or to comfort. One of the tragedies of life is that we so often fail to grasp these opportunities when they come. " There are three things which come not back—the spent arrow, the spoken word, and the lost opportunity."

(viii) We are to rejoice in hope. When Alexander the Great was setting out upon one of his eastern campaigns, he was distributing all kinds of gifts to his friends. In his generosity he had given away nearly all his possessions. " Sir," said one of his friends, " you will have nothing left for yourself." " Oh, yes, I have," said Alexander, " I have still my hopes." The Christian must be essentially an optimist. Just because God is God, the Christian is always certain that " the best is yet to be." Just because he knows of the grace that is sufficient for all things and the strength that is made perfect in weakness, the Christian knows that no task is too much for him. " There are no hopeless situations in life; there are only men who have grown hopeless about them." There can never be any such thing as a hopeless Christian.

(ix) We are to meet tribulation with triumphant fortitude. Someone once said to a gallant sufferer: " Suffering colours all life, doesn't it? " " Yes," said the gallant one, " it does, but I propose to choose the colour." When the dreadful affliction of complete deafness began to descend on Beethoven and life seemed to be one unbroken disaster, he said: " I will take life by the throat." As William Cowper had it:

> " Set free from present sorrow,
>   We cheerfully can say,
> ' Even let the unknown tomorrow
>   Bring with it what it may,
> It can bring with it nothing
>   But he will bear us through.' "

When Nebuchadnezzar cast Shadrach, Meshach and Abednego into the burning fiery furnace he was amazed that they took no harm. He asked if three men had not been cast into the flames. They told him it was so. He said, " But I see four men loose, walking in the midst of the fire, and they are not hurt; and the appearance of the fourth is like a son of the gods " (*Daniel* 3: 24, 25). A man can meet anything when he meets it with Christ.

(x) We are to persevere in prayer. Is it not the case that there are times in life when we let day add itself to day and week to week, and we never speak to God? When a man ceases to pray, he despoils himself of the strength of Almighty God. No man should be surprised when life collapses if he insists on living it alone.

(xi) We are to share with those in need. In a world bent on getting, the Christian is bent on giving, because he knows that " what we keep we lose, and what we give we have."

(xii) The Christian is to be given to hospitality. Over and over again the New Testament insists on this duty of the open door (*Hebrews* 13: 2; 1 *Timothy* 3: 2; *Titus* 1: 8; 1 *Peter* 4: 9). Tyndale used a magnificent word when he translated it that the Christian should have a *harborous* disposition. A home can never be happy when it is selfish. Christianity is the religion of the open hand, the open heart, and the open door.

THE CHRISTIAN AND HIS FELLOW MEN

Romans 12: 14–21

> Bless those who persecute you; bless them and do not curse them.
> Rejoice with those who rejoice, and weep with those who weep.
> Live in harmony with one another.
> Keep your thoughts from pride; and never refuse to be associated with humble people.
> Don't become conceitedly wise in your own estimation.
> Never return evil for evil.
> Take thought to make your conduct fair for all to see.
> If it is possible, as far as you can, live at peace with all men.
> Beloved, do not seek to revenge yourself on others; leave such vengeance to The Wrath, for it stands written: " Vengeance belongs to me; I will repay, says the Lord." Rather, if your enemy is hungry, give him food. If he is thirsty, give him drink. If you do this you will heap coals of fire on his head. Be not overcome by evil, but overcome evil with good.

PAUL offers a series of rules and principles wherewith to govern our relationships with our fellow men.

(i) The Christian must meet persecution with a prayer for those who persecute him. Long ago Plato had said that the good man will choose rather to suffer evil than to do evil; and it is always evil to hate. When the Christian is hurt, and insulted, and maltreated, he has the example of his Master before him, for he, upon his Cross, prayed for forgiveness for those who were killing him.

There has been no greater force to move men into Christianity than this serene forgiveness which the martyrs in every age have showed. Stephen died praying for forgiveness for those who stoned him to death (*Acts* 7: 60). Among those who killed him was a young man named Saul, who afterwards became Paul, the apostle to the Gentiles and the slave of Christ. There can be no doubt that the death scene of Stephen was one of the things that turned Paul to Christ. As Augustine said: " The Church owes Paul to the prayer of Stephen." Many a persecutor has become a follower of the faith he once sought to destroy, because he has seen how a Christian can forgive.

(ii) We are to rejoice with those who rejoice, and to weep with those who weep. There are few bonds like that of a common sorrow. A writer tells of the saying of an American negro woman. A lady in Charleston met the negro servant of a neighbour. " I'm sorry to hear of your Aunt Lucy's death," she said. " You must miss her greatly. You were such friends." " Yes'm," said the servant, " I is sorry she died. But we wasn't no friends." " Why," said the lady, " I thought you were. I've seen you laughing and talking together lots of times." " Yes'm. That's so," came the reply. " We've laughed together, and we've talked together, but we is just 'quaintances. You see, Miss Ruth, we ain't never shed no tears. Folks got to cry together before dey is friends."

The bond of tears is the strongest of all. And yet it is much easier to weep with those who weep than it is to rejoice with those who rejoice. Long ago Chrysostom wrote on this passage: " It requires more of a high Christian temper to rejoice with them that do rejoice than to weep with them that weep. For this nature itself fulfils perfectly; and there is none so hard-hearted as not to weep over him that is in calamity; but the other requires a very noble soul, so as not only to keep from envying, but even to feel pleasure with the person who is in esteem." It is, indeed, more difficult to congratulate another on his success, especially if his success involves disappointment to us, than it is to sympathize with his sorrow and his loss. It is only when self is dead that we can take as much joy in the success of others as in our own.

(iii) We are to live in harmony with one another. It was Nelson who, after one of his great victories, sent back a despatch in which he gave us the reason for it: " I had the happiness to command a band of brothers." It is a band of brothers that any Christian Church should be. Leighton once wrote: " The mode of Church government is unconstrained; but peace and concord, kindness and good will are indispensable." When strife enters into any Christian society, the hope of doing any good work is gone.

(iv) We are to avoid all pride and snobbishness. We have always to remember that the standards by which the world judges a man are not necessarily the standards by which God judges him. Saintliness has nothing to do with rank, or wealth, or birth. Dr James Black in his own vivid way described a scene in an early Christian congregation. A notable convert has been made, and the great man comes to his first Church service. He enters the room where the service is being held. The Christian leader points to a place. " Will you sit there please? " " But," says the man, " I cannot sit there, for that would be to sit beside my slave." " Will you sit there please? " repeats the leader. " But," says the man, " surely not beside my slave." " Will you sit there please? " repeats the leader once again. And the man at last crosses the room, sits beside his slave, and gives him the kiss of peace. That is what Christianity did; and that is what it alone could do in the Roman Empire. The Christian Church was the only place where master and slave sat side by side. It is still the place where all earthly distinctions are gone, for with God there is no respect of persons.

(v) We are to make our conduct fair for all to see. Paul was well aware that Christian conduct must not only be good; it must also look good. So-called Christianity can be presented in the hardest and most unlovely way; but real Christianity is something which is fair for all to see.

(vi) We are to live at peace with all men. But Paul adds two qualifications. (*a*) He says, *if it be possible*. There may come a time when the claims of courtesy have to submit to the claims of principle. Christianity is not an easy-going tolerance which will accept anything and shut its eyes to everything. There may come a time when some battle has to be fought, and when it does, the Christian will not shirk it. (*b*) He says, *as far as you can*. Paul knew very well that it is easier for some to live at peace than for others. He knew that one man can be compelled to control as much temper in an hour as another man in a lifetime. We would do well to remember that goodness is a great deal easier for some than for others; that will keep us alike from criticism and from discouragement.

(vii) We are to keep ourselves from all thought of taking revenge. Paul gives three reasons for that. (*a*) Vengeance does not belong to us but to God. In the last analysis no human being has a right to judge any other; only God can do that. (*b*) To treat a man with kindness rather than vengeance is the way to move him. Vengeance may break his spirit; but kindness will break his heart. " If we are kind to our enemies," says Paul, " it will heap coals of fire on their heads." That means, not that it will store up further punishment for them, but that it will move them to burning shame. (*c*) To stoop to vengeance is to be ourselves conquered by evil. Evil can never be conquered by evil. If hatred is met with more hatred it is only increased; but if it is met with love, an antidote for the poison is found. As Booker Washington said: " I will not allow any man to make me lower myself by hating him." The only real way to destroy an enemy is to make him a friend.

THE CHRISTIAN AND THE STATE

Romans 13: 1–7

Let everyone render due obedience to those who occupy positions of outstanding authority, for there is no authority which is not allotted its place by God, for the authorities which exist have been set in their places by God. So he who sets himself up against authority has really set himself up against God's arrangement of things. Those who do set themselves against authority will receive condemnation upon themselves. For the man who does good has nothing to fear from rulers, but the man who does evil has. Do you wish to be free of fear of authority? Do good and you will enjoy praise from authority, for any servant of God exists for your good. If you do evil, then you must fear. For it is not for nothing that the man set in authority bears the sword, for he is the servant of God, and his function is to vent wrath and vengeance on the man who does evil. So, then, it is necessary for you to submit yourself, not because of the wrath, but for the sake of your own conscience.

For this same reason you must pay your taxes too; for those set in authority are the servants of God, and continue to work for that very end. Give to all men what is due to them. Give tribute to those to whom tribute is due; pay taxes to those to whom taxes are due. Give fear to those to whom fear is due. Give honour to those to whom honour is due.

At first reading this is an extremely surprising passage, for it seems to counsel absolute obedience on the part of the Christian to the civil power. But, in point of fact, this is a commandment which runs through the whole New Testament. In 1 *Timothy* 2: 1, 2, we read: " I urge that supplications, prayers, intercessions, and thanksgivings be made for all men, for kings and for all who are in high positions; that we may lead a quiet and peaceable life, godly and respectful in every way." In *Titus* 3: 1 the advice to the preacher is: " Remind them to be submissive to rulers and authorities, to be obedient, to be ready for any honest work." In 1 *Peter* 2: 13–17 we read: " Be subject for the Lord's sake to every human institution, whether it be to the emperor as supreme, or to governors as sent by him to punish those who do wrong and to praise those who do right. For it is God's will that by doing right you should put to silence the ignorance of foolish men.... Honour all men. Love the brotherhood. Fear God. Honour the emperor."

We might be tempted to argue that these passages come from a time when the Roman government had not begun to persecute the Christians. We know, for instance, in the Book of Acts that frequently, as Gibbon had it, the tribunal of the pagan magistrate was often the safest refuge against the fury of the Jewish mob. Time and again we see Paul receiving protection at the hands of impartial Roman justice. But the interesting and the significant thing is that many years, and even centuries later, when persecution had begun to rage and Christians were regarded as outlaws, the Christian leaders were saying exactly the same thing.

Justin Martyr (*Apology* 1: 17) writes, " Everywhere, we, more readily than all men, endeavour to pay to those appointed by you the taxes, both ordinary and extraordinary, as we have been taught by Jesus. We worship only God, but in other things we will gladly serve you, acknowledging you as kings and rulers of men, and praying that, with your kingly power, you may be found to possess also sound judgment." Athenagoras, pleading for peace for the Christians, writes (chapter 37): " We deserve favour because we pray for your government, that you may, as is most equitable, receive the kingdom, son from father, and that your empire may receive increase and addition, until all men become subject to your sway." Tertullian (*Apology* 30) writes at length: " We offer prayer for the safety of our princes to the eternal, the true, the living God, whose favour, beyond all other things, they must themselves desire. . . . Without ceasing, for all our emperors we offer prayer. We pray for life prolonged; for security to the empire; for protection for the imperial house; for brave armies, a faithful senate, a virtuous people, the world at rest—whatever, as man or Caesar, an emperor would wish." He goes on to say that the Christian cannot but look up to the emperor because he " is called by our Lord to his office." And he ends by saying that " Caesar is more ours than yours because our God appointed him." Arnobius (4: 36) declares that in the Christian gatherings " peace and pardon are asked for all in authority."

It was the consistent and official teaching of the Christian Church that obedience must be given to, and prayers made for, the civil power, even when the wielder of that civil power was a Nero.

What is the thought and belief at the back of this?

(i) In Paul's case there was one immediate cause of his stressing of civil obedience. The Jews were notoriously rebellious. Palestine, especially Galilee, was constantly seething with insurrection. Above all there were the Zealots; they were convinced that there was no king for the Jews but God; and that no tribute must be paid to anyone except to God. Nor were they content with anything like a passive resistance. They believed that God would not be helping them unless they embarked on violent action to help themselves. Their aim was to make any civil government impossible. They were known as the dagger-bearers. They were fanatical nationalists sworn to terrorist methods. Not only did they use terrorism towards the Roman government; they also wrecked the houses and burned the crops and assassinated the families of their own fellow-Jews who paid tribute to the Roman government.

In this Paul saw no point at all. It was, in fact, the direct negation of all Christian conduct. And yet, at least in one part of the nation, it was normal Jewish conduct. It may well be that Paul writes here with such inclusive definiteness because he wished to dissociate Christianity altogether from insurrectionist Judaism, and to make it clear that Christianity and good citizenship went necessarily hand in hand.

(ii) But there is more than a merely temporary situation in the relationship between the Christian and the state. It may well be true that the circumstances caused by the unrest of the Jews are in Paul's mind, but there are other things as well. First and foremost, there is this—no man can entirely dissociate himself from the society in which he lives and has a part. No man can, in conscience, opt out of the nation. As a part of it, he enjoys certain benefits which he could not have as an individual; but he cannot reasonably claim all the privileges and refuse all the duties. As he is part of the body of the Church, he is also part of the body of the nation; there is no such thing in this world as an isolated individual. A man has a duty to the state and must discharge it even if a Nero is on the throne.

(iii) To the state a man owes protection. It was the Platonic idea that the state existed for the sake of justice and safety and secured for a man security against wild beasts and savage men. " Men," as it has been put, " herded behind a wall that they might be safe." A state is essentially a body of men who have covenanted together to maintain certain relationships between each other by the observance of certain laws. Without these laws and the mutual agreement to observe them, the bad and selfish strong man would be supreme; the weaker would go to the wall; life would become ruled by the law of the jungle. Every ordinary man owes his security to the state, and is therefore under a responsibility to it.

(iv) To the state ordinary people owe a wide range of services which individually they could not enjoy. It would be impossible for every man to have his own water, light, sewage, transport system. These things are obtainable only when men agree to live together. And it would be quite wrong for a man to enjoy everything the state provides and to refuse all responsibility to it. That is one compelling reason why the Christian is bound in honour to be a good citizen and to take his part in all the duties of citizenship.

(v) But Paul's main view of the state was that the Roman Empire was the divinely ordained instrument to save the world from chaos. Take away that Empire and the world would disintegrate into flying fragments. It was in fact the *pax Romana*, the Roman peace, which gave the Christian missionary the chance to do his work. Ideally men should be bound together by Christian love; but they are not; and the cement which keeps them together is the state.

Paul saw in the state an instrument in the hand of God, preserving the world from chaos. Those who administered the state were playing their part in that great task. Whether they knew it or not they were doing God's work, and it was the Christian's duty to help and not to hinder.

THE DEBTS WHICH MUST BE PAID AND THE DEBT WHICH NEVER CAN BE PAID

Romans 13: 8–10

> Owe no man anything, except to love each other; for he who loves the other man has fulfilled the law. The commandments, You must not commit adultery, You must not kill, You must not steal, You must not covet, and any other commandment there may be, are all summed up in this saying—You must love your neighbour as yourself. Love does no harm to its neighbour. Love is, therefore, the complete fulfilment of the law.

THE previous passage dealt with what might be called a man's public debts. Verse 7 mentions two of these public debts. There is what Paul calls *tribute*, and what he calls *taxes*. By *tribute* he means the tribute that must be paid by those who are members of a subject nation. The standard contributions that the Roman government levied on its subject nations were three. There was a *ground tax* by which a man had to pay, either in cash or in kind, one-tenth of all the grain, and one-fifth of the wine and fruit produced by his ground. There was *income tax*, which was one per cent of a man's income. There was a *poll tax*, which had to be paid by everyone between the ages of fourteen and sixty-five. By *taxes* Paul means the local taxes that had to be paid. There were customs duties, import and export taxes, taxes for the use of main roads, for crossing bridges, for entry into markets and harbours, for the right to possess an animal, or to drive a cart or wagon. Paul insists that the Christian must pay his tribute and his taxes to state and to local authority, however galling it may be.

Then he turns to *private* debts. He says, " Owe no man anything." It seems a thing almost unnecessary to say; but there were some who even twisted the petition of the Lord's Prayer, " Forgive us our debts, as we forgive our debtors," into a reason for claiming absolution from all money obligations. Paul had to remind his people that Christianity is not an excuse for refusing our obligations to our fellow men; it is a reason for fulfilling them to the utmost.

He goes on to speak of the one debt that a man must pay every day, and yet, at the same time, must go on owing every day, the debt to love each other. Origen said: " The debt of love remains with us permanently and never leaves us; this is a debt which we both discharge every day and for ever owe." It is Paul's claim that if a man honestly seeks to discharge this debt of love, he will automatically keep all the commandments. He will not commit adultery, for when two people allow their physical passions to sweep them away, the reason is, not that they love each other too much, but that they love each other too little; in real love there is at once respect and restraint which saves from sin. He will not kill, for love never seeks to destroy, but always to build up; it is always kind and will ever seek to destroy an enemy not by killing him, but by seeking to make him a friend. He will never steal, for love is always more concerned with giving than with getting. He will not covet, for covetousness (*epithumia*) is the uncontrolled desire for the forbidden thing, and love cleanses the heart, until that desire is gone.

There is a famous saying, " Love God—and do what you like." If love is the mainspring of a man's heart, if his whole life is dominated by love for God and love for his fellow men, he needs no other law.

THE THREAT OF TIME

Romans 13: 11–14

Further, there is this—realize what time it is, that it is now high time to be awakened from sleep; for now your salvation is nearer than when you believed. The night is far gone; the day is near. So, then, let us put away the works of darkness, and let us clothe ourselves with the weapons of light. Let us walk in loveliness of life, as those who walk in the day, and let us not walk in revelry or drunkenness, in immorality and in shamelessness, in contention and in strife. But put on the Lord Jesus Christ as a man puts on a garment, and stop living a life in which your first thought is to gratify the desires of Christless human nature.

LIKE so many great men, Paul was haunted by the shortness of time. Andrew Marvell could always hear " time's winged chariot hurrying near." Keats was haunted by fears that he might cease to be before his pen had gleaned his teeming brain. Robert Louis Stevenson wrote:

> " The morning drum-call on my eager ear
>   Thrills unforgotten yet; the morning dew
>   Lies yet undried along my fields of noon.
>   But now I pause at whiles in what I do
>   And count the bell, and tremble lest I hear
>   (My work untrimmed) the sunset gun too soon."

But there was more in Paul's thought than simply the shortness of time. He expected the Second Coming of Christ. The Early Church expected it at any moment, and therefore it had the urgency to be ready. That expectancy has grown dim and faint; but one permanent fact remains—no man knows when God will rise and bid him go. The time grows ever shorter, for we are every day one day nearer that time. We, too, must have all things ready.

The last verses of this passage must be forever famous, for it was through them Augustine found conversion. He tells the story in his *Confessions*. He was walking in the garden. His heart was in distress, because of his failure to live the good life. He kept exclaiming miserably, " How long? How long? To-morrow and tomorrow—why not now? Why not this hour an end to my depravity? " Suddenly he heard a voice saying, " Take and read; take and read." It sounded like a child's voice; and he racked his mind to try to remember any child's game in which these words occurred, but could think of none. He hurried back to the seat where his friend Alypius was sitting, for he had left there a volume of Paul's writings. " I snatched it up and read silently the first passage my eyes fell upon: ' Let us not walk in revelry or drunkenness, in immorality and in shamelessness, in contention and in strife. But put on the Lord Jesus Christ, as a man puts on a garment, and stop living a life in which your first thought is to gratify the desires of Christless human nature.' I neither wished nor needed to read further. With the end of that sentence, as though the light of assurance had poured into my heart, all the shades of doubt were scattered. I put my finger in the page and closed the book: I turned to Alypius with a calm countenance and told him." (C. H. Dodd's translation.) Out of his word God had spoken to Augustine. It was Coleridge who said that he believed the Bible to be inspired because, as he puts it, " It finds me." God's word can always find the human heart.

It is interesting to look at the six sins which Paul selects as being, as it were, typical of the Christless life.

(i) There is *revelry* (*kōmos*). This is an interesting word. Originally *kōmos* was the band of friends who accompanied a victor home from the games, singing his praises and celebrating his triumph as they went. Later it came to mean a noisy band of revellers who swept their way through the city streets at night, a band of roysterers, what, in Regency England, would have been called a *rout*. It describes the kind of revelry which lowers a man's self and is a nuisance to others.

(ii) There is *drunkenness* (*methē*). To the Greeks drunkenness was a particularly disgraceful thing. They were a wine-drinking people. Even children drank wine. Breakfast was called *akratisma*, and consisted of a slice of bread dipped in wine. For all that, drunkenness was considered specially shameful, for the wine the Greek drank was much diluted, and was drunk because the water supply was inadequate and dangerous. This was a vice which not only a Christian but any respectable heathen also would have condemned.

(iii) There was *immorality* (*koitē*). *Koitē* literally means a *bed* and has in it the meaning of the desire for the forbidden bed. This was the typical heathen sin. The word brings to mind the man who sets no value on fidelity and who takes his pleasure when and where he will.

(iv) There is *shamelessness* (*aselgeia*). *Aselgeia* is one of the ugliest words in the Greek language. It does not describe only immorality; it describes the man who is lost to shame. Most people seek to conceal their evil deeds, but the man in whose heart there is *aselgeia* is long past that. He does not care who sees him; he does not care how much of a public exhibition he makes of himself; he does not care what people think of him. *Aselgeia* is the quality of the man who dares publicly to do the things which are unbecoming for any man to do.

(v) There is *contention* (*eris*). *Eris* is the spirit that is born of unbridled and unholy competition. It comes from the desire for place and power and prestige and the hatred of being surpassed. It is essentially the sin which places self in the foreground and is the entire negation of Christian love.

(vi) There is *envy* (*zēlos*). *Zēlos* need not be a bad word. It can describe the noble emulation of a man who, when confronted with greatness of character, wishes to attain to it. But it can also mean that envy which grudges a man his nobility and his pre-eminence. It describes here the spirit which cannot be content with what it has and looks with jealous eye on every blessing given to someone else and denied to itself.

RESPECT FOR SCRUPLES

Romans 14: 1

> Welcome the man who is weak in the faith, but not with a view to passing judgment on his scruples.

IN this chapter Paul is dealing with what may have been a temporary and local problem in the Roman Church, but is also one continually confronting the Church and always demanding solution. In the Church at Rome there were apparently two lines of thought. There were some who believed that in Christian liberty the old *tabus* were gone; they believed that the old food laws were now irrelevant; they believed that Christianity did not consist in the special observance of any one day or days. Paul makes it clear that this in fact is the standpoint of real Christian faith. On the other hand, there were those who were full of scruples; they believed that it was wrong to eat meat; they believed in the rigid observance of the Sabbath tyranny. Paul calls the ultra-scrupulous man the man who is *weak in the faith*. What does he mean by that?

Such a man is weak in the faith for two reasons.

(i) He has not yet discovered the meaning of Christian freedom; he is at heart still a legalist and sees Christianity as a thing of rules and regulations.

(ii) He has not yet liberated himself from a belief in the efficacy of works. In his heart he believes that he can gain God's favour by doing certain things and abstaining from others. Basically he is still trying to earn a right relationship with God, and has not yet accepted the way of grace, still thinking more of what he can do for God than of what God has done for him.

Paul bids the stronger brethren to welcome such a person and not to besiege him with continual criticisms.

This problem is not confined to the days of Paul. To this day in the Church there are two points of view. There is the more liberal which sees no harm in many things and is well content that many an innocent pleasure should go on within the Church. And there is the narrower point of view, which is offended at many things in which the liberal person sees no harm.

Paul's sympathies are all with the broader point of view; but, at the same time, he says that when one of these weaker brethren comes into the Church he must be received with brotherly sympathy. When we are confronted with someone who holds the narrower view there are three attitudes we must avoid.

(i) We must avoid *irritation*. An impatient annoyance with such a person gets us nowhere. However much we may disagree, we must try to see the other person's point of view and to understand it.

(ii) We must avoid *ridicule*. No man remains unwounded when that which he thinks precious is laughed at. It is no small sin to laugh at another man's beliefs. They may seem prejudices rather than beliefs; but no man has a right to laugh at what some other holds sacred. In any event, laughter will never woo the other man to a wider view; it will only make him withdraw still more determinedly into his rigidity.

(iii) We must avoid *contempt*. It is very wrong to regard the narrower person as an old-fashioned fool whose views may be treated with contempt. A man's views are his own and must be treated with respect. It is not even possible to win a man over to our position unless we have a genuine respect for his. Of all attitudes towards our fellow man the most unChristian is contempt.

Before we leave this verse, it should be noted that there is another perfectly possible translation. " Welcome the man who is weak in the faith, but do not introduce him straight away to the discussion of questions which can only raise doubts." There are some people whose faith is so strong that no amount of debate and questioning will really shake it. But there are others who have a simple faith which is only needlessly disturbed by clever discussion.

It may well be that our own age is overfond of discussion for discussion's sake. It is fatal to give the impression that Christianity consists of nothing but a series of questions under debate. " We have found," said G. K. Chesterton, " all the questions that can be found. It is time we stopped looking for questions and started looking for answers." " Tell me of your certainties," said Goethe, " I have doubts enough of my own." There is one good rule which should guide the progress of any discussion, even if it has been a bewildered discussion, and even if it has been discussing questions to which there is no real answer, it should always finish with an *affirmation*. There may be many questions left unanswered, but there must be some certainty left unshaken.

TOLERANCE FOR ANOTHER'S POINT OF VIEW

Romans 14: 2–4

> One man has enough faith to believe that he can eat anything; but he who is weak in the faith eats vegetables. Let not him who eats contemptuously despise him who does not eat; and let not him who does not eat pass censorious judgment on him who does eat, for God has received him. Who are you to judge another man's servant? It is in his own master's judgment that he stands or falls—and he will stand, for the Master is able to make him stand.

HERE emerges one of the definite points of debate in the Roman Church. There were those who observed no special food laws and *tabus* at all, and who ate anything; and there were those who conscientiously abstained from meat, and ate only vegetables. There were many sects and religions in the ancient world which observed the strictest food laws. The Jews themselves did. *Leviticus* 11 gives its lists of the creatures which may and which may not be eaten. One of the strictest sects of the Jews was the Essenes. They had communal meals for which they bathed and wore special clothes. The meals had to be specially prepared by priests or they would not eat them. The Pythagoreans had their distinctive food laws. Pythagoras taught that the soul of man was a fallen deity confined to the body as to a tomb. He believed in reincarnation through which the soul might dwell in a man, an animal, or a plant in an endless chain of being. Release from this chain of being was found through absolute purity and discipline; and this discipline included silence, study, self-examination and abstention from all flesh. In almost any Christian congregation there would be those who observed special food laws and tabus.

It is the same problem. Within the Church there was a narrower party and there was a more liberal party. Paul unerringly pinpoints the danger that was likely to arise. Almost certainly the more liberal party would despise the scruples of the narrower party; and, still more certainly, the narrower party would pass censorious judgment on what they believed to be the laxity of the more liberal party. That situation is just as real and perilous in the Church today as it was in the time of Paul.

To meet it Paul lays down a great principle. No man has any right to criticize another man's servant. The servant is answerable to his master alone. Now all men are the servants of God. It is not open to us to criticize them, still less to condemn them. That right belongs to God alone. It is not in our judgment that a man stands or falls but in his. And, Paul goes on, if a man is honestly living out his principles as he sees them, God can make him able to stand.

Many a congregation of the Church is torn in two because those who hold broader views are angrily contemptuous of those whom they regard as die-hard conservatives; and because those who are stricter in their outlook are censorious of those who wish the right to do things which they think are wrong. It is not open to us to condemn each other. " I beseech you by the bowels of Christ," said Cromwell to the rigid Scots of his day, " think it possible that you may be mistaken." We must banish both censoriousness and contempt from the fellowship of the Church. We must leave the judgment of others to God, and seek only to sympathize and to understand.

DIFFERENT ROAD TO THE SAME GOAL

Romans 14: 5, 6

> One man rates one day beyond another; one regards all days alike. Let each man be fully convinced in his own mind. The man who observes a particular day observes it to the Lord. The man who eats, eats to the Lord, for he says his grace. The man who does not eat, does not eat to the Lord, for he too says his grace to God.

PAUL introduces another point on which narrower and more liberal people may differ. The narrower people make a great deal of the observance of one special day. That was indeed a special characteristic of the Jews. More than once Paul was worried about people who made a fetish of observing days. He writes to the Galatians: " You observe days, and months, and seasons, and years: I am afraid I have laboured over you in vain " (*Galatians* 4: 10, 11). He writes to the Colossians: " Let no man pass judgment on you in questions of food and drink or with regard to a festival or a new moon or a sabbath. These are only a shadow of what is to come; but the substance belongs to Christ " (*Colossians* 2: 16, 17). The Jews had made a tyranny of the sabbath, surrounding it with a jungle of regulations and prohibitions. It was not that Paul wished to wipe out the Lord's Day—far from it; but he did fear an attitude which in effect believed that Christianity consisted in observing one particular day.

There is far more to Christianity than Lord's Day observance. When Mary Slessor spent three lonely years in the bush she frequently got the days mixed up because she had no calendar. " Once she was found holding her services on a Monday, and again on Sunday she was discovered on the roof, hammering away, in the belief that it was Monday! " No one is going to argue that Mary Slessor's services were any less valid because they were held on Monday, or that she was in any sense breaking the commandment because she was working on the Sunday. Paul would never have denied that the Lord's Day is a precious day, but he would have been equally insistent that not even it must become a tyranny, still less a fetish. It is not the day that we ought to worship, but him who is the Lord of all days.

In spite of all that, Paul pleads for sympathy between the narrower and the more liberal brethren. His point is that, however different their practice may be, their aim is the same. In their different attitude to days, both believe that they are serving God; when they sit down to eat, the one eats meat and the other does not, but both say their grace to God. We do well to remember that. If I am trying to get from Glasgow to London there are many routes I may use. I could in fact get there without traversing one half mile of road that another man might use. It is Paul's plea that the common aim should unite us and the differing practice should not be allowed to divide us.

But he insists on one thing. Whatever course a man chooses, let him be fully convinced in his own mind. His actions should be dictated not by *convention*, still less by *superstition*, but altogether by *conviction*. He should not do things simply because other people do them; he should not do them because he is governed by a system of semi-superstitious tabus; he should do them because he has thought them out and reached the conviction that for him at least they are the right things to do.

Paul would have added something else to that—no man should make his own practice the universal standard for all other people. This, in fact, is one of the curses of the Church. Men are so apt to think that their way of worship is the only way. T. R. Glover somewhere quotes a Cambridge saying: " Whatsoever thy hand findeth to do, do it with thy might—but remember that someone thinks differently." We would do well to remember that, in a great many matters, it is a duty to have our own convictions, but it is an equal duty to allow others to have theirs without regarding them as sinners and outcasts.

THE IMPOSSIBILITY OF ISOLATION

Romans 14: 7–9

For none of us lives to himself, and none of us dies to himself. If we live, we live to the Lord; and if we die, we die to the Lord. Whether we live or die we belong to the Lord. It was for this purpose that Christ died and rose to life again—that he might be the Lord of the dead and of the living.

PAUL lays down the great fact that it is impossible in the nature of things to live an isolated life. There is no such thing in this world as a completely detached individual. That, in fact, is doubly true. " Man," said Macneile Dixon, " has an affair with the gods and an affair with the mortals." No man can disentangle himself either from his fellow men or from God.

In three directions a man cannot disentangle himself from his fellow men.

(i) He cannot isolate himself from *the past*. No man is self-made. " I am a part," said Ulysses, " of all that I have met." A man is a receiver of a tradition. He is an amalgam of all that his ancestors made him. True, he himself does something to that amalgam; but he does not start from nothing. For weal or for woe, he starts with what all the past has made him. The unseen cloud of witnesses do not only compass him about; they dwell within him. He cannot dissociate himself from the stock from which he springs and from the rock from which he is hewn.

(ii) He cannot isolate himself from *the present*. We live in a civilization which is daily binding men more and more closely together. Nothing a man does affects only himself. He has the terrible power of making others happy or sad by his conduct; he has the still more terrible power of making others good or bad. From every man goes out an influence which makes it easier for others to take the high way or the low way. From every man's deeds come consequences which affect others more or less closely. A man is bound up in the bundle of life, and from that bundle he cannot escape.

(iii) He cannot isolate himself from *the future*. As a man receives life so he hands life on. He hands on to his children a heritage of physical life and of spiritual character. He is not a self-contained individual unit; he is a link in a chain. Someone tells of a youth, who lived carelessly, who began to study biology. Through a microscope he was watching certain of these living things that you can actually see living and dying and begetting others in a moment of time. He rose from the microscope. " Now I see it," he said. " I am a link in the chain, and I will not be a weak link any more." It is our terrible responsibility that we leave something of ourselves in the world by leaving something of ourselves in others. Sin would be a far less terrible thing if it affected only a man himself. The terror of every sin is that it starts a new train of evil in the world.

Still less can a man disentangle himself from Jesus Christ.

(i) In this life Christ is forever a living presence. We do not need to speak of living as if Christ saw us; he does see us. All life is lived in his eye. A man can no more escape from the risen Christ than he can from his shadow. There is no place where he can leave Christ behind, and there is nothing which he can do unseen.

(ii) Not even death breaks that presence. In this world we live in the unseen presence of Christ; in the next we shall see him in his visible presence. Death is not the chasm that ends in obliteration; it is the gateway that leads to Christ.

No human being can follow a policy of isolation. He is bound to his fellow men and to Christ by ties that neither time nor eternity can break. He can neither live nor die to himself.

MEN UNDER JUDGMENT

Romans 14: 10–12

Who are you to judge your brother in anything? Or, who are you contemptuously to despise your brother? For we shall all stand at God's judgment seat; for it stands written: " As I live, God says, every knee shall bow to me, and every tongue shall confess its faith to God." So, then, each of us shall render account to God for himself.

THERE is one basic reason why we have no right to judge anyone else; and that is that we ourselves are men under judgment. It is the very essence of humanity that we are not the judges but the judged. To prove his point Paul quotes *Isaiah* 45: 23.

This was indeed a thought with which any Jew would agree. There was a rabbinic saying: " Let not thine imagination assure thee that the grave is an asylum; for perforce thou wast framed, and perforce thou wast born, and perforce thou livest, and perforce thou diest, and perforce thou art about to give account and reckoning before the King of kings, the Holy One, blessed is he." The only person who has the right to judge anyone is God; the man who stands at the bar of God's judgment has no right to judge a fellow who also stands at that bar.

Just before this Paul has been thinking of the impossibility of the isolated life. But there is one situation in which a man is isolated, and that is when he stands before the judgment seat of God. In the old days of the Roman Republic, in the corner of the Forum farthest from the Capitol stood the *tribunal*, the judgment seat, where the Praetor Urbanus had sat dispensing justice. When Paul wrote, Roman justice required more than one judgment seat; and so in the great basilicas, the colonnaded porches around the Forum, the magistrates sat dispensing justice. The Roman well knew the sight of a man standing before the judge's judgment seat.

That is what happens to every man; and it is a judgment which he must face alone. Sometimes in this world he can make use of the merits of someone else. Many a young man has been spared some penalty for the sake of his parents; many a husband has been given mercy for the sake of his wife or child; but in the judgment of God a man stands alone. Sometimes, when a great one dies, the coffin lies in front of the mourning congregation, and, on the top of it, there is arranged the gowns of his academic honours, or the insignia of his state dignities; but he cannot take them with him. Naked we come into the world, and naked we leave it. We stand before God in the awful loneliness of our own souls; to him we can take nothing but the character which in life we have been building up.

Yet that is not the whole truth. We do not stand alone at the judgment seat of God, for we stand with Jesus Christ. We do not need to go stripped of everything; we may go clad in the merits that are his. Collin Brooks, writer and journalist, writes in one of his books: " God may be kinder than we think. If he cannot say, ' Well done! good and faithful servant,' it may be that he will say at last, ' Don't worry, my bad and faithless servant: I don't altogether dislike you.' " That was a man's whimsical way of stating his faith; but there is more to it than that. It is not that God merely does not dislike us; it is that, sinners as we are, he loves us for the sake of Jesus Christ. True, we must stand before God's judgment seat in the naked loneliness of our own souls; but, if we have lived with Christ in life, we shall stand with him in death, and before God he will be the advocate to plead our cause.

A MAN AND HIS NEIGHBOUR'S CONSCIENCE

Romans 14: 13–16

So, then, let us stop passing judgment on each other, and rather let this be our only judgment—the determination not to put any hindrance or stumbling block in our brother's way. I know this, and I am firmly convinced of it in the Lord Jesus Christ, that there is nothing in itself which is unclean. All the same, if anyone thinks that anything is unclean, it is unclean to him. If your brother is grieved by something which you eat, you are no longer conducting yourself according to the principle that love lays down. Do not bring ruin by what you eat to that man for whom Christ died.

THE Stoics used to teach that there were a great many things which they called *adiaphora*, that is, *indifferent*. In themselves they were quite neutral, neither good nor bad. The Stoics put it this way—it all depends by what handle you pick them up. Now that is profoundly true. To a student of art, a certain picture might be a work of art, to someone else an obscene drawing. To one group of people a discussion might be an interesting and stimulating and mind-kindling experience, to someone else a succession of heresies, and even blasphemies. An amusement, a pleasure, a pastime might seem to one quite permissible, and to another prohibited. More, there are pleasures which are quite harmless to one man, which can, in fact, be the ruin of another. The thing itself is neither clean nor unclean; its character is determined by the person who sees it or does it.

That is what Paul is getting at here. There are certain things which a man strong in the faith may see no harm in doing; but, if a person with a more narrow outlook saw him doing them, his conscience would be shocked; and if such a person were persuaded to do them himself his conscience would be outraged. We may take a very simple example. One man will genuinely see no harm in playing some outdoor game on Sunday, and he may be right; but another man's conscience is shocked at such a thing, and, if he were persuaded to take part in it, all the time he would have the haunting feeling that he was doing wrong.

Paul's advice is clear. *It is a Christian duty to think of everything, not as it affects ourselves only, but also as it affects others.* Note that Paul is not saying that we must always allow our conduct to be dictated by the views of others; there are matters which are essentially matters of principle, and in them a man must take his own way. But a great many things are neutral and indifferent; a great many things are neither in themselves good or bad; a great many things are not essential parts of life and conduct but belong to what we might call the extras of life. It is Paul's conviction that in regard to such things we have no right to give offence to the more scrupulous brother by doing them ourselves, or by persuading him to do them.

Life must be guided by the principle of love; and when it is, we will think, not so much of our right to do as we like as of our responsibilities to others. We have no right to distress another man's conscience in the things which do not really matter. Christian freedom must never be used as an excuse for rough-riding over the genuine feelings of others. No pleasure is so important that it can justify bringing offence and grief, and even ruin, to others. Augustine used to say that the whole Christian ethic could be summed up in a saying: " Love God, and do what you like." In a sense it is true; but Christianity consists not only in loving God; it consists also in loving our neighbour as ourselves.

THE PERIL OF CHRISTIAN FREEDOM

Romans 14: 17–20

Do not allow that good gift of freedom which you possess to become a thing which gets you into disrepute. For the Kingdom of God does not consist of food and drink, but of righteousness and peace and joy, which are the gifts of the Holy Spirit. For the man who rules his life by this principle, and so becomes the slave of Christ, is well-pleasing to God and approved by men. So, then, let it be the things that make for peace that we pursue, and the things which build up one another. Do not destroy God's work for the sake of food. True, all things are pure; but it is wrong for a man to take life's road more difficult for someone else through what he eats.

IN essence, Paul is here dealing with the peril and the abuse of Christian freedom. To a Jew, Christian freedom has its dangers. All his life he had been compassed about by a multiplicity of rules and regulations. So many things were unclean and so many were clean. So many animals might not be eaten; so many purity laws must be observed. When the Jew came into Christianity he found that all the petty rules and regulations were abolished at one stroke, and the danger was that he might interpret Christianity as a freedom to do exactly as he liked. We must remember that Christian freedom and Christian love go hand in hand; we must hold fast to the truth that Christian freedom and brotherly love are bound up together.

Paul reminds his people that Christianity does not consist in eating and drinking what one likes. It consists in three great things, all of which are essentially *unselfish* things.

There is *righteousness*, and this consists in giving to men and to God what is their due. Now the very first thing that is due to a fellow man in the Christian life is sympathy and consideration; the moment we become a Christian the feelings of the other man become *more* important than our own; Christianity means putting others first and self last. We cannot give a man what is due to him and do what we like.

There is *peace*. In the New Testament peace does not mean simply absence of trouble; it is not a negative thing, but is intensely positive; it means everything that makes for a man's highest good. The Jews themselves often thought of peace as a state of right relationships between man and man. If we insist that Christian freedom means doing what we like, that is precisely the state we can never attain. Christianity consists entirely in *personal relationships* to man and to God. The untrammelled freedom of Christian liberty is conditioned by the Christian obligation to live in a right relationship, in *peace*, with our fellow men.

There is *joy*. Christian joy can never be a selfish thing. It does not consist in making ourselves happy; it consists in making others happy. A so-called happiness which made someone else distressed would not be Christian. If a man, in his search for happiness, brings a hurt heart and a wounded conscience to someone else, the ultimate end of his search will be, not joy, but sorrow. Christian joy is not individualistic; it is interdependent. Joy comes to the Christian only when he brings joy to others, even if it costs him personal limitation.

When a man follows this principle he becomes the slave of Christ. Here is the essence of the matter. Christian freedom means that we are free to do, not what we like, but what Christ likes. Without Christ a man is a slave to his habits, his pleasures, his indulgences. He is not really doing what he likes. He is doing what the things which have him in their grip make him do. Once the power of Christ enters into him he is master of himself, and then, and only then, real freedom enters his life. Then he is free not to treat men and not to live life as his own selfish human nature would have him do; he is free to show to all men the same attitude of love as Jesus showed.

Paul ends by setting out the Christian aim within the fellowship. (*a*) It is the aim of *peace*; the aim that the members of the fellowship should be in a right relationship with each other. A church where there is strife and contention, quarrels and bitterness, divisions and breaches, has lost all right to the name of church. It is not a fragment of the Kingdom of Heaven; it is simply an earthbound society. (*b*) It is the aim of *upbuilding*. The picture of the church as a building runs through the New Testament. The members are stones within the building. Anything which loosens the fabric of the church is against God; anything which makes that fabric stronger and more secure is of God.

The tragedy is that in so many cases it is little unimportant things which disturb the peace of the brethren, matters of law and procedure and precedent and prestige. A new age would dawn in the Church if we remembered that our rights are far less important than our obligations, if we remembered that, while we possess Christian liberty, it is always an offence to use it as if it conferred upon us the right to grieve the heart and conscience of someone else. Unless a church is a body of people who, in love, consider one another it is not a church at all.

RESPECT FOR THE WEAKER BROTHER

Romans 14: 21–23

> It is the fine thing neither to eat meat, nor to drink wine, nor to do anything which makes the road more difficult for your brother to walk. As far as you yourselves are concerned you have enough faith to know that these things do not matter—well, then, let that be a matter between yourself and God. Happy is the man who never has cause to condemn himself for doing what he has come to the conclusion it was right to do. But he who has doubts about eating something stands condemned if he does eat it, because his decision to eat is not the result of faith.

WE are back at the point that what is right for one man may be the ruin of another. Paul's advice is very practical.

(i) He has advice for the man who is strong in the faith. That man knows that food and drink make no difference. He has grasped the principle of Christian freedom. Well, then, let that freedom be something between him and God. He has reached this stage of faith; and God knows well that he has reached it. But that is no reason why he should flaunt his freedom in the face of the man who has not yet reached it. Many a man has insisted on the rights of his freedom, and then had cause to regret that he ever did so when he sees the consequences.

A man may come to the conclusion that his Christian freedom gives him a perfect right to make a reasonable use of alcohol; and, as far as he is concerned, it may be a perfectly safe pleasure, from which he runs no danger. But it may be that a younger man who admires him is watching him and taking him as an example. And it may also be that this younger man is one of these people to whom alcohol is a fatal thing. Is the older man to use his Christian freedom to go on setting an example which may well be the ruin of his young admirer? Or is he to limit himself, not for his own sake, but for the sake of the one who follows in his footsteps?

¨ Surely conscious limitation for the sake of others is the Christian thing. If a man does not exercise it, he may well find that something that he genuinely thought to be permissible has brought ruin to someone else! It is surely better to make this deliberate limitation than to have the remorse of knowing that what one demanded as a pleasure has become death to someone else. Again and again, in every sphere of life, the Christian is confronted with the fact that he must examine things, not only as they affect himself, but also as they affect other people. A man is always in some sense his brother's keeper, responsible, not only for himself, but for everyone who comes into contact with him. " His friendship did me a mischief," said Burns of the older man he met in Irvine as he learned the art of flax-dressing. God grant that none may say that of us because we misused the glory of Christian freedom!

(ii) Paul has advice for the man who is weak in the faith, the man with the over-scrupulous conscience. This man may disobey or silence his scruples. He may sometimes do something because everyone else is doing it and he does not wish to be different. He may do it because he does not wish to court ridicule or unpopularity. Paul's answer is that if a man defies his conscience he is guilty of sin. If a man believes a thing to be wrong, then, if he does it, for him it is sin. A neutral thing becomes a right thing only when it is done out of the real, reasoned conviction that it is right. No man is the keeper of another man's conscience, and each man's conscience, in things indifferent, must be the arbiter for him of what is right or wrong.

THE MARKS OF THE FELLOWSHIP

Romans 15: 1–6

It is the duty of us who are strong to bear the weaknesses of those who are not strong, and not to please ourselves. Let each one of us please our neighbour, but always for his good and always for his upbuilding in the faith. For the Anointed One of God did not please himself, but, as it stands written, " The insults of those who were insulting you fell upon me." All the things that were written long ago were written to teach us, so that, through our fortitude, and through the encouragement which the scriptures give, we may hold fast to our hope. May the God who inspires us with fortitude, and gives us encouragement, grant to you to live in harmony with one another as Christ Jesus would have you to do, so that your praise to the God and Father of our Lord Jesus Christ may rise from a united heart and a united voice.

PAUL is still dealing with the duties of those within the Christian fellowship to one another, and especially with the duty of the stronger to the weaker brother. This passage gives us a wonderful summary of the marks which should characterize that fellowship.

(i) The Christian fellowship should be marked by the *consideration* of its members for each other. Always their thoughts should be, not for themselves, but for each other. But this consideration must not degenerate into an easy-going, sentimental laxity. It must always be designed for the other person's good and for his upbuilding in the faith. It is not the toleration which tolerates because it is too lazy to do anything else. It is the toleration which knows that a man may be won much more easily to a fuller faith by surrounding him with an atmosphere of love than by attacking him with a battery of criticism.

(ii) The Christian fellowship should be marked by the *study of scripture*; and from that study of scripture the Christian draws *encouragement*. Scripture, from this point of view, provides us with two things. (*a*) It gives us the record of God's dealing with a nation, a record which is the demonstration that it is always better to be right with God and to suffer, than to be wrong with men and to avoid trouble. The history of Israel is the demonstration in the events of history that ultimately it is well with good and evil with the wicked. Scripture demonstrates, not that God's way is ever an easy way, but in the end it is the only way to everything that makes life worth while in time and in eternity. (*b*) It gives us the great and precious promises of God. It is said that Alexander Whyte sometimes had a habit of uttering one text when he left some home during his pastoral visitation; and, as he uttered it, he would say: " Put that under your tongue and suck it like a sweetie." These promises are the promises of a God who never breaks his word. In these ways scripture gives to the man who studies it comfort in his sorrow and encouragement in his struggle.

(iii) The Christian fellowship should be marked by *fortitude*. Fortitude is an attitude of the heart to life. Again we meet this great word *hupomonē*. It is far more than patience; it is the triumphant adequacy which can cope with life; it is the strength which does not only accept things, but which, in accepting them, transmutes them into glory.

(iv) The Christian fellowship should be marked by *hope*. The Christian is always a realist, but never a pessimist. The Christian hope is not a cheap hope. It is not the immature hope which is optimistic because it does not see the difficulties and has not encountered the experiences of life. It might be thought that hope is the prerogative of the young; but the great artists did not think that. When Watts drew " Hope " he drew her as a battered and bowed figure with one string left upon her lyre. The Christian hope has seen everything and endured everything, and still has not despaired, because it believes in God. It is not hope in the human spirit, in human goodness, in human achievement; it is hope in the power of God.

(v) The Christian fellowship should be marked by *harmony*. However ornate a church may be, however perfect its worship and its music, however liberal its giving, it has lost the very first essential of a Christian fellowship if it has lost harmony. That is not to say that there will not be differences of opinion; it is not to say that there will be no argument and debate; but it means that those who are within the Christian fellowship will have solved the problem of living together. They will be quite sure that the Christ who unites them is greater by far than the differences which may divide them.

(vi) The Christian fellowship should be marked by *praise*. It is no bad test of a man to ask whether the main accent of his voice is that of grumbling discontent or cheerful tha ksgiving. " What can I do, who am a little old lame man," said Epictetus, " except give praise to God? " The Christian should enjoy life because he enjoys God. He will carry his secret within him, for he will be sure that God is working all things together for good.

(vii) And the essence of the matter is that the Christian fellowship takes its example, its inspiration and its dynamic from Jesus Christ. He did not please himself. The quotation which Paul uses is from *Psalm* 69: 9. It is significant that when Paul speaks of *bearing* the weaknesses of others he uses the same word as is used of Christ bearing his Cross (*bastazein*). When the Lord of Glory chose to serve others instead of to please himself, he set the pattern which every one who seeks to be his follower must accept.

THE INCLUSIVE CHURCH

Romans 15: 7–13

So, then, welcome one another as Christ welcomed you, that God may be praised. What I mean is this—Christ became a servant of the Jewish race and way of life for the sake of God's truth, not only to guarantee the promises which the fathers received, but also that the Gentiles should praise God for his mercy. As it stands written: " Therefore I will offer praise to God among the Gentiles and I will sing to your name." And, again it says: " Rejoice, O Gentiles with his people." And, again: " Praise the Lord, all you Gentiles, and let all the peoples praise him." And again Isaiah says: " There shall live the scion of Jesse, even he who rises up to rule the Gentiles; in him the Gentiles set their hopes." May the God of hope fill you with all joy and peace in your faith, so that by the power of the Holy Spirit you may overflow with hope.

PAUL makes one last appeal that all people within the Church should be bound into one, that those who are weak in the faith and those who are strong in the faith should be one united body, that Jew and Gentile should find a common fellowship. There may be many differences but there is only one Christ, and the bond of unity is a common loyalty to him. Christ's work was for Jew and Gentile alike. He was born a Jew and was subject to the Jewish law. This was in order that all the great promises given to the fathers of the Jewish race might come true and that salvation might come first to the Jew. But he came, not only for the Jew, but for the Gentile also.

To prove that this is not his own novel and heretical idea Paul cites four passages from the Old Testament; he quotes them from the Septuagint, the Greek version of the Old Testament, which is why they vary from the translation of the Old Testament as we know it. The passages are *Psalm* 18: 50; *Deuteronomy* 32: 43; *Psalm* 117: 1; *Isaiah* 11: 10. In all of them Paul finds ancient forecasts of the reception of the Gentiles into the faith. He is convinced that, just as Jesus Christ came into this world to save all men, so the Church must welcome all men, no matter what their differences may be. Christ was an inclusive Saviour, and therefore his Church must be an inclusive Church.

Then Paul once again goes on to sound the notes of the Christian faith. The great words of the Christian faith flash out one after another.

(i) There is *hope*. It is easy in the light of experience to despair of oneself. It is easy in the light of events to despair of the world. Someone tells of a meeting in a certain church at a time of emergency. The meeting was constituted with prayer by the chairman. He addressed God as " Almighty and eternal God, whose grace is sufficient for all things." When the prayer was finished, the business part of the meeting began; and the chairman introduced the business by saying: " Gentlemen, the situation in this church is completely hopeless, and nothing can be done." Either his prayer was composed of empty and meaningless words, or his statement was untrue.

It has long ago been said that there are no hopeless situations; there are only men who have grown hopeless about them. It is told that there was a cabinet meeting in the darkest days of the last war, just after France had capitulated. Mr Churchill outlined the situation in its starkest colours. Britain stood alone. There was a silence when he had finished speaking, and on some faces was written despair, and some would have given up the struggle. Mr Churchill looked round that dispirited company. " Gentlemen," he said, " I find it rather inspiring."

There is something in Christian hope that not all the shadows can quench—and that something is the conviction that God is alive. No man is hopeless so long as there is the grace of Jesus Christ; and no situation is hopeless so long as there is the power of God.

(ii) There is *joy*. There is all the difference in this world between pleasure and joy. The Cynic philosophers declared that pleasure was unmitigated evil. Anthisthenes made the strange statement that he would " rather be mad than pleased." Their argument was that " pleasure is only the pause between two pains." You have longing for something, that is the pain; you get it, the longing is satisfied and there is a pause in the pain; you enjoy it and the moment is gone; and the pain comes back. In truth, that is the way pleasure works. But Christian joy is not dependent on things outside a man; its source is in our consciousness of the presence of the living Lord, the certainty that nothing can separate us from the love of God in him.

(iii) There is *peace*. The ancient philosophers sought for what they called *ataraxia*, the untroubled life. They wanted all that serenity which is proof alike against the shattering blows and the petty pinpricks of this life. One would almost say that today serenity is a lost possession. There are two things which make it impossible.

(*a*) There is *inner tension*. Men live a distracted life, for the word *distract* literally means *to pull apart*. So long as a man is a walking civil war and a split personality, there can obviously be for him no such thing as serenity. There is only one way out of this, and that is for self to abdicate to Christ. When Christ controls, the tension is gone.

(*b*) There is *worry about external things*. Many are haunted by the chances and the changes of life. H. G. Wells tells how in New York harbour he was once on a liner. It was foggy, and suddenly out of the fog loomed another liner, and the two ships slid past each other with only yards to spare. He was suddenly face to face with what he called the general large dangerousness of life. It is hard not to worry, for man is characteristically a creature who looks forward to guess and fear. The only end to that worry is the utter conviction that, whatever happens, God's hand will never cause his child a needless tear. Things will happen that we cannot understand, but if we are sure enough of God's love, we can accept with serenity even those things which wound the heart and baffle the mind.

(iv) There is *power*. Here is the supreme need of men. It is not that we do not know the right thing; the trouble is the doing it. The trouble is to cope with and to conquer things, to make what Wells called " the secret splendour of our intentions " into actual facts. That we can never do alone. Only when the surge of Christ's power fills our weakness can we master life as we ought. By ourselves we can do nothing; but with God all things are possible.

THE WORDS REVEAL THE MAN

Romans 15: 14–21

Brothers, I myself am quite sure that you, as you are, are full of goodness and replete with all knowledge and well able to give good advice to one another. I write to you with a certain amount of boldness, as it were, with the purpose of reminding you of what you already know. My ground for doing so is the God-given grace which made me the servant of Christ Jesus to the Gentiles, and gave me the sacred task of telling the good news, and my aim in doing so is to make the Gentiles an offering acceptable to God, an offering consecrated by the Holy Spirit. Now, in Christ, I have good reason to take a legitimate pride in my work in God's service. I can say this for I will not venture to speak of anything other than the things which Christ has wrought in me, by word and deed, by the power of signs and wonders, and by the power of the Holy Spirit, to bring the Gentiles into obedience to him. Thus from Jerusalem right round to Illyricum, I have completed the announcing of the good news of God's Anointed One. But it has always been my ambition to announce the good news, not where Christ's name has already been preached, because I want to avoid building on another man's foundation, but as it stands written: " Those to whom the good news has not been told shall see; and those who have not heard will understand."

FEW passages reveal Paul's character better than this. He is coming to the end of his letter and is wishing to prepare the ground for the visit that he hopes soon to pay to Rome. Here we see something at least of his secret in winning men.

(i) Paul reveals himself as *a man of tact*. There is no rebuke here. He does not nag the brethren at Rome nor speak to them like some angry schoolmaster. He tells them that he is only reminding them of what they well know, and assures them that he is certain that they have it in them to render outstanding service to each other and to their Lord. Paul was much more interested in what a man could be than in what he was. He saw faults with utter clarity, and dealt with them with utter fidelity; but all the time he was thinking, not of the wretched creature that a man was, but of the splendid creature that he might be.

It is told that once when Michelangelo began to carve a huge and shapeless block of marble, he said that his aim was to release the angel imprisoned in the stone. Paul was like that. He did not want to knock a man down and out; he did not criticize to cause pain; he spoke with honesty and with severity but always because he wished to enable a man to be what he could be and never yet attained to being.

(ii) The only glory that Paul claimed was that he was *the*

servant of Christ. The word he uses (*leitourgos*) is a great one. In ancient Greece there were certain state duties called *liturgies* (*leitourgiai*) which were sometimes laid upon and sometimes voluntarily shouldered by men who loved their country. There were five of these voluntary services which patriotic citizens used to undertake.

(*a*) There was *chorēgia*, which was the duty of supplying a chorus. When Aeschylus and Sophocles and Euripides were producing their immortal dramas, in each of them a verse-speaking chorus was necessary. There were great festivals like the City Dionysia when as many as eighteen new dramatic works were performed. Men who loved their city would volunteer to collect, maintain, instruct and equip such a chorus at their own expense.

(*b*) There was *gumnasiarchia*. The Athenians were divided into ten tribes; and they were great athletes. At certain of the great festivals there were the famous torch-races in which teams from the various tribes raced against each other. We still speak of *handing on the torch*. To win the torch-race was a great honour, and there were public-spirited men who at their own cost would select and support and train a team to represent their tribe.

(*c*) There was *hestiasis*. There were occasions when the tribes met together to share in a common meal and a common rejoicing; and there were generous men who undertook the task of meeting the expense of such a gathering.

(*d*) There was *archetheōria*. Sometimes the city of Athens sent an embassy to another city or to consult the oracle at Delphi or Dodona. On such an occasion everything had to be done in such a way that the honour of the city was maintained; and there were patriotic men who voluntarily defrayed the expenses of such an embassy.

(*e*) There was *triērarchia*. The Athenians were the great naval power of the ancient world. And one of the most patriotic things that a man could do was voluntarily to undertake the expenses of maintaining a trireme or warship for a whole year.

That is the background of this word *leitourgos*. In later days, as patriotism died, such liturgies became compulsory and not voluntary. Later the word came to be used of any kind of service; and later still it came to be used especially of worship and service rendered in the temple of the gods. But the word always had this background of generous service. Just as a man in the ancient days laid his fortune on the altar of the service of his beloved Athens, and counted it his only glory, so Paul laid his everything on the altar of the service of Christ, and was proud to be the servant of his Master.

(iii) Paul saw himself, in the scheme of things, as *an instrument in the hands of Christ*. He did not talk of what he had done; but of what Christ had done with him. He never said of anything: " I did it." He always said: " Christ used me to do it." It is told that the change in the life of D. L. Moody came when he went to a meeting and heard a preacher say: " If only one man would give himself entirely and without reserve to the Holy Spirit, what that Spirit might do with him! " Moody said to himself: " Why should I not be that man? " And all the world knows what the Spirit of God did with D. L. Moody. It is when a man ceases to think of what he can do and begins to think of what God can do with him, that things begin to happen.

(iv) Paul's ambition was to be *a pioneer*. It is told that when Livingstone volunteered as a missionary with the London Missionary Society they asked him where he would like to go. " Anywhere," he said, " so long as it is forward." And when he reached Africa he was haunted by the smoke of a thousand villages which he saw in the distance. It was Paul's one ambition to carry the good news of God to men who had never heard it. He takes a text from *Isaiah* 52: 15 to tell his aim.

> " Ye armies of the living God,
>   His sacramental host,
>   Where hallowed footstep never trod,
>   Take your appointed post."

PLANS PRESENT AND FUTURE

Romans 15: 22–29

> And that is why on many occasions I found the way to come to
> you blocked. But now, since I have no longer a sphere for work in
> these areas, and since for many years back I have had a great
> desire to come to you, when I shall go to Spain I hope to see you
> on my way through; and, I hope, after I have first enjoyed your
> company for a while, to be sped on my way by you. But at the
> moment I am on my way to Jerusalem, to render some service to
> God's dedicated people there. For Macedonia and Achaea re-
> solved to make a contribution to the poor among God's dedicated
> people in Jerusalem. For that was their resolve and indeed they
> owe a debt to them. For if the Gentiles have received a share in
> spiritual blessings they also owe a debt to render service to them
> in material things. When I have completed this business, and
> when I have duly delivered the gifts to them intact, I will leave for
> Spain by way of you. I know that when I do come to you, I will
> come bringing a full blessing from Christ.

HERE we have Paul telling of an immediate and of a future plan.

(i) His future plan was to go to Spain. There were two
reasons why he should wish to go there. First, Spain was at the
very western end of Europe. It was in one sense the then limit of
the civilized world, and the very fact that it was such would lure
Paul on to preach there. He would characteristically wish to
take the good news of God so far that he could not take it
farther.

(ii) At this time Spain was experiencing a kind of blaze of
genius. Many of the greatest men in the Empire were Spaniards.
Lucan, the epic poet, Martial, the master of the epigram,
Quintilian, the greatest teacher of oratory of his day, were all
Spaniards. Above all, Seneca, the great Stoic philosopher, who
was first the guardian and afterwards the prime minister of
Nero, was a Spaniard. It may well be that Paul was saying to
himself that if only he could touch Spain for Christ tremendous
things might happen.

(iii) His immediate plan was to go to Jerusalem. He had had a plan which was very dear to his heart. He had arranged for a collection to be taken from his young churches for the poor in the Church of Jerusalem. There is no doubt that that collection would be necessary. In a city like Jerusalem much of the available employment must have been connected with the Temple and its needs. All the priests and the Temple authorities were Sadducees, and the Sadducees were the supreme enemies of Jesus. It must therefore have happened that many a man, when he became a Christian in Jerusalem, lost his job and was in sore need. The help the younger churches could give was much needed. But there were at least three other great reasons why Paul was so eager to take this gift to Jerusalem.

(*a*) For himself it was the payment of a debt and a duty. When it had been agreed that Paul should be the apostle to the Gentiles, one injunction had been laid upon him by the leaders of the Church—that he would remember the poor (*Galatians* 2: 10). " Which very thing," said Paul, " I was eager to do." He was not the man to forget a debt, and now that debt was about to be paid, at least in part.

(*b*) There was no better way of demonstrating in the most practical way the unity of the Church. This was a way of teaching the young churches that they were not isolated units but members of a great Church extending throughout all the world. The value of giving to others is that it makes us remember that we are not members of a congregation but of a Church which is worldwide.

(*c*) There was no better way of putting Christianity into practical action. It was easy enough to talk about Christian generosity; here was a chance to turn Christian words into Christian deeds.

So Paul is on the way to Jerusalem, and he is planning a journey to Spain. As far as we know he never got to Spain, for in Jerusalem he encountered the trouble which led to his long imprisonment and his death. It would seem that this was one plan of the great pioneer which never was worked out.

OPEN-EYED INTO DANGER

Romans 15: 30–33

> Brothers, I call upon you by the Lord Jesus Christ, and by the love of the Spirit, to strive along with me in prayer to God for me; for I need your prayers that I may be rescued from those in Jerusalem who do not believe, and that the help that I am bringing to Jerusalem may prove acceptable to God's dedicated people there. I want you to pray that by God's will I may come to you with joy, and enjoy a time of rest with you. The God of peace be with you all. Amen.

WE came to the end of the las passage by saying that as far as we know Paul's plans to go to Spain were never realized. We know for a certainty that when he went to Jerusalem he was arrested and spent the next four years in prison, two in Caesarea and two in Rome. Here again his great character comes out.

(i) When Paul went to Jerusalem he knew what he was doing and was well aware of the dangers that lay ahead. Just as his Master steadfastly set his face to go to Jerusalem (*Luke* 9: 51) so also did Paul. The highest courage is to know that something perilous awaits us and still to go on. That is the courage that Jesus showed; that is the courage that Paul showed; and that is the courage that all Christ's followers must show.

(ii) In such a situation Paul asked for the prayers of the Christian Church at Rome. It is a great thing to go on knowing that we are wrapped in the warmth of the prayers of those who love us. However far we are separated from those we love, we and they can meet around the mercy-seat of God.

(iii) Paul leaves them his blessing as he goes. It was no doubt all that he had to give. Even when we have nothing else, we can still bear our friends and loved ones in prayer to God.

(iv) It was the blessing of the God of peace that Paul sent to Rome and it was with the presence of the God of peace that he himself went to Jerusalem with all its threats. The man who has the peace of God in his heart can meet all life's perils unafraid.

A LETTER OF COMMENDATION

Romans 16: 1, 2

> I commend to you our sister Phoebe, who is a servant of the
> Church which is in Cenchreae. I want you to welcome her in the
> Lord in the way that God's people should welcome one another;
> and I want you to help her in whatever way she needs your help,
> for she has been a helper to many, and to me, too.

WHEN a person is applying for a new job, he usually gets a
testimonial from someone who knows him well and who can
pay tribute to his character and ability. When a person is going
to live in some strange town, he often takes with him a letter of
introduction from someone who knows people in that town. In
the ancient world such letters were very common. They were
known as *sustatikai epistolai*, letters of commendation or
introduction. We still possess many of these letters, written on
papyrus and recovered from the rubbish heaps buried in the
desert sands of Egypt.

A certain Mystarion, for instance, an Egyptian olive-planter,
sends his servant on an errand to Stotoetis, a chief priest, and
gives him a letter of introduction to take with him.

> Mystarion to his own Stotoetis, many greetings.
> I have sent my Blastus to you for forked sticks for my olive-
>   gardens.
> See then that you do not detain him, for you know how I need him
>   every hour.
> To Stotoetis, chief priest at the island.

That is a letter of commendation to introduce the Blastus who
has gone upon the errand. So Paul writes to introduce Phoebe
to the Church at Rome.

Phoebe came from Cenchreae which was the port of Corinth.
Sometimes she is called a *deaconess*, but it is not likely that she
held what might be called an official position in the Church.
There can have been no time in the Christian Church when the
work of women was not of infinite value. It must have been

specially so in the days of the early Church. In the case of baptism by total immersion, as it then was, in the visitation of the sick, in the distribution of food to the poor, women must have played a big part in the life and work of the Church, but they did not at that time hold any official position.

Paul bespeaks a welcome for Phoebe. He asks the people at Rome to welcome her as God's dedicated people ought to welcome each other. There should be no strangers in the family of Christ; there should be no need for formal introductions between Christian people, for they are sons and daughters of the one father and therefore brothers and sisters of each other. And yet a church is not always the welcoming institution that it ought to be. It is possible for churches, and still more possible for church organizations, to become almost little closed societies which are not really interested in welcoming the stranger. When a stranger comes amongst us, Paul's advice still holds good—welcome such a one as God's dedicated people ought to welcome each other.

A HOUSEHOLD WHICH WAS A CHURCH

Romans 16: 3, 4

Give my greetings to Prisca and to Aquila, my fellow-workers in Christ Jesus, who risked their own necks to save my life. It is not only I who have cause to be thankful to them, but all the churches of the Gentiles; and give my greetings to the church that is in their house.

THERE is no more fascinating pair of people in the New Testament than Prisca and Aquila. Sometimes Prisca is also called Priscilla which is an affectionate diminutive form of her name. Let us begin with the facts about them of which we are sure.

They appear first in *Acts* 18: 2. From that passage we learn that they had previously been resident in Rome. Claudius had issued an edict in A.D. 52 banishing the Jews. Anti-semitism is no new thing, and the Jews were hated in the

ancient world as they so often are today. When they were
banished from Rome, Prisca and Aquila settled in Corinth.
They were tent-makers which was Paul's own trade, and he
found a home with them. When he left Corinth and went to
Ephesus, Prisca and Aquila went with him and settled there
(*Acts* 18: 18).

The very first incident related of them is characteristic. There
came to Ephesus that brilliant scholar Apollos; but he had not
at this time anything like a full grasp of the Christian faith; so
Aquila and Prisca took him into their house and gave him
friendship and instruction in that faith (*Acts* 18: 24–26). From
the very beginning Prisca and Aquila were people who kept an
open heart and an open door.

The next time we hear of them they are still in Ephesus. Paul
wrote his first letter to the Corinthians from Ephesus and in it
he sends greetings from Prisca and Aquila and from the church
that is in their house (1 *Corinthians* 16: 19). This was long
before the days when there was any such thing as a church
building; and the home of Prisca and Aquila served as a
meeting place for a group of Christian folk.

The next time we hear of them they are in Rome. The edict of
Claudius which had banished the Jews had ceased to be
effective and no doubt Prisca and Aquila like many another
Jew drifted back to their old homes and their old business. We
discover that they are just the same—again there is a group of
Christian people meeting in their house.

For the last time they emerge in 2 *Timothy* 4: 19, and once
again they are in Ephesus; and one of the last messages Paul
ever sent was a greeting to this pair of Christians who had come
through so much with him.

Prisca and Aquila lived a curiously nomadic and unsettled
life. Aquila himself had been born in Pontus in Asia Minor
(*Acts* 18: 2). We find them resident first in Rome, then in
Corinth, then in Ephesus, then back in Rome, and then finally
again in Ephesus; but wherever we find them, we find their
home a centre of Christian fellowship and service. Every home
should be a church, for a church is a place where Jesus dwells.

From the home of Prisca and Aquila, wherever it was, radiated friendship and fellowship and love. If one is a stranger in a strange town or a strange land, one of the most valuable things in the world is to have a home from home into which to go. It takes away loneliness and protects from temptation. Sometimes we think of a home as a place into which we can go and shut the door and keep the world out: but equally a home should be a place with an open door. The open door, the open hand, and the open heart are characteristics of the Christian life.

So much is certain about Prisca and Aquila; but it may be that there is even greater romance in their story. To this day in Rome there is a Church of St Prisca on the Aventine. There is also a cemetery of Priscilla. This cemetery is the burying place of the ancient Roman Acilian family. In it lies buried Acilius Glabrio. He was consul of Rome in A.D. 91 which was the highest office Rome could offer him; and it seems extremely likely that he died a martyr's death as a Christian. He must have been one of the first of the great Romans to become a Christian and to suffer for his faith. Now when people received their freedom in the Roman Empire they were enrolled in one of the great families and took one of the family names as theirs. One of the commonest female names in the Acilian family was Prisca; and Acilius is sometimes written Aquilius, which is very close to Aquila. Here we are faced with two fascinating possibilities.

(i) Perhaps Prisca and Aquila received their freedom from some member of the Acilian family, in which it may be that once they were slaves. Can it be that these two people sowed the seeds of Christianity into that family so that one day a member of it—Acilius Glabrio, no less a person than a Roman consul—became a Christian?

(ii) There is an even more romantic possibility. It is an odd thing that in four out of the six mentions of this pair in the New Testament Prisca is named *before* her husband, although normally the husband's name would come first, as we say " Mr and Mrs." There is just the possibility that this is because Prisca was not a freedwoman at all but a great lady, a member by birth of the Acilian family. It may be that at some meeting of the Christians this great Roman lady met Aquila, the humble Jewish tentmaker, that the two fell in love, that Christianity destroyed the barriers of race and rank and wealth and birth, and that these two, the Roman aristocrat and the Jewish artisan, were joined for ever in Christian love and Christian service.

Of these speculations we can never be sure, but we can be sure that there were many in Corinth, in Ephesus and in Rome, who owed their souls to Prisca and Aquila and to that home of theirs which was also a church.

TO EVERY NAME A COMMENDATION

Romans 16: 5–11

> Give my greetings to my beloved Epaenetus, who was the first convert to Christ in Asia.
> Give my greetings to Mary who has toiled hard among you.
> Give my greetings to Andronicus and Junias, my kinsmen and my fellow-prisoners. They are of high mark among the apostles, and they were Christians before I was.
> Give my greetings to Ampliatus, my beloved in the Lord.
> Give my greetings to Urbanus, our fellow-worker in Christ, and to my beloved Stachys.
> Give my greetings to Apelles, a man of sterling worth in Christ.
> Give my greetings to those who are of the household of Aristobulus.
> Give my greetings to Herodion, my kinsman.
> Give my greetings to those of the household of Narcissus who are in the Lord.

No doubt behind every one of these names there is a story which is a romance in Christ. None of these stories do we know, but at some of them we can guess. In this chapter there are twenty-four individual names and there are two interesting things to note.

(i) Of the twenty-four, six are women. That is worth remembering, for often Paul is accused of belittling the status of women in the Church. If we really wish to see Paul's attitude, it is a passage like this that we should read, where his appreciation of the work that women were doing in the Church shines through his words.

(ii) Of the twenty-four names, thirteen occur in inscriptions or documents which have to do with the Emperor's palace in Rome. Although many are very common names, this fact is nonetheless suggestive. In *Philippians* 4: 22 Paul speaks of the saints of Caesar's household. It may be that they were for the most part slaves, but it is still important that Christianity seems to have penetrated even thus early into the imperial palace.

Andronicus and Junias form an interesting pair, because it is most likely that Junias is a female name. That would mean that in the early Church a woman could be ranked as an apostle. The apostles in this sense were people whom the Church sent out to tell the story of Jesus at large. Paul says that Andronicus and Junias were Christians before he was. That means that they must go right back to the time of Stephen; they must have been a direct link with the earliest Church at Jerusalem.

Behind the name of Ampliatus may well lie an interesting story. It is a quite common slave name. Now in the cemetery of Domatilla, which is the earliest of the Christian catacombs, there is a decorated tomb with the single name *Ampliatus* carved on it in bold and decorative lettering. The fact that the single name *Ampliatus* alone is carved on the tomb—Romans who were citizens would have three names, a nomen, a praenomen, and a cognomen—would indicate that this Ampliatus was a slave; but the elaborate tomb and the bold lettering would indicate that he was a man of high rank in the Church. From that it is plain to see that in the early days of the Church the distinctions of rank were so completely wiped out that it was possible for a man at one and the same time to be a slave and a prince of the Church. Social distinctions did not exist. We have no means of knowing that Paul's Ampliatus is the Ampliatus in the cemetery of Domatilla, but it is not impossible that he is.

The household of Aristobulus may also be a phrase with an interesting history. In Rome *household* did not describe only a man's family and personal relations; it included also his servants and slaves.   In Rome for long there had lived a grandson of Herod the Great whose name was Aristobulus. He had lived always as a private individual and had inherited none of Herod's domains; but he was a close friend of the Emperor Claudius. When he died his servants and slaves would become the property of the Emperor, but they would form a section of his establishment known as *the household of Aristobulus*. So this phrase may well describe Jewish servants and slaves who had once belonged to Aristobulus, Herod's grandson, and had now become the property of the Emperor. This is made the more probable by the name mentioned on each side of the phrase. *Apelles* may quite well be the Greek name that a Jew called *Abel* would take, and *Herodion* is a name which would obviously suit one who had some connection with the family of Herod.

The household of Narcissus may have still another interesting story behind it. Narcissus was a common name; but the most famous Narcissus was a freedman who had been secretary to the Emperor Claudius and had exercised a notorious influence over him. He was said to have amassed a private fortune of almost £4,000,000. His power had lain in the fact that all correspondence addressed to the Emperor had to pass through his hands and never reached him unless he allowed it to do so. He made his fortune from the fact that people paid him large bribes to make sure that their petitions did reach the Emperor. When Claudius was murdered and Nero came to the throne, Narcissus survived for a short time, but in the end he was compelled to commit suicide, and all his fortune and all his household of slaves passed into Nero's possession. It may well be his one-time slaves which are referred to here. If Aristobulus really is the Aristobulus who was the grandson of Herod, and if Narcissus really is the Narcissus who was Cladius's secretary, this means that many of the slaves at the imperial court were already Christians. The leaven of Christianity had reached the highest circles in the Empire.

HIDDEN ROMANCES

Romans 16: 12—16

> Give my greetings to Tryphaena and Tryphosa who toil in the
>   Lord.
> Give my greetings to Persis, the beloved, who has toiled hard in
>   the Lord.
> Give my greetings to Rufus, chosen in the Lord, and to his mother
>   who was a mother to me too.
> Give my greetings to Asyncritus, to Phlegon, to Hermes, to
>   Patrobas, to Hermas, and to the brothers who are with them.
> Give my greetings to Philologos and to Julias, to Nereus and to
>   his sister, to Olympas, and to all God's dedicated people who
>   are with them.
> Greet each other with the kiss that God's dedicated people use.
> All the Churches of Christ send you greetings.

No doubt behind all these names lies a story; but it is only
about a few of them that we can guess and reconstruct.

(i) When Paul wrote his greetings to Tryphaena and Tryphosa—who were very likely twin sisters—he wrote them with
a smile, for the way in which he put it sounds like a complete
contradiction in terms. Three times in this list of greetings Paul
uses a certain Greek word for Christian toil. He uses it of Mary
(verse 6), and of Tryphaena and Tryphosa and of Persis in this
passage. It is the verb *kopian*, which means *to toil to the point
of exhaustion*. That is what Paul said that Tryphaena and
Tryphosa were in the habit of doing; and the point is that
Tryphaena and *Tryphosa* mean respectively *dainty* and *delicate*! It is as if he were saying: " You two may be called *dainty*
and *delicate*; but you belie your names by working like Trojans
for the sake of Christ." We can well imagine a twinkle in Paul's
eye as he dictated that greeting.

(ii) One of the great hidden romances of the New Testament
lies behind the name of Rufus and his mother, who was also a
mother to Paul. It is obvious that Rufus is a choice spirit and a
man well-known for saintliness in the Roman Church; and it is

equally obvious that Paul felt that he owed a deep debt of gratitude to the mother of Rufus for the kindness he had received from her. Who was this Rufus?

Turn to *Mark* 15: 21. There we read of one Simon a Cyrenian who was compelled to carry the Cross of Jesus on the road to Calvary; and he is described as the *father of Alexander and Rufus.* Now if a man is identified by the names of his sons, it means that, although he himself may not be personally known to the community to whom the story is being told, his sons are. To what Church, then, did Mark write his gospel? He wrote it to the Church of Rome, and he knew that it would know who Alexander and Rufus were. Almost certainly here we find Rufus again, the son of that Simon who carried the Cross of Jesus.

That must have been a terrible day for Simon. He was a Jew, from far-off Cyrene in North Africa. No doubt he had scraped and saved for half a lifetime to celebrate one Passover in Jerusalem. As he entered the city on that day, with his heart full of the greatness of the Feast he was going to attend, suddenly the flat of a Roman spear touched him on the shoulder; he was impressed into the Roman service; he found himself carrying a criminal's cross. How the resentment must have blazed in his heart! How angry and bitter he must have been at this terrible indignity! All the way from Cyrene for this! To have come so far to sit at the glory of the Passover and to have had this dreadful and shameful thing happen! No doubt he meant, as soon as he reached Calvary, to fling the cross down and stride away with loathing in his heart.

But something must have happened. On the way to Calvary the spell of the broken figure of Jesus must have laid its tendrils round his heart. He must have stayed to watch, and that figure on the Cross drew Simon to himself for ever. That chance encounter on the road to Calvary changed Simon's life. He came to sit at the Jewish Passover and he went away the slave of Christ. He must have gone home and brought his wife and sons into the same experience as he had himself.

We can weave all kinds of speculations about this. It was men from *Cyprus and Cyrene* who came to Antioch and first preached the gospel to the Gentile world (*Acts* 11: 20). Was Simon one of the men from Cyrene? Was Rufus with him? Was it they who took the first tremendous step to make Christianity the faith of a whole world? Was it they who helped the Church burst the bonds of Judaism? Can it be that in some sense we today owe the fact that we are Christians to the strange episode when a man from Cyrene was compelled to carry a cross on the road to Calvary?

Turn to Ephesus when there is a riot raised by the people who served Diana of the Ephesians and when the crowd would have lynched Paul if they could have got at him. Who stands out to look that mob in the face? A man called Alexander (*Acts* 19: 33). Is this the other brother facing things out with Paul?

And as for their mother—surely she in some hour of need must have brought to Paul the help and the comfort and the love which his own family refused him when he became a Christian. It may be guesswork, for Alexander and Rufus are common names; but maybe it is true and maybe the most amazing things followed from that chance encounter on the way to Calvary.

(iii) There remains one other name which may have a perhaps even more amazing story behind it—that of Nereus. In A.D. 95 an event occurred which shocked Rome. Two of the most distinguished people in the city were condemned for being Christians. They were Flavius Clemens, who had been consul of Rome, and his wife Domatilla, who was of royal blood. She was the grand-daughter of Vespasian, a former Emperor, and the niece of Domitian the reigning Emperor. In fact the two sons of Flavius Clemens and Domatilla had been designated Domitian's successors in the imperial power. Flavius was executed and Domatilla was banished to the island of Pontia where years afterwards Paula saw the cave where " she drew out a long martyrdom for the Christian name."

The point is this—the name of the chamberlain of Flavius and Domatilla was Nereus. Is it possible that Nereus the slave had something to do with the making into Christians of Flavius Clemens the ex-consul and Domatilla the princess of the royal blood? It may be an idle speculation, for Nereus is a common name, but, on the other hand, it may be true.

There is one other fact of interest to add to this story. Flavius Clemens was the son of Flavius Sabinus, who had been Nero's city prefect when Nero sadistically persecuted the Christians after charging them with being responsible for the appalling fire which devastated Rome in A.D. 64. As city prefect Flavius Sabinus must have been Nero's executive officer in that persecution. It was then that Nero ordered the Christians to be rolled in pitch and set alight to form living torches for his gardens, to be sewn into the skins of wild beasts and flung to savage hunting dogs, to be shut up in ships which were sunk in the Tiber. Is it possible that thirty years before he died for Christ, the young Flavius Clemens had seen the dauntless courage of the martyrs and wondered what made men able to die like that?

Five verses of names and of greetings—but they open vistas which thrill the heart!

A LAST LOVING APPEAL

Romans 16: 17–20

> Brothers, I urge you to keep your eye on those who, contrary to the teaching which they have received, cause dissensions and put in your way things which would trip you up. Steer clear of them. Such men are not real servants of Christ, our Lord; they are the servants of their own greed. By their plausibility and their flattery they deceive the hearts of innocent folk. I know that you will deal with such people, for the story of your obedience has reached all men. So, then, I rejoice over you. I want you to be wise in what is good, and untainted with what is evil. The God of peace will soon overthrow Satan so that you may trample him under your feet. The grace of the Lord Jesus Christ be with you.

ROMANS was a letter which Paul found very difficult to bring to an end. He has sent his greetings; but before he closes he makes one last appeal to the Christians in Rome to keep themselves from every evil influence. He picks out two characteristics of men hurtful to the Church and to the Christian fellowship.

(i) They are men who cause dissensions among the brethren. Any man who does anything which disturbs the peace of a church has much to answer for. A minister was once talking to a man newly come to his congregation from another town. The man had obviously little of the love of Christ upon him. He said to the minister: " You know such and such a congregation? " naming that of which he had formerly been a member. " Yes," said the minister. " Well," said the man with a certain evil relish. " I wrecked it! " There are people who take a pride in making trouble and who like nothing better than to sow the poisonous seeds of strife. The man who has brought strife to any band of brothers will answer for it some day to him who is the King and Head of the Church.

(ii) They are men who put hindrances in the way of others. The man who makes it harder for someone else to be a Christian also has much to answer for. The man whose conduct is a bad example, whose influence is an evil snare, whose teaching dilutes or emasculates the Christian faith which he pretends to teach, will someday bear his own punishment; and it will not be light, for Jesus was stern to any man who caused one of his little ones to stumble.

There are two interesting words in this passage. There is the word we have translated *plausibility* (*chrēstologia*). The Greeks themselves defined a *chrēstologos* as " a man who speaks well and who acts ill." He is the kind of man who, behind a façade of pious words, is a bad influence, who leads astray, not by direct attack, but by subtlety, who pretends to serve Christ. but in reality is destroying the faith. There is the word we have translated *untainted with what is evil*. It is the word *akeraios* and it is used of metal which has no suspicion of alloy, of wine and of milk which are not adulterated with water. It describes something which is absolutely pure of any corruption. The Christian is a man whose utter sincerity must be beyond all doubt.

One thing is to be noted in this passage—it is clear that the latent trouble in the Church at Rome has not yet flared into action. Paul, indeed, says that he believes that the Roman Church is well able to deal with it. He was a wise pastor, because he believed firmly that prevention was better than cure. Often in a church or a society a bad situation is allowed to develop because no one has the courage to deal with it; and often, when it has fully developed, it is too late to deal with it. It is easy enough to extinguish a spark if steps are taken at once, but it is almost impossible to extinguish a forest fire. Paul had the wisdom to deal with a threatening situation in time.

The passage closes with a most suggestive thing. Paul says that the *God of peace* will soon crush and overthrow Satan, the power of evil. We must note that the peace of God is the peace of action and of victory. There is a kind of peace which can be had at the cost of evading all issues and refusing all decisions, a peace which comes of lethargic inactivity. The Christian must ever remember that the peace of God is not the peace which has submitted to the world, but the peace which has overcome the world.

GREETINGS

Romans 16: 21–23

> Timothy, my fellow-worker, sends you his greetings, as do Lucius, Jason and Sosipater, my kinsmen. I Tertius, who wrote this letter, send you my greetings in the Lord. Gaius, whose hospitality I and the whole Church enjoy, sends you his greetings, as does brother Quartus.

IT is tempting to try to identify the group of friends who send their greetings along with Paul's. Timothy was Paul's right hand man, the man whom Paul saw as his successor and of whom he later said that no one knew his mind so well (*Philippians* 2: 19, 20). Lucius may be the Lucius of Cyrene, who was one of the prophets and teachers of Antioch who first sent Paul and Barnabas on their missionary journeys (*Acts* 13: 1). Jason may be the Jason who gave Paul hospitality at Thessalonica and suffered for it at the hands of the mob (*Acts*

17: 5–9). Sosipater may be the Sopater of Beroea who took his Church's share of the collection to Jerusalem with Paul (*Acts* 20: 4). Gaius may be the Gaius who was one of the two people whom Paul baptized at Corinth (1 *Corinthians* 1: 14).

For the first and only time, we know the name of the amanuensis who actually penned this letter to Paul's dictation, for Tertius slipped in his own greeting. No great man can do his work without the aid that humble helpers give him. Paul's other secretaries are anonymous, so that Tertius is the representative of those humble unknowns who were penmen for Paul.

One of the most interesting things in the whole chapter is the way in which again and again Paul characterizes people in a single sentence. Here there are two great summaries. Gaius is the man of hospitality; Quartus is the brother. It is a great thing to go down to history as the man with the open house or as the man with the brotherly heart. Some day people will sum us up in one sentence. What will that sentence be?

THE END IS PRAISE

Romans 16: 25–27

> Now unto him who is able to make you stand firm, in the way that the gospel I preach promises and the message Jesus brought offers, in the way which is now unveiled in that secret, which was for long ages wrapped in silence, but which is now full-disclosed, and made known to all the Gentiles—as the writings of the prophets said it would be, and as the command of God now orders it to be—that they might render to him a submission born of faith, to the only wise God, through Jesus Christ, be glory for ever. Amen.

THE letter to the Romans comes to an end with a doxology which is also a summary of the gospel which Paul preached and loved.

(i) It is a gospel which makes men able to stand firm. " Son of man," said God to Ezekiel, " stand upon your feet and I will speak with you " (*Ezekiel* 2: 1). The gospel is a power which enables a man to stand foursquare against the shocks of the world and the assaults of temptation.

A journalist relates a great incident of the Spanish Civil War. There was a little garrison of beleaguered men. The end was near and some wished to surrender and so to save their lives; but others wished to fight on. The matter was settled when a gallant soul declared: " It is better to die upon our feet than to live upon our knees."

Life can be difficult; sometimes a man is beaten to his knees by the battering that it gives to him. Life can be perilous; sometimes a man is like to fall in the slippery places of temptation. The gospel is God's power to save; that power which keeps a man erect, even when life is at its worst and its most threatening.

(ii) It is a gospel which Paul preached and which was offered by Jesus Christ. That is to say, the gospel takes its source in Christ and is transmitted by men. Without Jesus Christ there can be no gospel at all; but without men to transmit it, other men can never hear of it. The Christian duty is that when a man is himself found of Christ, he should straightway go and find others for him. After Andrew was found of Jesus, John says of him: " He first found his brother Simon, and said to him, ' We have found the Messiah ' " (*John* 1: 40, 41).

Here is the Christian privilege and the Christian duty. The Christian privilege is to appropriate the good news for ourselves; the Christian duty is to transmit that good news to others. A famous story tells how Jesus, after the Cross and the Resurrection, returned to his glory, still bearing the marks of his sufferings. One of the angels said to him, " You must have suffered terribly for men down there." " I did," said Jesus. " Do they all know about what you did for them? " asked the angel. " No," said Jesus, " not yet. Only a few know about it so far." " And," said the angel, " what have you done that they should all know? " " Well," said Jesus, " I asked Peter and James and John to make it their business to tell others, and the others still others, until the farthest man on the widest circle has heard the story." The angel looked doubtful, for he knew well what poor creatures men were. " Yes," he said, " but what if Peter and James and John forget? What if they grow weary of the telling? What if, away down in the twentieth century, men fail to tell the story of your love for them? What then? Haven't you made any other plans? " Back came the answer of Jesus, " I haven't made any other plans. *I'm counting on them*." Jesus died to give us the gospel; and now he is counting on us to transmit it to all men.

(iii) It is a gospel which is the consummation of history. It is something which was there from all ages and which at the coming of Christ was revealed to the world. With the coming of Jesus something unique happened, eternity invaded time and God emerged on earth. His coming was the event to which all history was working up and the event from which all subsequent history flows. After the coming of Christ the world could never be the same again. It was the central fact of history, so that men date time in terms of before and after Christ's birth. It is as if with his coming life and the world began all over again.

(iv) It is a gospel which is meant for *all* men and which was *always* meant for all men. It is not a gospel which was meant for the Jews only; its going out to the Gentiles was not an afterthought. The prophets, perhaps scarcely knowing what they were saying, had their hints and forecasts of a time when all men of all nations would know God. That time is not yet; but it is the dream of God that some day the knowledge of him will cover the earth as the waters cover the sea, and it is the glory of man that he can help make God's dream come true.

(v) It is a gospel which issues in an obedient world, a world where God is King. But that obedience is not founded on submission to an iron law, which breaks the man who opposes it; it is an obedience founded on faith, on a surrender which is the result of love. For Paul the Christian is not a man who has surrendered to an ineluctable power; he is a man who has fallen in love with the God who is the lover of the souls of men and whose love stands for ever full-displayed in Jesus Christ.

And so the long argument of the letter to the Romans comes to an end in a song of praise.

FURTHER READING

C. H. Dodd, *The Epistle of Paul to the Romans* (MC; *E*)
A. M. Hunter, *The Epistle to the Romans: The Law of Love*
  (Tch; *E*)
W. Sanday and A. C. Headlam, *Romans* (Sixth edition, in two
  volumes, revised by C. E. B. Cranfield) (ICC; *G*)

Abbreviations

ICC : International Critical Commentary
MC : Moffatt Commentary
Tch : Torch Commentary

  E : English Text
  G : Greek Text

THE DAILY STUDY BIBLE

Published in 17 Volumes